FEMALE SEXUAL PREDATORS

FEMALE SEXUAL PREDATORS

Understanding Them to Protect Our Children and Youths

Karen A. Duncan

Forensic Psychology
Duane L. Dobbert, series editor

PRAEGER

AN IMPRINT OF ABC-CLIO, LLC
Santa Barbara, California • Denver, Colorado • Oxford, England

Library of Congress Cataloging-in-Publication Data

Duncan, K. A. (Karen A.)
Female sexual predators : understanding them to protect our children and youths / Karen A. Duncan.
p. cm. — (Forensic psychology)
Includes bibliographical references and index.
ISBN 978-0-313-36629-1 (alk. paper) — ISBN 978-0-313-36630-7 (ebook)
1. Female sex offenders—Psychology. 2. Child sex offenders—Psychology. 3. Child sexual abuse—Prevention. 4. Sex crimes—Prevention. I. Title.
HV6557.D86 2010
364.15'3082—dc22 2010014498

ISBN: 978-0-313-36629-1
EISBN: 978-0-313-36630-7

14 13 12 11 10 1 2 3 4 5

This book is also available on the World Wide Web as an eBook.
Visit www.abc-clio.com for details.

Praeger
An Imprint of ABC-CLIO, LLC

ABC-CLIO, LLC
130 Cremona Drive, P.O. Box 1911
Santa Barbara, California 93116-1911

This book is printed on acid-free paper ∞

Manufactured in the United States of America

To Tom
A husband who makes the world a safe and joyous place

To
All Children and Teens
May Your World Be Safe and Loving
www.theright2besafe.org

Contents

Acknowledgments

Every author owes a debt of gratitude to the people who support her throughout the writing of a book. The support and encouragement of others is particularly welcomed when a book is focused on a subject matter that tends to be surrounded more by silence than acknowledgment of its reality, where existing gender stereotypes are challenged and dominant sociopolitical theories are questioned. The subject of women sex offenders is certainly one such topic. Therefore I extend a sincere thank-you and a debt of gratitude to Amy, Laura, Nancy, and Joanna for their courage in sharing their childhood experiences of being sexually abused by women they knew and trusted. Each of these women shared their stories to raise awareness about female sexual predators and to help each of us realize that it is not only boys who are sexually abused by women, but girls are too. Their hope is that in sharing what happened to them as young girls that adults will take action to protect all children from women intent on committing child sexual abuse and that in doing so, society will come to recognize, rather than dismiss, the tangible harm that arises from sexual crimes committed by women.

To Victoria Johnson, graduate student at Indiana University, School of Library and Information Science, whose ability, skill, and timeliness at locating numerous research articles saved me a tremendous amount of time while helping me to assure that the book would be grounded in current information. Thank you Victoria! I could not have completed this work without you. To Andrew Duncan, graduate of New York University, for fact checking media reports on female sexual offenders along with his engaging discussions on human sexuality within contemporary society. To Anthony Richey, who worked with Andrew Duncan to research and compile media reports on women convicted of child sexual abuse within schools. Anthony and Andrew along with some of the male college students in my human sexuality classes were invaluable in helping to gain the male perspective on women who sexually abuse adolescent boys and provided helpful insights on the male response to female sexual coercion.

To Kevin Fagan, with the *San Francisco Chronicle,* for sharing his experience as a journalist who writes about sexual crimes that as he said "are always painful to cover" but that he manages with compassion and sensibility. It was Kevin's story about the arrest of Melissa Huckaby for the kidnapping, rape, and murder of eight-year-old Sandra Cantu that prompted me to interview Kevin about how the media covers female sex offenders. I appreciated Kevin's perspective of sexual crimes committed by women and of how the media will at times exploit these cases. Kevin's perspective on the ethics that are required by journalists when reporting on sexual crimes was grounded in concern for the victims and pointed in his common sense approach for reporters. To Circuit and Family Court Judge K. Mark Loyd, who provided the opportunity to discuss the criminal justice response to female sex offenders within the history of the law regarding the prosecution of male sex offenders and how the law evolved over time as information about male sex offenders became available. I appreciate the time Judge Loyd extended to me, which in turn improved my understanding of the dynamics of criminal justice and the integral role it serves in child protection cases.

To Melissa Sisco, graduate student at the University of Arizona, Department of Psychology, for sharing her research on campus-based sexual aggression, Lauren Duncan at Smith College for responding to my inquires regarding her previous study on the sexual victimization of African American boys by females; Jeffrey Sandler at the University of Albany, School of Criminal Justice, for discussing the research on emerging typologies for female sexual offenders; and Jim Hopper for responding to my questions about the pathway from victimization to offending.

Debbie Carvalko, editor at ABC-CLIO Publishing, for her diligence in preparing the manuscript and for her continuing belief in the work that I do. Thank you Debbie for your support, understanding, and your intuitive editorial sense.

As always my husband, Tom, who makes me coffee, cinnamon rolls, and keeps me grounded. Thank you for being there to keep me going through the long days, and nights, of writing.

Introduction

Sexual crimes are among the most disturbing acts committed by one human being against another. They are disturbing not only because of the sexual nature of the crime but because of the psychological and emotional consequences that follow in their aftermath and because they are most often committed by someone the victim knows. Historically, there has been less acknowledgment and little attention given to females who commit sexual crimes even though females have been documented as committing sexual offenses as early as the 1930s (see Chideckel, 1935). This lack of attention has hindered the information that is needed about female sex offenders in order to prevent their criminal behavior. The same lack of attention has also afforded less recognition, understanding, and support to the people—adults, teens, and children—who are the victims of female sex offenders.

Even though there has been less research of female sexual offenders, what is known from the information that is available is that females commit the same types of sexual crimes as males do. Sexual stalking, sexual harassment, sexual assault, rape, and child sexual abuse are among the types of sexual crimes that both males and females are known to commit. There are, however, also differences. One of the differences between male and female sex offenders is that due to the potential for gender bias, female sexual crimes are more likely to be obscured. Female sexual crimes are obscured due in part to the cultural norms that define female sexual behavior and by the gender stereotypes that define who society identifies as a sex offender. A consequence of this obscurity is that victims are less protected. Victims are less protected because females are less likely to be identified, reported, prosecuted, and convicted when gender bias and cultural stereotypes prevail and camouflage their sexual offense. When and if females are convicted for their sexual crimes, they might not receive the same level of judicial accountability and social sanctioning as a male who has committed the same or similar crime. A consequence of less accountability is that females are given license to continue their sexual offending, thereby creating more victims and continuing the harm they cause to others. An additional outcome of gender bias and cultural stereotypes regarding females who commit sexual crimes are that they are not afforded the same opportunities for rehabilitation and treatment and a reliable level of law enforcement oversight when living in the community. This outcome of gender bias happens when a majority of the research, treatment, and criminal justice funding goes toward male sex offenders because female sex offenders are thought to commit fewer sexual crimes because fewer reports are made to law enforcement or because fewer cases are prosecuted (see Levine, 2006).

Female Sexual Predators is a response to the growing need for comprehensive information about females who commit sexual crimes that corresponds with the emerging research about female sex offenders. It is also in part a response to addressing the gender bias regarding female sex offenders that many of us who work in the field of child sexual abuse and family violence have come to recognize over the years. The idea, let alone the reality, that there are women who intentionally and with a sense of purpose act in a violent, aggressive, and coercive manner is not an acceptable idea in some social, political, and professional circles. As stated by Lori Girshick in writing about sexual violence within lesbian relationships, "The idea that women might be violent is not palatable; we don't know quite how to place it, and as feminists, we are worried about possible consequences to our patriarchal analysis. The thought of a woman rapist is even more removed from our sensibility. A woman sexually harming another woman? Penetrating her with an object or her fingers? Tying her up and anally raping her? Holding her down? Verbally harassing her? Her against her? This is tough stuff. Just ask the women it happens to" (see Girshick, 2002, p. 3). Similar responses can be found when discussing women who commit acts of sexual aggression in their heterosexual relationships with men or against adolescents and children.

The fact that there are mothers who through their own volition harm their children and in some cases contribute to a significant number of child deaths is not a reality that some people want to admit unless there is a man around to blame for the mother's violence. This denial is equally strong when it comes to accepting that there are mothers who sexually abuse their children and that the abuse can continue for a number of years, even into adulthood and in the absence of a male offender. The reality of being sexually abused by your mother is not a reality that sons and daughters want to necessarily acknowledge either; however, the denial of maternal sexual abuse does not erase its existence. What anyone who denies and minimizes maternal sexual abuse and other types of violence committed by mothers needs to realize is that a resistance to admit to female violence, and sexual violence in particular, prevents the possibility to provide a safe home to the children who remain in the care of this group of mothers and fails to address the needs of women who cause such incredible harm to a generation of our young.

A similar resistance holds true when discussing the need to recognize that there are young women on college campuses who commit acts of sexual coercion and sexual assault against their male dating partners and that they do so in a similar manner and by similar means, as do young men who commit these offenses. To advocate for this acknowledgement and for the prevention of sexual coercion and assault by females, goes against the gender stereotypes that can exist on college campuses and challenges the gender politics that can be found within the research about sexual violence, as it is reported to occur on college campuses. However, if we fear to make these challenges or fail to recognize that within contemporary society acts of sexual coercion and aggression may be more about how personal boundaries are violated by the individual rather than about the aggressor's gender, we risk not teaching an entire generation the basic human value that violating someone's personal boundaries is not acceptable whether you are a male or a female.

Promoting healthy, mutually respectful and life-affirming relationships is the overarching goal of all prevention education programs. It is important to remember that prevention efforts began with the recognition that the silence surrounding sexual violence was no longer acceptable. Within this basic premise of "no more silence" was the requirement that men and women across societies no longer deny that these traumatic crimes happen. Perhaps the time has come to thoughtfully consider that in order to achieve the overarching goal of preventing all sexual crimes that the day has come to acknowledge that in contemporary society the question of who commits sexual crimes is not determined by gender alone. In doing so, we begin the process of acknowledging that people who commit sexual crimes may have commonalities that include the abuse and exploitation of another human being; a belief in sexual entitlement rather than the belief in sexual consent; feelings of hostility and anger that often include an adherence to adversarial feelings against another gender; the acceptance of interpersonal violence that provides permission for violence; and an inherent denial of the harm sexual aggression in all its many forms cause to another human being. The outcome of such a paradigm shift is that we may actually provide the opportunity to move beyond the gender stereotypes that permeate the societal denial of female sex offenders and move toward the fulfillment of identifying, understanding, and preventing sexual crimes that are committed by females as well as males.

Female Sexual Predators covers a wide range of predatory sexual behaviors and offending patterns by women. It examines women employed in caretaking positions who commit sexual offenses against children and teens; mothers who commit sexual offenses against their sons and daughters; and college-age women who commit acts of sexual aggression and coercion within their heterosexual dating relationships. Women who sexually exploit male and female high school students are included along with a discussion of how widespread sexual harassment is within high schools, and how this type of behavior between educators and students can set the stage for more intrusive sexual acts that are both illegal and unethical. The book is unique in that it provides a worldview of female sexual predators with studies from the United States, England, South Africa, Australia, Poland, Canada, Sweden, and other countries. Chapter 1 is an in-depth discussion about female sexual offending that reviews studies from the United States and other countries in order to place female sexual offending within a broader context. The chapter discusses the underreporting of sexual offenses committed by females because of gender bias and cultural stereotypes and how sexist beliefs about female sexuality contribute to the continuation of sexual crimes committed by females. The types of sexual crimes females commit, along with the frequency and type of violence that females use during their sexual offending, are presented so that the reader has a clear understanding of the severity of sexual crimes committed by females and the level of harm that female sex offenders cause to their victims. The debate about whether females commit their sexual crimes alone or because of coercion by males is addressed, and the reader may be surprised by the findings. In particular, the physiological response that a male or female victim can experience as a result of sexual victimization by a woman is discussed to dispel the myth of the sexually invulnerable male and to clarify the human sexual response that can occur during sexual victimization.

Chapter 2 discusses maternal sexual abuse and the consequences to children sexually abused by their mothers or other women who assume a maternal role with children. Maternal sexual abuse is devastating to the sons and daughters who have been the victims of their mothers' sexual deviance and who have been silenced by a society unwilling to accept or discuss the existence of maternal sexual offenders. Children sexually abused by mothers describe a deep sense of betrayal and a personal loss that at times seems impossible to reconcile. The impact of maternal sexual abuse is presented, as is the resilience of adult children who have endured sexual abuse and other types of childhood abuses at the hands of their mothers. Characteristics of maternal sexual offenders are presented along with the types and context of sexual abuse that mothers commit so that the reader has an understanding of how maternal sexual abuse can differ from sexual offenses committed by fathers, and how they can also be similar. Further research on women who commit maternal sexual abuse is needed in order to provide greater protection to children and teens and to support the healing and recovery of children sexually abused by a female parent.

Chapter 3 delves into the research and the reality of sexual aggression and coercion committed by college women in the context of their dating relationships and social interaction with college men. This chapter challenges the stereotype that only college males commit acts of sexual aggression. Contemporary studies regarding sexual aggression and coercion on college campuses indicate that there is a greater amount of mutual sexual aggression between young adult men and women that takes place during dating than perhaps previous research suspected or reported. The relationship between alcohol consumption and sexual aggression is discussed with studies from Harvard and Columbia substantiating the fact that the amount of alcohol consumed by college students contributes to sexual aggression, although alcohol consumption in of itself is not the cause of coercive sexual behavior. Sexual aggression, intoxication, and the culture that is found within some sororities and fraternities is discussed, since this group of college students is at particular risk for alcohol-related sexual violence. The role of adversarial beliefs and a history of childhood sexual abuse are discussed since both are found to have a relationship for college-age females who commit sexual aggression against their male dating partner. Recent research on the role of love styles is also presented as another avenue of understanding how the types of attitudes a person holds toward their dating relationships can contribute to sexual coercion. Prevention of sexual violence on college campuses is discussed within the context of helping young women and men to develop mutually respectful relationships at this stage of their adult development and so that both young men and young women can learn to avoid becoming victims or offenders of sexual coercion and assault.

Chapter 4 turns to the topic of how a students' age and stage of cognitive and sexual development, as well as a students' social inexperience in responding to an adult intent on committing this type of child sexual abuse, is exploited by adult sex offenders who work in the school environment. Sexual harassment in the high school environment is a particular focus since sexual harassment that goes unchecked can become the social norm in schools. When sexual harassment becomes the cultural norm, it can then set the stage for more intrusive and illegal sexual behavior. Studies indicate that sexual harassment in the high school environment occurs across age groups and gender. Students report that they engage in the sexual harassment of each other, experience sexual harassment from the adults employed at their schools, commit sexual harassment against adults at their schools, and witness sexual harassment between the adults in their school. Chapter 5 concludes with a discussion of female sexual deviance, the emerging typologies for female sexual offenders, assessment and treatment of female sexual offenders, and the possibility of preventing child sexual abuse and sexual exploitation by women.

While *Female Sexual Predators* covers a spectrum of female sexual offending, it is primarily about raising awareness in order to help prevent the sexual abuse of children and teens by adult women. It is my sincere hope that all adults who care about children and teens will challenge the stereotypes they may hold about females who commit sexual crimes and thereby make a conscious choice to speak and act on the behalf of children and teens to ensure that their world is free of abuse and exploitation. I hope you will share this book with other adults you know. I especially ask that you share this information with women whom you suspect may not be that safe and nurturing adult that children and teens deserve—women who may not have that inner voice or a moral compass to guide them in knowing the difference between what is right and what is wrong when it comes to how adults are to speak and behave with children and teens. Perhaps through your sharing, one woman will stop, think, and consider the harm she may have already caused or could cause, and then choose a different path to follow. Thank you.

1

Female Sexual Offenders: A Changing Perspective

> Few behaviors deviate as far from cultural norms and deep-seated beliefs as those committed by women who sexually abuse children.
>
> —Craig Allen, *Women and Men Who Sexually Abuse Children*[1]

Societies are becoming increasingly aware that women do in fact commit sexual crimes.[2] Studies from the United States,[3] Australia,[4] Canada,[5] England,[6] South Africa,[7] and Sweden[8] have begun to place the sexual offenses that women commit into a broader social and public context by confirming that females perpetrate sexual crimes across societies and cultures. The information from this diverse group of cross-cultural studies documents that women commit a broad range of sexual offenses, that their sexual offenses are both similar to and different from those committed by men,[9] and that the harm women cause from their sexual crimes can exact a toll on a victim's physical health, emotional well-being, and ability to function effectively in relationships.[10]

A recent study by Dube et al. (2005) from the United States on the results of a large-scale longitudinal study that was sponsored by the Centers for Disease Control indicated that 40 percent of the men and 6 percent of the women who reported experiencing childhood sexual abuse disclosed that the sexual offender was a female.[11] The experience of child sexual abuse significantly increased the risk of negative health outcomes and social/relational problems across the life span of this group of adults. Individuals in this study who had experienced childhood sexual abuse had an increase risk for a suicide attempt, depression, and alcohol and drug problems. As studies continue to substantiate that sexual abuse by females is a significant social and public health problem, it becomes evident that education on the identification and detection of female sexual crime is important in the training of law enforcement personnel, child protection workers, educators, and health professionals (Bunting, 2005; Denov, 2003b; Gannon, Rose, & Ward, 2008; Turton, 2007).

Information on female sexual offending is also essential in programs that focus on the prevention of sexual victimization, such as those funded through the Centers for Disease Control and Injury Prevention,[12] the National Sexual Violence Prevention Resource Center,[13] and the National Coalition to Prevent Child Sexual Exploitation.[14] National, state, and community organizations that provide information in response to sexual victimization can enhance their effectiveness by including information regarding female sex offenders. In doing so, they help to raise awareness of the risk for victimization by females and aid in the detection and reporting of female sexual offenders in the

KEY POINTS

International studies indicate that sexual offenses committed by females occur across societies and cultures.

A majority of female sex offenders commit sexual offenses against their own children or other youth in their care.

Stereotypes about sexual offending and gender bias against viewing women as potential sex offenders can prevent the recognition and reporting of sexual crimes committed by females.

Children and teens benefit when law enforcement and child protection services are trained in the recognition and investigation of sexual offenses committed by females.

There are females who commit acts of physical violence in the commission of their sexual crimes that is equal to and at times exceeds that of some males.

The negative health outcomes and overall adverse consequences to victims of female sexual abuse are similar to those experienced by victims sexually abused by males.

Current education programs to prevent sexual victimization need to include accurate and up-to-date information about female sex offenders.

home, schools, day care centers, religious organizations, and the community at large. Education programs, media campaigns, and prevention strategies are recommended to go beyond the gender stereotypes and sensationalism that can sometimes surround the media reports of females who commit sexual crimes. Kevin Fagan, an award-winning reporter with the *San Francisco Chronicle*, offers his colleagues a reminder that "sex crimes are always potentially explosive and this can be especially true when the offender is a female. So we, in the legitimate media, have a greater responsibility to keep that in mind and try to be informative, responsible, and educational in our coverage of such stories [female sex crimes]."[15] When individuals, organizations, and the media work together to improve public education, public safety can also improve.

A recent study in South Africa by Andersson and Ho-Foster (2008) reported on the sexual abuse of boys. This study was in response to laws in South Africa that have been revised and updated to extend equal protection to boys against rape,[16] giving support to the changing view that sexual victimization is not only a crime committed against females and that offenders are not always male. The South African study is significant in that it surveyed a total of 126,696 boys across 1,191 schools in nine provinces. The survey identified 13,915 boys as experiencing forced sex in the year the survey took place. Boys identified that the sexual assaults they experienced occurred most often in their schools and that *women* were the predominant perpetrators. Boys indicated that 42 percent of the sexual offenders were female and that 32 percent were male, while 27 percent of the boys identified that both male and female perpetrators had sexually offended against them. Furthermore, the authors found that by the age of 18, two in every five schoolboys reported being forced to have sex and that most of the people who forced them to have sex were female offenders. The South African study brings attention to the frequency and severity of female sexual abuse along with the number of victims touched by sexual crimes committed by women and confirms that the range of offenses that females commit are substantial and have been occurring for a number of years.

A 2007[17] study sponsored by the McCarty Centre Society[18] in Vancouver, British Columbia, on marginalized and street youth surprised researchers when they learned that a substantial number of females engaged in the sexual exploitation of this vulnerable population of youth. One of the principal researchers noted that females accounted for 79 percent of the sexual exploitation of boys who participated in the study and a smaller percentage of the girls. The study defined sexual exploitation as "the exchange of sexual activity for money, goods or resources such as shelter and food" (p. 40). This means that women were approaching this group of young people to solicit sex, knowing that these youths were on the street, homeless, and without adult protection. This finding is even more staggering when you consider the fact that this group of youth, a majority of whom are Aboriginal, are among the most vulnerable of youth in this region of Canada, often coming from homes where they have already experienced multiple traumas that include sexual abuse and physical violence. Considering that women are stereotypically viewed as the gender that is protective of youth, not exploitive of them, the surprise of the researchers is understandable. The study also demonstrates that adult women are willing to sexually exploit children at a tremendous cost to the child they exploit. What do women who treat our young people in such a manner teach children about their place and value in the world?

In Australia, Child Wise[19] (2006) authorized a study to determine the extent of child sexual abuse in organizations that employ primarily females to care for children and in organizations that engage in other types of youth services where females are employees. The study found that adolescent and adult females employed in youth organizations or as individual caretakers to children sexually abused both male and female children. This is one aspect of female sexual abuse that is both similar to and different from male sexual abuse. Females, unlike males, do not seem to target one gender over the other (or what is referred to as a gender preference in victims); rather, females are likely to victimize males and females equally (Vandiver & Kercher, 2004). This means that children of both genders are at risk for sexual abuse by a female offender.[20] Child Wise emphasizes that organizations need to recruit and screen employees conscientiously in spite of the "traditional view that women are non-predatory" (p. 40) and realize that stereotypes about females will not protect children from a female intent on committing child sexual abuse. A lack of knowledge about female sex offenders can result in fewer restrictions placed on females in their physical contact with children and give females easy access to children without proper supervision and oversight (Hunt, 2006). The conviction of Vanessa George[21] on child pornography, a female who worked at Little Ted's nursery in England, is a prime example of how children can be exploited by female sexual offenders when female workers are not properly supervised and their behavior with children is not readily questioned.

The report from Child Wise suggests that it is highly beneficial for professionals responsible for the care and education of children to receive training on female sex offenders as part of their formal education. This recommendation for employee and staff training is echoed by the Centers for Disease Control and Prevention in Atlanta, Georgia. In their guidelines for preventing child sexual abuse in youth-serving organizations, the report states that "youth-serving organizations strive to create a safe environment for youth, employees, and volunteers so that youth can grow, learn, and have fun. Part of creating a safe environment is making sure that youth are not harmed in any way while participating in organization-sponsored activities. One risk in any organization working directly with youth is child sexual abuse. It is vital that organizations create a culture where child sexual abuse is discussed, addressed, and prevented."[22] It is equally important that organizations, in their efforts to protect children, expand beyond the traditional stereotypes of males as the offender and females as victims and be willing to recognize that it is not practical in the protection of children and teens to assume that females cannot or will not commit sexual offenses. As stated by Olive Wolfers (1993), "Agencies that provide care, generally speaking, are not geared toward detecting women's involvement in child sexual abuse and, consequently, frequently leave children unprotected" (p. 93).

A special report published by the U.S. Department of Justice (Beck, Adams, & Guerino, 2008)[23] on sexual crimes committed against youth in state and local juvenile correctional facilities that included private facilities where youth are in residential programs and the state may be paying for the housing and rehabilitation services for juveniles, indicated that females accounted for 46 percent of substantiated sexual offenses against this population of vulnerable youth and that female offenders included adult female staff employed at the facilities and adolescents residing in these facilities. The authors of the report indicated that 51 percent of the female offenders were white, 40 percent were African American, and 9 percent were Hispanic, indicating that female sex offenders cross racial and ethnic groups. A majority of the adult female offenders were employed in staff positions where they were responsible for the supervision and care of youth they sexually victimized. It was also of interest to note that while 45 percent of the male offenders were arrested and/or were referred for prosecution, only 34 percent of the female offenders were arrested and/or referred for prosecution.[24] No data on prosecution outcomes for males or females were available in the report, but this aspect of the report does suggest that the females were less likely to experience legal sanctions to prevent their reoffending. Nonlegal sanctions that were imposed against female offenders employed in a staff position were that 91 percent of the female staff experienced the loss of their job, and 12 percent were reprimanded or disciplined. The report did not indicate whether any of the females who remained employed were required to participate in specific interventions, such as mandated training or sex offense specific treatment to *decrease their risk* of reoffending, and whether written documentation of the females who victimized youth followed the reprimands, disciplinary actions, and loss of employment.

CLARIFYING CRIME REPORTS AND PREVALENCE STUDIES

Crime reports are limited in the information that they provide to the public regarding sexual crimes, whether the crimes are committed by males or females.[25] This is because for a crime to be included in crime statistics, the crime must first be reported to law enforcement, and then the law enforcement group at the state or county level must actually report the crime into national databases that track crime rates.[26] Additionally, sexual crimes are the least likely group of crimes to be reported to law enforcement because the offender often is someone in the victim's family or someone close to the victim; this is especially true of crimes against children.[27] Female sexual crimes are even less likely to be reported because of the stigma that victims experience, cultural stereotypes that have helped to obscure sexual crimes by females, and feminist frameworks that have dominated the public's view that females are victims while ignoring sexual crimes committing by females, especially those committed by mothers.[28]

Information from national crime reports in the United States indicates that both adult and adolescent females are entering the criminal justice system at higher rates than ever before for violent and nonviolent crimes, including sexual crimes.[29] As of 2005, women offenders represented 23 percent of adult probationers and 12 percent of parolees in communities (Glaze & Bonczar, 2006). National crime statistics on violent crimes in the United States (Rand, 2009) indicate that females represent 7 percent of all reported arrests for sexual offenses against people *12 years and older*, placing the number of victims of female sexual offending at approximately 14,265 victims during 2008. Given that sexual crimes are not readily reported and that female sexual crimes are even less likely to be detected or reported, the number of victims of female sex offenders is considered much higher than what is reported in official crime statistics.[30] Craig Allen (1991) estimated that, on the basis of population figures and prevalence rates of sexual abuse at the time of his analysis, an accumulative total of 1.5 million females and 1.6 million males would have been sexually abused by females in their childhood. Within the *juvenile court system, adolescent females* are responsible for 3 percent of forcible rape cases and 5 percent of other violent sex offenses.[31] More specifically according to the Center for Sex Offender Management (2007a), between 1997 and 2002, "juvenile cases involving female-perpetrated forcible rape and other violent sex offenses, and non-violent sex offenses rose by 6%, 62% and 42% respectively" (p. 2).[32] Similar to adult females, a majority of adolescent females victimize children entrusted in their care (siblings, other child family members, and children in the community), committing acts of sexual abuse that include penetration, forcible oral sex, and genital fondling.[33]

A U.S. Department of Justice Report (Snyder, 2000) on the sexual assault of children *11 years of age and younger* indicates that female offenders are most common in sexual assault against victims *under age 6*. For these youngest victims, females were 12 percent of their offenders.[34] Females also accounted for 6 percent of sexual assaults for child victims in the age range of 6 to 12 years old.[35] The majority of these young victims are children (defined as 11 years of age and younger) and older youth (defined as 12 to 17 years of age) in the direct care of females who are their mother or other family member or females employed in the role of day care/home care provider, educator, or youth worker.[36] Among the types of sexual crimes committed by women against children are forcible rape (oral, anal, and vaginal penetration) that includes sexual assault with an object, sexual fondling, and sexual exploitation that includes pornography and prostitution (Snyder, 2000).

In Great Britain, Vanessa George and Angela Allen were convicted in December 2009[37] of possessing, making, and distributing indecent images (i.e., child pornography) and committing sexual assaults on children, some under the age of one year; this is an example of the type of sexual offenses and level of exploitation that females can commit against children. Vanessa George worked in a day care center where she had access to children to make the pornographic images and commit the sexual assaults depicted in the images. She then distributed the pornographic images to a man she met on Facebook who in turn introduced George to Angela Allen. Together the three of them exchanged pornographic images of children. Police suspect that up to 30 children in the day care center where Vanessa George was employed were abused and exploited in this manner; however, at the time of her conviction, George refused to identify the children she had victimized. Police investigators emphasize that neither of the two women was groomed, coerced, or forced by Colin Blanchard, the male involved in the criminal acts . Rather, all three adults were equal participants, and George in particular violated the trust of the children in her care and that of their parents.[38]

Females fulfill various roles as caretakers to children as parents, teachers, nurses, and youth workers. The caretaking roles that are often held by women allow a female intent on committing sexual abuse to manipulate a victim in a similar manner that a male offender would in a similar position of authority and trust. Mothers have no need to groom their child victims given that they have control over the children in their homes. However, because of a lack of information regarding human sexuality and stereotypes surrounding female sexuality, along with the prominent view that sexual abuse is more likely to come from a man than a woman, and the greater physical contact and freedom that females are given with children, maternal sex offenders have a greater capacity to camouflage their sexual crimes in their caretaking relationships and to exonerate or excuse themselves simply on the fact that they are female.[39] Mothers cause considerable harm when they commit sexual abuse against their sons and daughters. Mothers often commit sexual abuse against their children alongside other abuses, such as emotional, verbal, and physical abuse.[40] Mothers also place their children at additional risk when they establish relationships with other adults who share their sexual offending beliefs and deviant sexual behavior.[41] When mothers are single, children who are sexually abused by them may have no other parent available to tell about their mother's abuse.[42] A study in Sweden found that among female sex offenders, 69 percent were single, 69 percent were mothers, and 32 percent had committed violent crimes other than sexual crimes.[43]

Female sexual offenders outside the family violate the trust they are given to protect and care for children. They exploit a younger child's physical dependency and need for affection, and can take advantage of a teen's curiosity and excitement about their developing sexuality. Females who sexually abuse children and teens are acting on their sexual deviance (i.e., sexual behavior with children) and predatory needs in a similar manner as male offenders—but with a greater ability to fool the public.[44] Females are able to manipulate and deceive not only the children they sexually abuse but also the adults around them. They, like male sex offenders, commit their sexual crimes rather than choosing to seek help to prevent their sexual offending and the harm they cause to those they abuse (Duncan, 2004).

Official *crime reports* for sexual offenses provide only partial insight into the characteristics of the crimes committed by female sexual offenders. Because of the low number of reported sexual crimes into law enforcement, researchers conduct prevalence studies among the general population[45] or in specific targeted groups, such as school-age youth,[46] to gain a better understanding of the frequency of sexual victimization and offending. *Prevalence studies* indicate higher victimization rates for sexual offenses when compared to crime reports since they are designed to focus on information gained primarily through surveys of the general population.[47] Prevalence studies ask questions regarding the experience of sexual victimization regardless of whether the victimization experience was reported to law enforcement.[48] Prevalence studies are limited because of researchers not specifically asking about female sexual offenders when surveys are conducted or not designing specific questions that cover the types of sexual offenses that are committed by females.[49] Even with their limitations, prevalence studies confirm that females are involved in a greater number of child sexual abuse cases than what is reported to law enforcement and reflected in crime statistics, and they commit a greater amount of sexual aggression in adult populations than what is indicated in crime reports.[50] For example, an early population study by Russell (1984) that was conducted in San Francisco was one of the first to identify female relatives (primarily mothers) as sexual offenders against children.

Bumby and Bumby (1997) reviewed retrospective studies of specialized population samples that included college students and incarcerated males and found that specialized samples yielded a wider range (between 2% and 78%) of adults having been sexually abused in childhood by a female. Johnson et al. (2006) identified that among 100 incarcerated males reporting child sexual abuse, 70 percent of the reported perpetrators were female. Within this incarcerated population of males, 59 percent of the men reported experiencing some form of sexual abuse before puberty with the first episode of sexual abuse beginning at an average age of 9.6 years. The females who committed sexual abuse against the men when they were boys were identified by the inmates as either friends or family members. Kaplan and Green (1995) found that self-report studies on adult survivors of child sexual abuse indicated that between 4 and 60 percent of sexual perpetrators had been female. Condy, Templer, Brown, and Veaco (1987) found a higher prevalence for adult female sexual contact with younger boys when they surveyed male college students and incarcerated men offenders.[51] The study also found that incarcerated women in their survey sample reported sexual intercourse with children that they had sexually abused and that these women's penetration of youth was more frequent than what is usually reported by male sex offenders. The women in the Condy et al. study were not necessarily incarcerated for sexual offenses, indicating that there is a group of female offenders convicted for crimes other than sexual offenses and whose sexual crimes against children are not being detected or reported. Penetration of victims or having victims penetrate them has been found in other studies reporting on the types of offenses committed by females (Andersson & Ho-Foster, 2008). Kaufman, Wallace, Johnson, and Reeder (1995), in their study of 53 victims of female sexual offenders, found that 23 of the children victimized by female offenders had been penetrated with foreign objects. Penetration with objects appears to be a sexual offense particular to female sex offenders and is something that investigators should ask about when interviewing victims and that researchers should include in their population surveys.

There is also a growing body of research that indicates that college-age females use a range of sexually aggressive behavior to coerce their dating partners into sexual behavior. Female sexual aggression is decidedly different than female sexual assertiveness, but this distinction may not be evident in the studies by researchers who report on college-based sexual violence and aggression. In addition, researchers need to be aware of a personal bias to perhaps consider female aggression as "assertiveness" rather than as coercive, nonconsensual sexual behavior. Female sexual aggression includes sexual stalking through Internet social network sites; taking advantage of a male's incapacitated state to have sexual intercourse (what is referred to as "date rape"); psychological coercion against males, such as threats of self-harm and suicide; spreading rumors of sexual impotency if a male does not comply with the sexual coercion; threatening to tell that a young man had sex outside a committed relationship, whether he did or not, in order to gain sexual compliance; using or threatening the use of physical force, especially against a male who, through his own socialization, is taught not to hit or harm a female.[52] This finding has implications for federally funded educational programs that are mandated to focus on the prevention of sexual assault to women on college campuses so consequently the focus may not include the prevention of female sexual aggression.[53] A lack of recognizing the victimization of college males by females has the potential to impede men to join in the efforts on college campuses to end sexual violence against females. In addition, programs that ignore the mutual sexual aggression that occurs between males and females may be less likely to achieve their overall goal of prevention if they are not addressing the full spectrum of sexual violence as it occurs in contemporary society.[54] It is important to consider that where sexual violence prevention programs began 30 years ago may not be where they need to be today in terms of addressing the reality of sexual crimes committed by females (Levine, 2006). Prevention education and awareness programs that lack current information on female sexual offending may inadvertently perpetuate female sexual crimes not only on college campuses but in the broader communities in which young people reside, socialize, attend school, and work.[55]

DIVERSE CHARACTERISTICS OF FEMALE SEX OFFENDERS

A broader context of female sexual offending allows for a more complete understanding of the sexual crimes committed by women that includes identifying the victims they target, what methods females use to control their victims, the level of violence committed during their sexual crimes and the resulting harm to victims, and the location where female sexual offenses occur. This depth of information is critical to identifying what criminologists refer to as "modus operandi," which is the predictable pattern of behavior that a perpetrator displays during the period prior to, during, and following the commission of a crime.[56] Research on the modus operandi of female sex offenders is seriously lacking, impeding the identification, reporting, and prosecution of female sexual offenders.[57] Not understanding the offending process of female sex offenders and the risk factors that contribute to and maintain female sexual crime impedes the development of valid risk assessment instruments for female sex offenders and the development of sex offender treatment for females in order to prevent reoffending.[58] Prevention is the key to establishing a society free of sexual violence and its effects on human beings.

A study by Kaufman et al. (1995) is one of the few that looked at comparing the modus operandi of female and male sexual offenders against children. Kaufman and colleagues compared 53 children sexually abused by females with 53 children sexually abused by males. They found that there were similarities and differences in the offending patterns of females when compared to males. Similarities between male and female offenders were in the types of sexual abuse committed, such as fondling by the abuser, genital contact without penetration, and oral contact by the assailant. However, female sex offenders were more likely to penetrate with objects, allow other adults to use the child, and force children or teens to commit sexual acts against other children. Sexual exploitation of victims and forcing sexual acts between children was also found in a study by Faller (1987) where the majority of child offenders were mothers and other family members. Whether this offending pattern is true of a majority of female child sex offenders is not yet known with any certainty.

It is important to keep in mind that while the sexual crimes committed by females are most often targeted toward children and teens, females also commit sexual crimes against adults, both males and females, in heterosexual and same-sex partner relationships.[59] Equally important is to remember that not all states in the United States or other countries have laws that address female sexual offending. For example, Great Britain recently updated its laws to include oral penetration in the definition of rape and made significant changes in defining consent to improve prosecution of reported sexual offenders; however, British law still defines rape as penetration with a penis.[60] Therefore, sexual offenses committed by females may or may not be covered under laws and statutes in a given state or country.[61]

A recent study from England by Gannon, Rose, and Ward (2008) on the offending processes of convicted female sex offenders documented that females will sexually offend against other females. The study identified that the female sex offenders were motivated by revenge and the desire to humiliate a victim and to teach the victim a lesson.[62] While group (gang) sexual assault is also found to occur by males,[63] the idea that females will also commit sexual assault in a group or with a single female co-offender is another characteristic of female sexual offending not previously considered, even though females, sexually assaulting in this manner, have been documented in previous studies. For example, Kaplan and Green (1995), in their study on female sex offenders, reported a participant who, during her incarceration, "had been raped by two female prisoners with an object on two occasions" (p. 293). Nelson (1994) referred to an incident reported by Evert (1987) of a female prisoner who "had her clitoris chewed off by another female prisoner." Female-to-female sexual violence in lesbian relationships is also documented by Girshick (2002) who noted that "denial of female perpetrators means they are free to move on to the next victim" (p. 10).

Sarrel and Masters (1982) were among the first to publish on the sexual assault of men by women. Their case studies included: (a) A 37-year-old white married male assaulted by two African American women who forced him to have intercourse and performed fellatio on him at gunpoint and (b) a 17-year-old male involved being entrapped by a group of two older men and three older women who threatened him with physical violence if he tried to get away. He was masturbated manually and fellated three times, resulting in forced erection and ejaculation. All of the males included in the case reports suffered enduring adverse effects as a consequence of their sexual victimization by women that lasted between two and seven years after the sexual assaults. A third case presented by Sarrel and Masters is typical of what has been described as "date rape" in the literature when women experience sexual violence from male acquaintances and dating partners. This case involved a 27-year-old, male truck driver. The case, as it was presented by Sarrel and Masters, is summarized here as an example of the extent of sexual assault that adult men can experience by women and the adverse effects that occur in its aftermath. The man described how, after arriving at a motel with a woman he had met in a bar, he was given a drink, shortly thereafter fell asleep, and, when he awoke, found himself "naked, tied hand and foot to a bedstead, gagged and blindfolded. As he listened to voices in the room, it was evident that several women were present." Sarrel and Masters reported that during his captivity, perhaps "four different women used him sexually, some of them a number of times," and that the man was "manipulated to erection and mounted" until he ejaculated. He described how he was repeatedly restimulated to erection against his will. Following the first two coercive sexual episodes, he did not ejaculate. As it became increasingly difficult for him to maintain an erection, "he was threatened with castration and felt a knife held to his scrotum." This level of sexual assault and aggression continued, according to the man, for "more than 24 hours." When the women decided to release him, "his feet were untied and he was dressed and taken by automobile to an isolated area where, still blindfolded with hands loosely tied, he was pushed from the car" (pp. 120–121). He suffered long-term sexual dysfunction following the rape. When the man eventually married, he was not able to consummate his marriage, and it was at this point in his life that he sought professional support.

His wife was unaware of the history of her husband's sexual assault by a group of women offenders.

Women sexually assaulting men and committing group sexual crimes against men and women are but two examples from the literature that challenge stereotypes surrounding female sexual offending. From these case reports and other studies on female sexual offenders it is being confirmed that female sexual crimes are diverse; potentially involve violence; occur in a variety of situations and in different relationships, including family members, strangers, and acquaintances; and involve victims across age-groups, gender, and ethnicity.

DO MEN COERCE WOMEN TO COMMIT SEXUAL CRIMES?

The early literature on female sexual offenders identified that the offense patterns of some females committing sexual crimes might potentially include a male partner, while other females commit their sexual offenses independently of another person (Faller, 1987; Matthews, 1989; McCarty, 1986). As a result of these early studies, researchers proposed three categories to identify this potential matrix in the offending patterns of females to include (a) *independent offender*, a female who commits sexual offenses on her own without a male partner; (b) *accomplice offender*, a female who commits sexual offenses in cooperation with a partner without coercion; and (c) *coerced offender*, a female who commits sexual offenses with a dominant partner, often identified as a male who is viewed as the primary instigator of the sexual offense and coerces a female (particularly a mother) into sexual offending, most often in the context of domestic violence (Matthews, 1989; McCarty, 1986).

There are concerns and questions that arise regarding the proposed *coerced offender* category. These include (a) exclusion of the possibility of a female coercing a male (or another female), which may indicate the possibility of heterosexism or an inflexible view of offending roles between offending partners, and (b) that a standardized male coerced offender criterion has not been substantiated for the specific cases where researchers have suggested that male coercion occurred. Given the potential for deception among individuals charged with sexual crimes and child sexual crimes in particular, it is critical that the female offender's report by itself not be the basis for substantiating a report of coercion.[64] This becomes a particularly important question regarding maternal sexual offenders who claim male coercion, because as women and mothers, they are aware of the social stereotypes available to them to place blame for their sexual offending onto a male offender and to deny their own deviant sexual interest in children.[65]

The coerced offender category also has the potential to reflect a particular sociopolitical or biased view of sexual offending and victimization rather than the reality of a particular sexual crime committed by a particular individual. Jackie Turton (2007) cautions against the assumption of a male coercer and shares that "it is hard to avoid the general assumption of male coercion, and there are still some professionals who explain all female perpetrators as male-coerced. For instance, Julia manages a therapeutic unit for abused children and their families. She suggested that men influence women, not necessarily in terms of individual coercion but as a group, and that women have been changed and perhaps coerced by patriarchy into behaving abusively" (p. 48).

The view that a male partner can psychologically, economically, or physically coerce a woman partner into sexual offending or that the mother is unable (rather than unwilling) to report the sexual abuse of her child is grounded in the early literature on father–daughter incest where a mother was viewed as a covictim or a coconspirator (rather than a co-offender) in the sexual abuse of her child (primarily a daughter). This dominant view of mothers in the context of child sexual abuse has continued in current studies on nonoffending parents where the main focus of research and treatment intervention remains on mothers and seldom includes fathers as non-offending parents directly.[66] It is also important to keep in mind that the view of females as *victims of dominant males* was developed in the historical context and sociopolitical view arising from radical feminist scholarship.[67] This particular feminist framework has been a significant influence in the literature on child sexual abuse and adult rape for several years.[68] It may be that this traditional framework, even with its apparent limitations and possible bias, continues to have an influence on how female violence is viewed and child sexual abuse in particular is framed (i.e., coercion of a female by a dominant male). This sociopolitical framework of violence may influence some groups of the public, law enforcement, and professional opinions in spite of the evidence indicating that females are capable and willing to exert violence against others without the influence or presence of a male, and perhaps under the influence of another female, and that they do so beginning in the early stages of their social development (e.g., sibling abuse, female bullies, and teen dating violence).[69]

What is critical to this discussion is that a potential to view women as less accountable for the sexual abuse they commit creates a risk of providing less protection to victims and children in particular. Additionally, when females are not reported, investigated, and prosecuted for their crimes, there is the potential that some of their offense beliefs are reinforced (e.g., "The kid wasn't hurt if no one touched them" and "It happened to me and I lived through it" or "The church knew it was going on so it must be okay"[70] and

"The victim is young and so won't remember this" or "If I do this, it will be less harmful than if he messes with her" and even "I suppose I thought well I've been left to bring her up on my own, he knows more about kids than I do"[71]), and therefore their sexually abusive behavior continues. In addition, without prosecution and conviction, there is no potential for monitoring by law enforcement of the female offender. When accountability is not specifically attributed, intervention by Child Protective Services (CPS) may not be sufficient to address the ongoing harm to children from parental offenders who are at risk of continuing a lifestyle that contributes to future sexual offenses and other forms of child maltreatment.[72]

Catherine Faller (1995) addressed the absence of protection to children in her study of 72 females identified for the sexual abuse of 332 children. Faller found that only 3 of the 72 women had criminal charges filed against them and that attempts to prosecute the women were unsuccessful. Faller identified that the most common legal intervention was an investigation by CPS and that protective action took place primarily through the juvenile court system (not criminal court) and that this level of protective action occurred only in "almost half the cases" (p. 24), leaving the rest of the children with *no action* for protection. Faller also examined the records where legal intervention took place to determine what level of protection was afforded to this group of children. Faller defined the protection that was provided to children as protected, some protected/some not protected and unprotected. Examples of the protection categories include: (a) *protected*—a mother's parental rights were terminated, a day care center's license was revoked, or a child care worker was fired; (b) *some protected/some not*—the woman did not have access to some of her victims but did have access to others; when the offender no longer had contact with identified victims but had ready access to other children (this category of protection was applied to cases where a mother had supervised visits with her victims but was allowed to have stepchildren in her care); a mother lost custody of her child victim but gave birth to another child and was allowed to retain custody; and identified victims were removed from an abusive child care situation, but the woman continued to provide care for children in other day care centers that she owned where those licenses were not revoked; and (c) *unprotected*—when a female offender continued to have unsupervised access to her victims after intervention.

Faller provides the following observation on the protection (and lack of it) to children sexually victimized by females; despite the general severity of these cases, remarkably few women suffered serious consequences because of their behavior. About a third had continued access to their victims or other potential victims. Moreover, there was an apparent reluctance to criminally prosecute these women, and there were no successful prosecutions. The lack of punitive intervention in our sample may be another indication of denial of female perpetration highlighted by Allen (1990, 1991). Alternatively, such behavior by women may not be seen by authorities as very harmful.

When reviewing the category of "coerced female sex offender" in the context of providing protection to children, it becomes imperative that researchers not obscure the harm inflicted by mothers who commit sexual crimes or automatically deflect the accountability for female sexual offenses onto males. Equally important is the recognition that children, sexually victimized by parents and other caregivers in co-offending relationships, are suffering multiple abuses from multiple offenders.[73] It may be that it is this group of child victims that endure the most adverse outcomes of sexual abuse as a result of multiple traumas by multiple offenders across stages of their development and where a mother is central to the sexual offending.[74]

Bunting (2005) suggests that "co-offending is an important issue which can impact professional responses because it raises questions over the degree of involvement and responsibility females have for their behavior" (p. 258). Given that female sexual offending is a new and developing field of inquiry, it would be prudent for clinicians and researchers alike not to assume male coercion as a precursor to female sexual offending. It is also important to be aware of a tendency to reframe female sexual offending into a more culturally scripted construct, such as male coercion. Johansson-Love and Fremouw (2009) found that both female sex offenders and female offenders of nonsexual crimes had coperpetrators, suggesting that for some females committing criminal acts with other people may simply be a part of their offending pattern or that females "may justify-excuse their behavior by having an accomplice" (p. 374). Caution therefore is warranted when considering male coercion as it might (or might not) relate to female sexual offending until specific and measurable criteria can be established to support this determination. Such criteria would allow an objective evaluation as to whether coercion by a partner actually took place, under what circumstances, for how long, and in what manner and whether options were available to a mother other than engaging in sexual offenses against a child.[75]

As research on female sexual offenders becomes available, a reality is that a majority of known females commit sexual offenses *without male or female partners*. Ferguson and Meehan (2005) analyzed the case records of 279 female sex offenders convicted of 940 separate offenses in the state of Florida and found that 97.3 percent of the females were solo offenders, acting alone. Additionally, they found that 43 of the female sex offenders who were given probation or parole had committed previous sexual crimes, indicating that females do reoffend even after conviction from their first sexual crime, placing potential future victims at risk when female sex offenders are in the community and not sufficiently monitored by law enforcement. A history of previous sex crimes has been found to be a significant risk factor in the likelihood of reoffending in females (Sandler & Freeman, 2009)[76] as it has for males.[77]

Sgroi and Sargent (1993) found that among the 10 female sex offenders in their study, three of the females acted alone. Of interest to the question of male coercion and female sexual offending were the findings by Sgroi and Sargent that females who were initially male coerced began to offend alone. This indicates that even when male coercion does exist, it may not always be the reason that females continue their criminal behavior; female sexual offenders may have more diverse and interchangeable offending patterns in a co-offender relationship. Nathan and Ward (2002) reported that among the women in their study who co-offended with a male, less than half the women reported being coerced. Instead, the women reported offending because of motivations of jealousy, rejection, and revenge, all independent motivations. These types of motivations were also found among female sex offenders in a recent study in England where the females identified that they sexually offended in a group.[78] These findings are not that surprising, especially in the context that male and female sexual offenders may be more similar in their sexual offending behavior than previously thought.[79]

Vandiver (2006b), accessing the 2001 National Incident-Based Reporting System (NIBRS),[80] a database on reported crimes from 21 states and Washington, D.C., identified that females acting alone comprised 54 percent of the total number of female sex offenders reported into the database. Vandiver was able to collect information only on females where offenses were known to law enforcement at the time of her study. Since not all states report into the NIBRS, this database was not representative of the number of female sex offenders in the criminal justice system at the time of Vandiver's study. Vandiver noted that because co-offending females are thought to come to the attention of law enforcement more often because of their involvement with a male offender, it was significant to find that females committing sexual crimes independent of a male offender composed the larger percentage of female sex offenders.

A study by Bader, Scalora, Casady, and Black (2008) compared female perpetrators litigated by Child Protective Services (CPS) to female perpetrators litigated in the criminal justice system and found a higher number of female sex offenders in the CPS system (n = 179) when compared to female sex offenders in the *criminal justice system* (n = 57). Bader et al. also found that in the CPS sample, a majority of the child victims were under the age of 12 (74.9%), while a majority of the victims in the criminal justice system were between the ages of 13 and 19 (73.8%). The study also found that CPS had a higher number of sexual abuse cases that were incest (*intrafamilial*) cases (97.8%), while the criminal justice sample had a majority of nonincest (*extrafamilial*) cases (63.3%). In further comparison of the two samples of female sex offenders, *CPS had a higher number of girl victims* (63.7%), *while the criminal justice sample had a majority of boy victims* (62.1%); with both groups indicating that female sex offenders abuse both boys and girls. The child protection sample indicated that females acted independently of a co-offender in 71.4 percent of the sexual abuse cases and with a co-offender in 28.6 percent of the cases. The criminal justice sample indicated that females acted independently of a co-offender in 75.4 percent of sexual abuse cases and with a co-offender in 24.6 percent of the cases. This study indicates that *independent female sex offenders* may be the greater number of female sexual offenders across both the criminal justice system and the child protective system. Bader and colleagues concluded that "cases in the criminal justice system sample tended to include older, male victims who were not related to the female perpetrator, while the cases in the CPS sample tended to involve younger, female victims who were related to the female perpetrator" (p. 116). As explained by Circuit Court Judge K. Mark Loyd, "Females in the child protection system would primarily be mothers, maybe a step-mother, but given that child protection only works with families, then most likely the females are a parent that committed the sexual offense."

Bader et al. (2008) also respond to the issue of male coercion regarding female sexual offending stating that "although earlier research suggested that women were often coerced into sexual offending by a male co-offender both the CPS sample and the criminal justice sample had approximately three quarters of the women perpetrating alone. This finding is consistent with more recent studies that show a majority of women acting alone" (p. 177) in committing sexual offenses. Regarding what database researchers draw on in their studies of female sexual offenders Bader and colleagues offer this insight:

> In conclusion, these findings have important implications for both research and clinical practice. Significant differences between criminal justice and CPS samples highlight the importance of examining samples that have been drawn from both sources to describe the true nature of female sexual offending. The finding that most cases of female perpetrated sexual assault did not lead to criminal justice involvement also suggests that clinicians will most often encounter perpetrators and victims in clinical settings rather than forensic or correctional ones. (p. 117)

Unfortunately, the Vandiver (2006b) study did not provide analysis regarding the relationship between victim and female offender in terms of identifying intrafamilial female offenders from extrafamilial female offenders as did the Bader et al. (2008) study. However, the two studies are compatible in terms of indicating that a majority of female sex offenders appear to be committing their crimes alone and in the absence of a male offender. Therefore, male coercion of female sexual offenders should not be immediately assumed or readily anticipated in studies of female sexual offenders or in treatment programs working with female perpetrators of sexual crimes.

FEMALE SEX OFFENDERS AND VIOLENCE

A much-quoted phrase when discussing what has prevented the acknowledgment of the harm that females cause to their victims is credited to Mathis (1972) in his book *Clear Thinking About Sexual Deviation*. In reference to female sexual abuse, Mathis stated, "That she might seduce a helpless child into sex play is unthinkable, and even if she did so, what harm could be done without a penis?" (p. 54). Thirty-seven years later, this view of female sexual abuse can still permeate societal beliefs about female sex offenders, the injuries they commit, and the resulting harm they cause to their victims.[81] Mathis, like others, view sexual abuse as "rape" when in fact rape (traditionally defined as forced penetration of the vagina by a penis) is but one type of sexual offense that can be committed against a human being and the use of a penis but one way to penetrate a victim. Studies have not yet been conducted to indicate if the harm is greater to a victim when penetrated with objects or if the emotional repercussions are longer lasting when compared to traditional rape. Several years later, it would be interesting to hear what Mathis might say knowing what we now know about female sexual offending. While some male sexual offenders are known to be sadistic and violent when committing rape and other types of sexual offenses,[82] females commit sadistic and violent acts in the commission of their sexual offenses as well.[83] Ferguson and Meehan (2005) conducted an analysis of the criminal records of 279 convicted female sex offenders in the criminal justice system in the state of Florida. They were surprised by the level of violence this group of females had committed during their sexual crimes. The authors noted that the rate of female violence "exceeded those observed in general male samples of child sexual abusers" (p. 86). The authors considered whether females who committed physical violence during their sexual crimes were more likely to be incarcerated. Allen (1991) suggested that only the most serious offenses committed by females result in judicial action, which is one explanation for a higher level of violence in this group of females. Ferguson and Meehan (2005) also proposed that "female sexual offenders may gradually become more aggressive over time, increasing the amount of force directed toward their victims" (p. 83), but they did not offer an explanation as to the reason female sex offenders might become more aggressive, nor did they consider that there simply may be a group of female sex offenders who begin their sexual offense histories with violence and continue this pattern as part of their offending. The violence committed by this group of convicted female sex offenders occurred across 940 separate criminal offenses. The acts of violence included mutilation and disfigurement (severe genital damage and permanent scarring), aggravated assault (hitting and kicking resulting in visible physical injury), simple assault (pushing, holding down, and restraining with no visible physical injury), and threats of violence.

Similar to the Florida study, other studies indicate that female sex offenders use violence and physical force at the same or similar level as males.[84] A recent study by Miller, Turner, and Henderson (2009) found that when comparing a group of incarcerated female sexual offenders with a group of incarcerated male sexual offenders, the two groups did not differ significantly on their rate of violent offenses. Sgroi and Sargent (1993) found in their investigation of victims sexually abused by females that among the offenses committed against victims were forcing sexual acts with animals, bondage, routine insertion of enemas, penetration with objects, and forcing children to witness sexual acts. Sgroi and Sargent also found that victims reported experiencing physical and emotional abuse by the female offender when the sexual abuse was not occurring, and that victims experienced these other abuses during the sexual abuse. Female sex offenders committing multiple types of child abuse was also found by Elliot (1993a, 1993b), Finkelhor (1994), Finkelhor and Russell (1984), Krug (1989), Lisak (1994), Mitchell and Morse (1998), Ogilvie (2004), and Rosencrans (1997). Child sexual abuse occurring in the context of other types of family violence has also been cited by Duncan (2004), so it is not a surprise that female sex offenders commit multiple abuses, particularly against children.

Saradjian (1996), in her report on 50 females who sexually abused at least 68 children, confirms the sexual deviance of females who commit sexual abuse. Among the findings by Saradjian was that 14 of the women admitted *gaining sexual arousal* from the children's pain. Regarding the length of time that the sexual abuse occurred, Saradjian identified a range of 2.3 years to 4.1 years before the sexual abuse was detected. The women in Saradjian's study tended to abuse children beginning when the children were quite young, and the abuse continued over a long period of time, and this was especially true if the female offenders were the biological mothers of the child victims. The author states that "this finding goes a long way to dispelling the myth that sexual abuse by women is misconstrued as inappropriate expressions of affection" (p. 31). Saradjian's study also gives support to the view by Plummer (1981) that female sexual deviance can be a part of the sexual offending patterns of females and that a pedophilic tendency by females should not be so easily dismissed. Sexual motivations for female sexual offending is seldom discussed in the literature or investigated in studies on female sexual offenders.

The findings also suggest that female sexual offending is not a single incident and that the detection and reporting of female sexual abuse is important to ending the sexual abuse and disrupting the adverse outcomes to children.

Finkelhor and Russell (1984) found in their national study on child sexual abuse that maternal sexual abuse often occurred along with physical abuse and that the children sexually abused by females were younger than the child victims of males. In 1996, a study by the National Center on Child Abuse and Neglect indicated in the United States that females accounted for 25 percent of reported child sexual abuse.[85] This group of children, victimized primarily by mothers, equated to approximately 36,000 children having experienced sexual crimes by their primary female caretaker. Together, these reports refute previous claims that child sexual abuse by females is rare and provide support to developing a more current perspective on the prevalence of female sexual offending and increasing awareness that female sexual abuse may often co-occur with physical abuse when perpetrated by a mother or other primary female caretaker (e.g., stepmother, adopted mother, or foster mother). Sexual abuse should be investigated when other types of child abuse are reported, and other types of abuses should be investigated when child sexual abuse is reported.

As stated previously, females are known to use objects in the penetration of their victims causing severe physical injury that includes genital mutilation, hymeneal, and anal tears; sexually transmitted infections are also known to occur from female sexual abuse.[86] Rosencrans (1997), in a comprehensive study of 93 female and 9 male survivors of maternal incest, listed all the objects this group of maternal sex offenders used against their children. The objects identified by Rosencrans included enema devices, sticks, candles, vibrators, pencils, keys, hairbrushes, hairbrush handles, lightbulbs, soapy washcloths, wooden spoons, various fruits and vegetables, knives, scissors, lit cigarettes, sock-darning tools, surgical knives, hair rollers, religious medals, vacuum cleaner parts, and goldfish (and I would add soda bottles and Barbie dolls as reported by a female client sexually abused by her mother in this manner).

How often a woman might murder her victim is relatively unknown, but there are confirmed cases where a woman has killed during the commission of a sex crime. A woman in the Correctional Service of Canada (1995)[87] and one incarcerated at a Florida prison (2005)[88] are documented as murdering their victims during the commission of their sex crimes. In the charges against Melissa Huckaby indicted in April 2009 for the kidnapping and murder of eight-year-old Sandra Cantu in San Joaquin County, California, are included charges of rape with a foreign object indicative of "genital trauma consistent with forcible penetration."[89]

An important variable that can help explain the levels of violence by female sex offenders and is missing among studies on female sexual offenders and their use of violence is assessment of psychopathy. Psychopathy is identified in the literature as a characteristic of an individual's personality construct and character that has the potential to distinguish male sex offenders in the general categories of sex offender typologies for males (Rosenberg, Abel, & Mackie, 2005). Psychopathy has direct clinical application regarding risk assessment, legal disposition (e.g., incarceration, community supervision), and treatment parameters (Rosenberg et al., 2005). While all child sexual abuse is a violation of a child's personal boundaries and an act of aggression, research indicates that sex offenders who engage in both sexual violation and other types of violence are more psychopathic than sex offenders who do not and that sex offenders with elevated measures of psychopathy indicate greater sexual deviance (as cited by Rosenberg et al., 2005), and with increased violence and sexual deviance comes a greater risk for reoffending and, most important, a greater level of harm to the potential victim that would include sexual murders.[90]

Cleckley (1988) provided indicators of psychopathy as including a superficial charm and manner, egocentricity and lack of regard for others, inability to tell the truth, insincerity and deceit, poverty of affect, lack of insight, a general absence of remorse, and antisocial behavior. Hare (1996) defined characteristics of psychopathy as including egocentricity as indicated by selfishness and self-absorption, lack of genuine remorse, lack of empathy, pathological lying, manipulativeness, and the persistent violations of social norms. A study by Rosenberg et al. (2005) using the Psychopathy Checklist—Revised (PCL-R) found a relationship between *psychopathy and physical violence* and that this relationship distinguished among three groups of male sex offenders (same-sex extrafamilial offenders, opposite-sex extrafamilial offenders, and incest offenders). The results of the study indicate that male sex offenders who use physical violence against the children they sexually abused were significantly more psychopathic than those who did not. The use of violence and psychopathy as measured by the PCL-R was found across the three groups of *male child sex offenders.* The results of the study also indicate that physical violence and sexual abuse can occur to child victims whether the offender is related to the child or not related and whether the child victim is male, female, or a family member. The studies also found that psychopathy may indicate which individual sex offender is at greater risk for violent recidivism in the commission of sexual offenses. Rosenberg and colleagues offered the following insight and recommendation:

> Clinicians and other individuals who deal with child sexual offenders may well want to consider the psychopathy levels of the men they encounter clinically, because more psychopathic offenders appear to be both more violent and more criminally versatile. Knowledge of this tendency may make it easier for clinicians to make accurate

judgments about this population. One of the most difficult questions when dealing with child sexual offenders is how to assess their dangerousness, and a multi-faceted evaluation of risk is likely to be necessary. (p. 64)

The recommendation by Rosenberg et al. can also apply to female sex offenders and is especially important in the context of crime reports that indicate that females are more likely to commit sexual crimes against children 12 years old and younger and that children 6 years old and younger may be particularly vulnerable to a female/mother with psychopathic tendencies committing physical violence against the child along with sexual violence. This finding may also have relevancy to the higher rate of child deaths/murders committed by mothers when compared to fathers or other adults.[91] Given the characteristics of psychopathy and the prevailing stereotypes that can still confound the perspectives on female violence and sexual offending, it would be useful for mental health professionals working in cooperation with the criminal justice system and CPS to assess female sex offenders for psychopathy. It is most likely that the previous study in Florida that found high rates of violence among the female sexual offenders considered a group of psychopathic female sexual offenders, a much more dangerous group of female sex offenders than might have been considered by the authors of the study.

PRIOR SEXUAL VICTIMIZATION AND FEMALE SEXUAL OFFENDING

The experience of childhood sexual abuse has been found to be significant in the lives of females seeking mental health services,[92] substance abuse treatment,[93] and medical services.[94] The trauma of childhood sexual abuse has also been found to be prominent in the lives of mothers involved in the child protection system whose children have been sexually abused (Duncan, 2004). Because sexual victimization is prominent in the lives of females, it should not come as a surprise that studies examining the social histories and characteristics of females convicted for nonsexual crimes[95] and studies examining social histories and characteristics of female sexual offenders[96] have found that both groups of female offenders report sexual victimization in their social histories.[97] Prior sexual victimization has also been found among incarcerated male sex offenders and males committing nonsexual crimes.[98] Together, these findings have raised the question of whether there is a relationship between prior sexual victimization and sexual offending.[99] At this point in time, the studies are inconclusive; however, as studies become more refined, they may help to shed light on this seemingly interrelated pathway from sexual victimization to sexual offending.

Susan Strickland (2008) completed a study that compared incarcerated female sexual offenders with females incarcerated for nonsexual offenses (female offenders). Both groups of women were incarcerated in three women's prison in the state of Georgia. Strickland did not identify the relationship of the sex offender to her victim, which is a drawback to the study, nor did she identify the *original sex offender* (the person who sexually offended against the female sex offender as a child). Strickland did compare the two groups of female offenders on measures of childhood trauma, including sexual trauma, sexual orientation, personality disorder, chemical dependency, emotional neediness, cognitive distortions, and social competence. Regarding childhood trauma, Strickland found that while both groups of female offenders reported high rates of childhood victimization, the female sex offender group differed in terms of the severity of the childhood trauma they experienced. Strickland concluded that women who became sexual abusers suffered greater overall trauma as children in terms of multiple traumas that included physical abuse, emotional and sexual abuse, and physical neglect than did the female offenders of nonsexual crimes. Strickland suggests that it is not childhood sexual victimization per se that is the risk for future sexual offending but rather the severity and duration of sexual trauma in the context of multiple traumas and that it is this combination of traumas that creates a risk for future sexual offending. Strickland did not find significant differences for personality disorders between the two groups. Christopher, Lutz-Zois, and Reinhardt (2007) found similar findings when comparing female sex offenders with female offenders from a Midwest women's prison. The authors did not find differences between the two groups of female offenders on measures of antisocial or borderline personality disorder, similar to Strickland's study. However, like Strickland, they did find that the sex offender group experienced childhood sexual abuse for a greater duration. Kaplan and Green (1995) found similar results in terms of both groups of incarcerated female offenders reporting prior sexual victimization. The female sex offender group indicated a higher incidence of sexual victimization and physical abuse in childhood and indicated that their childhood sexual victimization was perpetrated exclusively by family members.

A study by Johansson-Love and Fremouw (2009) comparing case files and chart notes of male and female sex offenders with male and female offenders of nonsexual crimes in the West Virginia Department of Corrections found that sexual victimization in the history of female sex offenders was "only partially supported," with 45 percent of the female sex offenders reporting prior sexual victimization and 33 percent of the female offenders of nonsexual crimes also reporting prior sexual abuse. Additionally, the study found that 39 percent of the male sex offenders and 3 percent of the male offenders of nonsexual crimes reported sexual abuse.[100] The female sex offender group did not indicate differences in reported anxiety disorders, such as posttraumatic stress disorder, as compared to the other groups. A limitation of this study is that the information was not determined by standardized measures and the diagnoses cited were not made by mental health professionals since information for all groups of offenders came from case files.

When considering the previously mentioned studies together, it may be that (a) a measure of psychopathy would have discriminated among the groups of male and female sex offenders and the male and female offenders; (b) the personality measures and/or the statistical analysis used in the studies were not able to *distinguish personality structure/disorders* in female offenders of either group;[101] (c) some female offenders incarcerated for nonsexual crimes may have a history of sexual offending that has not been detected or included in the crimes for which they are currently incarcerated, which is a reason for similarities to female sexual offenders and not necessarily that both groups of female offenders experienced prior sexual victimization; and (d) childhood sexual victimization may be *influencing the types of sexual crimes that females commit* and acting as an influence to commit sexual crimes.

McCarty (1986) identified that sexual acts committed by maternal offenders are similar to the sexual acts they reported occurring against them as children. Trauma reenactment from sexual victimization has also been cited by Duncan (2004) to explain women who commit self-injurious behaviors and who appear to be reenacting the original sexual trauma to their own bodies as a result of a deep sense of shame. In the case of female sexual offenders, they may be reenacting the sexual offenses committed against them as children onto their child victims but for different reasons and motivations that may include rage or sexual arousal. Additionally, simply because "trauma reenactment" occurs in other victim groups does not mean that female sexual offending is trauma reenactment. Alternatively, female sexual offenders may commit sexual acts that are familiar to them (i.e., those experienced as a child victim) as suggested by Albert Bandura (1986)[102] in his model of how social behavior and cognitive schemas are learned through modeling.[103] Therefore, sexual offending as a social behavior (e.g., antisocial) and the cognitive schemas (e.g., sex-offending beliefs)[104] are learned by an individual child through experiencing a specific set of circumstances during childhood sexual abuse coupled with the establishment or reinforcement of deviant sexual arousal that has an early onset and repeated over a period of time, and where the sexual abuse along with other abuses are allowed to continue without intervention because of child maltreatment that goes undetected or unreported, or, if child abuse is detected and reported, then adequate intervention is not provided to deter the sexual offending pathway from developing.

In addition, deviant sexual arousal should not be discounted simply because an offender is a female. Therefore, the sexual arousal of females toward their child victims or the arousal they experience from rage, power, and abuse may also serve as a pathway to female sexual offending that may have originated from the sexual abuse and/or was reinforced from the sexual abuse in their childhood. This is a more complex explanation that considers early trauma on the developing brain, learning theory, cognitive schemas, family values, sexual arousal, establishment and reinforcement of deviant sexual arousal, and intrapersonal motivations for sexual offending. What has to be considered in any theoretical framework of a pathway from sexual victimization to sexual offending is that the majority of children, male and female, who experience child sexual abuse do not become offenders, so what delineates the sexual offenders who have experienced sexual victimization?[105]

Alcohol and drug abuse is commonly reported for female offenders of nonsexual crimes and for females in clinical populations reporting a history of childhood sexual abuse; therefore, it has been included in some studies on female sexual offenders.[106] Regarding drug and alcohol abuse, Johansson-Love and Fremouw (2009) found that female sex offenders were the group with the *least* drug and alcohol abuse history when compared to male sex offenders and female offenders of nonsexual crimes. Strickland (2008) also found *no differences* in the abuse of substances between the two groups of female offenders in her study. This finding was also indicated in a Swedish study by Fazel, Sjostedt, Grann, and Langstrom (2007) that found *no significant differences* in substance abuse when comparing female sex offenders and female offenders of nonviolent crimes.

It may be that (a) alcohol and drug use, especially illicit drugs, is but one aspect of the characteristics of female offenders who commit criminal behavior, including sexual crimes; (b) dealing in illicit drugs is another type of criminal behavior that female offenders of both groups engage in for economic reasons; and (c) drugs and alcohol are an outcome of coping long term with sexual victimization but not a causal factor for females who commit sexual crimes. Johansson-Love and Fremouw (2009) suggest that "substance abuse may not play as large of a role in the sex offender population as in other criminal groups because sex offenses may be motivated by sexual drives while 'other' crimes are often motivated/related to substance abuse/addiction" (p. 374). Additionally, female sexual offenders as a diverse group may experience a variety of outcomes because of prior sexual victimization (i.e., depression, psychotic episodes, obsessive-compulsive disorders, posttraumatic stress disorder, and so on) that are unrelated to their sexual offending.[107] This suggested explanation is consistent with findings that some female offenders (incarcerated not for sexual crimes but for other violent and nonviolent crimes) who have experienced sexual victimization use drugs and alcohol to dissociate from the memories of sexual abuse, that is, to avoid the reexperiencing aspects of prior sexual abuse.[108] The use of alcohol and drugs is also documented among females with prior histories of sexual trauma who seek mental health and substance abuse services.[109] Collectively, these findings suggest that there is a group of female victims, a group of female offenders, and a group of female sex offenders who use drugs and alcohol, and while all three groups of females may be engaging in drug and alcohol use as a result of sexual victimization, this does not imply that alcohol and drug use is an antecedent to sexual offending. It is also important to remember that there is also a group of victims of sexual crimes who do not engage in drug and alcohol abuse and a group of female sex offenders who do not engage in drug and alcohol use.

Strickland (2008) found similarities between the female sexual offenders and female offenders in terms of lacking a personal accountability for their crimes and a persistent tendency to "blame the victim" (p. 482). This finding is similar to Johansson-Love and Fremouw's (2009) study that found that female sex offenders had the fewest admissions of guilt for their sexual crimes and "were the least likely to admit guilt when compared to male and female offenders of violent crimes" (p. 372). In examining the results further, it was indicated that *45.2 percent of female sex offenders* and *25.8 percent of male sex offenders* gave *no admission of guilt* to their sexual offenses. Kaplan and Green (1995) found similar results in their study where the female sexual offenders either denied their offenses or greatly minimized the consequences of harm they caused to their victims. These findings are similar to what Craig Allen (1991) reported in his study indicating that female sex offenders were less likely to admit guilt regarding their sexual offenses. Similar findings were also found in a study by Faller (1995) showing that female sex offenders either denied their crimes or only partially admitted to their crimes. Adult children of maternal sexual offenders also indicate that their mothers seldom, if ever, admit to their sexual offenses or apologize for them (Denov, 2004a; Ogilvie, 2004; Reckling, 2004; Rosencrans, 1997). This characteristic of female sex offenders may be an indication of a type of psychopathy along a continuum of psychopathy specific to females and in the absence of physical violence or where physical violence has not been detected.[110]

UNDERSTANDING FEMALE SEXUAL OFFENDING

From the literature review on women sex offenders, it appears that a majority of female sex offenders are mothers and other females in caretaking roles who commit their sexual offenses under their own volition and in the absence of male offender. There is also a minority of female sex offenders who commit their sexual offenses with other sex offenders, either in pairs or as a group, and these other offenders may be male or female. There is also the female sex offender who coerces, manipulates, or forces a child or adolescent into committing sexual offenses against other youth and who coerce children into prostitution and use children in pornography for economic gain (Vandiver & Kercher, 2004). Female sex offenders can commit their sexual offenses over a long period of time if not detected or reported and are unlikely to admit to their sexual offenses on their own, and do not readily show remorse about their sexual crimes or seek help to prevent their offending behavior.

It does appear that a majority of known female sexual offenders who are incarcerated or otherwise supervised in the criminal justice system have experienced prior sexual victimization that was severe and enduring across their early development. So far, studies have been able to identify this level of trauma in the social histories of a group of female sexual offenders; whether these dynamics hold true for other groups of female sexual offenders not under criminal justice supervision is not yet known, and whether this single factor is a predictor for sexual offending by females remains to be seen. It may be that other variables *in the context of the prior sexual victimization* are the greater risk factors for later sexual offending. These variables may include (a) adversarial beliefs about relationships, parenting, and a particular gender; (b) the relationship and emotional closeness the female offender had with the person who offended against her; (c) a lack of protective adults in the environment; (d) a lack of nonabusive role models due to isolation in the family and the stigma of sexually deviant behavior beyond childhood; (e) the impact of trauma on specific structures in the brain, such as the limbic system and frontal lobes; and (f) all or some of the these variables for a particular female sex offender.

Researchers need to expand their studies on female sexual offenders to include female sex offenders in the child protection system and clinical populations. It may be that for maternal sexual offenders, this prior history of severe and enduring sexual victimization in the context of other abuses has extended a pathway for later sexual offending, particularly against their own children. However, what *specific factors* in the context of prior sexual victimization might contribute to sexual offending have not yet been identified. Additionally, given that female sexual offenders are known to commit their sexual offenses against children they know, this suggests that maternal sexual offenders make up a significant number of female sex offenders in the studies presented. Therefore, studies and the developing typologies need to include a separate category for maternal sexual offenders in order to differentiate the characteristics of this particular group of female sexual offenders. Studies that are focused on the clinical application of risk assessment, supervision, evaluation, and treatment are needed.[111] These applications will in turn assist with the prevention of female sexual offending.[112]

There are a group of female sex offenders who commit a high level of violence and physical aggression against their victims that equals or exceeds that of male sexual offenders. Maternal sexual offenders are known to commit sexual abuse and other types of maltreatment against their children that compound the injuries and harm inflicted on this group of children. Psychopathic characteristics are indicated among a group of female sexual offenders because of the level of violence they use and the lack of remorse they verbalize regarding the offenses they commit. Reoffending and revictimization are particular risks for children of maternal sexual offenders and other potential child victims when female offenders are allowed access to children are not restricted in their contact with youth, or are not appropriately supervised when released or residing in communities whether their offense patterns include acting on their own or with another offender. Standardized measures of psychopathy are warranted for female sexual offenders as part of their risk assessment and when referred to treatment programs to prevent reoffending. Psychopathy as a characteristic of a group of female sexual offenders would also help in the development of typologies of female sexual offenders that have been emerging from the literature on female sexual offenders.[113]

While alcohol and drug use may be an outcome of prior sexual victimization, it does not present as a reliable predictor for sexual offending against children. Alcohol and drug use may be an indicator of other types of criminal activities that female sex offenders commit outside the crime of sexual offending. As mentioned previously, the lack of remorse and acknowledgment for their sexual crimes along with a persistent tendency to blame victims and to minimize the harm caused to their victims and a propensity toward violence may indicate a higher degree of psychopathy than previously considered among female sexual offenders and should be considered in future studies and in the assessment of convicted female sex offenders referred for sex offender treatment. These particular characteristics of female sexual offenders are consistent with the indicators of psychopathy described by Cleckley (1988) and Hare (1996) that include lack of regard for others, inability to tell the truth, insincerity and deceit, lack of insight, general absence of remorse, antisocial behavior, selfishness and self-absorption, lack of genuine remorse, lack of empathy, pathological lying, manipulativeness, and persistent violations of social norms (sexual offending and violence).

THE RISK TO AFRICAN AMERICAN BOYS BY FEMALE SEX OFFENDERS

Information is needed on the prevalence of female sexual offending that is committed against males, especially adult women against boys. One reason that this research is needed is that male children have been neglected in studies on sexual victimization, and what studies exist focus on the traditional role of the male offender and not on the contemporary knowledge of female sexual offenders who sexually victimize boys inside and outside the family. A second reason that research is warranted is that with the growing awareness that females sexually offend against boys and that some males turn to sexual offending in adolescence, there is a need to answer the question, "What is the role of female sexual offenders in creating a pathway to male sexual offending against females?" Additionally, a second question is, "What is the role of female sexual offenders in creating a sexualized view of female relationships among males who have been sexually exploited by females during their childhood?" While these questions may be viewed as controversial, they are evident as needing to be answered in order to prevent female sexual offenders from harming male children and to educate society that the sexual victimization and sexual exploitation of boys is not acceptable or without harmful consequences.

The radio program *Tell Me More*, hosted by Michelle Norris and broadcasted, on National Public Radio,[114] aired a segment called "Behind Closed Doors" on July 13, 2009, titled "Sexual Abuse Often Taboo for Black Boys." Norris introduced the topic of the show by stating, "Several prominent African-American women, such as Oprah Winfrey and Queen Latifah, have disclosed being sexually abused as girls. In contrast, many well-known African-American males frame their childhood sexual experiences with adult women as a source of pride or a rite of passage, instead of abuse." The segment then went on to discuss what Norris framed as a double standard in the African-American community regarding how males and females define their experiences of childhood sexual abuse. The discussion focused on the way in which males, in this case, African American males, avoid labeling themselves as "victims" in reference to child sexual abuse and that they do so in the context of gender stereotypes of masculinity, race, and sexuality.

In one of the few longitudinal studies available on the long-term effects of childhood sexual abuse on males and African American men in particular, Duncan and Williams (1998)[115] examined the experiences of 106 mainly African American working-class men.[116] The authors divided the men into groups based on their experience of sexual contact as children with adult males and females. They then grouped the men in terms of coercion (coerced, noncoerced) and by gender of the offender (male, female) and identified three groups: (a) coerced male on male (CM), (b) coerced female on male (CF), and (c) noncoerced female on male (NF). They then measured the effect of coerced and noncoerced sexual contact on male attitudes and behavior in adult heterosexual relationships with a particular interest on childhood sexual victimization and later adult violence.

Duncan and Williams (1998) identified the victim group from medical records obtained during the 1970s on children brought to the emergency room of a city-owned hospital for collection of forensic evidence and treatment due to reported sexual abuse. Each sexually abused boy was matched with a comparison boy on race and age. The comparison group had been seen at the same emergency room for injuries or ailments not related to sexual abuse within one year of the date the victim group was seen at the hospital. The comparison group was selected from the records of the pediatric outpatient department of the hospital. The male children in the comparison group had no known history of sexual abuse that was indicated in their medical records. The boys ranged in age from 2 to 15 years at the time they were seen at the hospital. This was a young group of children given that the mean age of the boys was eight years old. The boys were contacted 20 years after being seen at the hospital as children; a total of 106 males of the original 145 boys were successfully contacted and interviewed. The interviews were conducted by three female interviewers (two white and one African American[117]) either at a private office or, for those men who were currently incarcerated, in private rooms at correctional institutions (22% of the men were in correctional institutions).

The authors defined sexual abuse as any sexual contact from fondling or touching to oral, anal, or vaginal intercourse. Duncan and Williams (1998) used original police reports to substantiate sexual abuse. Police reports were then supplemented with information gained from the men during individual interviews. CM was defined as "incidents that were perpetrated against boys 0–17 years of age by males of any age where there was unwanted or forced sexual contact." CF was defined as "incidents where sexual contacts perpetrated against boys 0–17 years of age when such contact involved force, threat, coercion or was unwanted by the male"; additionally, the authors included all incidents involving "boys under the age of 13 and a female perpetrator 5 or more years older than the victim" and classified these as coerced female incidents, even if the boy reported that the contact was consensual because of the young age of the boys. The third category, NF, was defined as incidents "involving a female perpetrator 5 or more years older than the male victim aged 13–17, but where no force or coercion was reported and where the boy reported that he did not consider the contact to have been abuse" (p. 772).

What was surprising to the authors was the number of men who disclosed additional incidences of sexual abuse during their childhood to researchers during the interview portion of the study. These delayed disclosures of sexual abuse occurred in both the research sample and the control sample of men. These additional disclosures of sexual abuse had not previously been reported to authorities when the men were children. The authors found that 81 percent of the total number of men participating in the current study (sexual abuse sample and comparison group) reported experiencing sexual abuse in their childhood and that a female offender was reported by 51 percent of the boys.[118] The finding of unreported child sexual abuse lends support to the premise that males are less likely to report sexual abuse to authorities, that a survivor of child sexual abuse is less likely to disclose sexual abuse until the person is an adult, and that asking children about sexual abuse increases disclosure and the opportunity for protection (Paine & Hansen, 2000).

In the majority of cases where the men (as boys) had been sexually coerced by a male, 51 percent of the abuse was from someone the boy knew, an older schoolmate, or an adult from the neighborhood where the boy resided; 40 percent of the abusers were total strangers (several of these sexual abuse incidences were reported as occurring by gang members); family members perpetrated 10 percent of the sexual abuse (older brothers, uncles, grandfathers, or cousins, with no fathers reported as perpetrators). A majority of the sexual abuse incidences involved anal or oral penetration.

In the majority of cases where the men (as boys) had been sexually coerced by a female, 81 percent of the female offenders were acquaintances or friends (an older female friend of the family or babysitter) who touched, fondled, or had the boy vaginally penetrate her. Additionally, female family members accounted for 9 percent of female coercion cases (older aunts, cousins, or sisters); none of the female perpetrators in this group of boys were mothers or total strangers.

In all but one of the cases defined as noncoercion of sexual abuse by a female, the female offenders were friends or acquaintances of the teenager (ages 13 to 17 years). The relationship between female offender and boy victim was identified as an older female family friend or babysitter who encouraged the boy's sexual interest in her. The authors noted that in many of the female noncoerced sexual contact cases, the man claimed to be the initiator when he was a teenager. This view of a boy's sexual victimization follows the *male stereotype* of child sexual abuse mentioned by Michelle Norris of *Tell Me More* and found in studies where it is not uncommon for some male victims to reframe the abuse committed against them as consensual rather than as exploitation or victimization by a female.[119] Duncan and Williams (1998) found that in almost all the noncoerced female cases of child sexual abuse, there was an age differential between the boy and the female of five or more years, which is the legal definition of child sexual abuse in a majority of states.[120]

The following is a summary of the research results:[121]

- Overall: In adolescence, 13 percent of the men had been arrested for sex offenses or self-reported offending behavior.
- Overall: In adulthood, 10 percent of the men had been arrested for self-reported sex offenses.

- CM child sexual abuse survivors were more likely to report higher levels of violence in their adult intimate relationships than were men with no sexual victimization.
- Victims of CM sexual abuse were the least likely to commit sex offenses as adults.
- CF child sexual abuse survivors had high levels of violence in their adult intimate relationships when compared to men with no sexual victimization.
- CF sexual abuse survivors were more likely to commit sexual offenses as teens and more likely to commit sexual offenses as adults.
- CF sexual abuse survivors were more likely to compulsively masturbate as teens.
- Victims of both CM and CF (multiple offenders) were the most likely to commit sexual offenses as adults.
- Noncoerced female victims did not differ significantly from the nonabused comparison group on any of the measured variables (hypermasculinity, compulsive masturbation, and violence in relationships) but did report being more shy and awkward when NF victimization occurred with CM victimization.
- Male-abused participants did not score higher on homophobia than the nonabused sample or the female-abused sample.
- Sixty percent of the comparison group, which had no record of sexual abuse, reported instances of sexual abuse to the interviewers.

The finding by Duncan and Williams (1998) that boys sexually coerced by females were more likely than nonabused males to have committed sexual offenses as teens and as adults has significant implications in our understanding of a pathway from male victimization to later male offending for males victimized in childhood by females. The findings in Duncan and Williams study have also been found in studies by Glasser et al. (2001), Groth (1979a, 1979b), Groth and Burgess (1980), Peluso and Putnam (1996), and Petrovich and Templer (1984) where sexual abuse by females has been identified in the histories of convicted male sex offenders (child sexual offenders and adult rapists). Collectively, these findings help to provide direction to future studies attempting to understand the connection between prior sexual victimization in the lives of males who commit sexual offenses. These findings also indicate the importance of identifying the gender and relationship of the original offender to the current offender when he was a child.[122]

The importance of these two mediating factors in understanding and, preventing male sexual offending is explained by Duncan and Williams (1998): "negative effects are more likely when abuse is perpetrated by someone to whom the victim is emotionally close (e.g., family members)" (p. 768). Given that females who sexually offend against boys are more likely to be in a caretaking role while male perpetrators of boys are more likely to be same-age peers or strangers, "it is probable that the long-term negative effects of childhood sexual abuse on heterosexual relationships may be more pronounced when this abuse is perpetrated by female care-givers than when perpetrated by male acquaintances or strangers" (p. 768). Furthermore, the findings indicate that boys sexually abused by a female and sexually abused by a male are at further risk of sexual offending and/or committing physical violence into adulthood.

Therefore, it may very well be that female sexual offenders are one of the mediators (influences) that creates an increased risk for a group of boys to commit sexual offenses in early or late adolescence and that this mediator (i.e., sexual victimization by a female) remains a predictable factor for some male adolescents to continue their sexual offense patterns into adulthood and in particular the sexual offenses that they commit against females. Sexual victimization by females that occurs in the context of other types of traumatic experiences, such as domestic violence, emotional abuse, parental neglect, and physical abuse, and that can also involve females may factor as additional risk factors or compound risk factors for sexual offending and physical violence.[123] The sexual victimization of males by females may help to explain the propensity for some males to offend against a greater number of females (Duncan, 2006). As suggested by Duncan and Williams (1998), "Physical aggression and violence are modeled for boys who are victims of sexual coercion, regardless of whether the perpetrator is male or female" (p. 780), confirming that both male and female child sexual offenders have the potential to influence developing attitudes, beliefs, and behaviors toward violence, whether the violence is physical, sexual, or both.[124] The thesis of a relationship between male victimization by females as a risk for male sexual offending against females is further supported by Glasser et al. (2001) in their review of 747 case files from a forensic outpatient clinic in England. Glasser and colleagues reviewed case files in an effort to evaluate the relationship between sexual victimization in childhood with later adult sexual offending for males. Glasser et al. found that "a high percentage of male subjects abused in childhood by a female relative became perpetrators" (p. 482) and that the "abuse of males by female relatives may be more likely to contribute to the male victim becoming an abuser than abuse by male relatives or persons outside the family" (p. 485).

Recognizing the potential for female sex offenders to place a group of boys at risk of later sexual offending is not suggesting that a majority of boy victims are at risk of becoming male sexual offenders or perpetrators of other types of interpersonal violence. Crime reports indicate that a low percentage of the total male population actually commit violence against females; crime reports also indicate that males are more likely to commit physical violence against each other than against females.[125] Rather, the purpose of this discussion is to acknowledge that the sexual victimization of males and by females and male sexual offending against females may have a closer relationship than previously considered and that this potential relationship is relevant to the prevention of sexual offending by females against boys, which in turn has the potential to prevent male violence toward females. The outcome is that one cycle of violence, when identified and interrupted, prevents the intergenerational transmission of violence. This is accomplished through the early detection of female sex offenders, screening boys for victimization by females, expanding prevention education programs that include awareness of female sexual offenders and the harm they cause to the children they victimize, and including female offending against males as an integral part of the treatment programs with male sexual offenders (as well as female sexual offenders). Additionally, recognizing sexual victimization as a public health problem requires regular screening for children across the medical community, including screening specifically related to sexual victimization by females.[126]

PROFESSIONAL BIAS AND GENDER STEREOTYPES

The feminist writer bell hooks (2000)[127] offers a thoughtful view that reminds us of what can happen when society views violence of any kind in sexist terms and allows gender bias and stereotypes to prevail. She states,

> It lends credibility to stereotypes that suggest men are violent, women are not; men are abusers, women are victims. This type of thinking allows us to ignore the extent to which women (with men) in this society accept and perpetuate the idea that it is acceptable for a dominant group to maintain power over the dominated by using coercive force. It allows us to overlook or ignore the extent to which women exert coercive authority over others or act violently. The fact that women may not commit violent acts as often as men does not negate the reality of female violence. (p. 118)

Specific sex role stereotypes of masculinity and femininity can influence individual expectations of behavior where preferential treatment is granted to one sex over the other.[128] Sex role stereotypes[129] as a form of gender bias can create barriers that impede the detection and reporting of female sexual offenders. In turn, they have the potential to influence the response of professionals who investigate sexual crimes and provide services to victims.[130] Hetherton and Beardsall (1998), along with other authors (Allen, 1990; Banning, 1989; Bunting, 2007; Denov, 2003a, 2003b; Longdon, 1994; Nelson, 1994), have asserted that professional bias in the form of gender stereotypes obscures sexual crimes committed by females. For example, gender bias regarding female sexual crimes may create a tendency to disregard the harm that females cause to their victims (Nelson, 1994).

Susan Robinson (1998) identified gender as a factor in the response by professions to victim reports of sexual abuse when the offender is female.

Robinson shares that "victims have consistently reported difficulty in getting child protection services, police and therapists to believe them" when the perpetrator is a female. Responses based on the gender of a reported offender rather than the crime being reported can lead to sexual offenses by females "not being recorded and therefore not appearing in official crime statistics" (p. 68). Allen (1987) found that professionals tended to pardon female sex offenders by viewing females as having no malicious intent to cause harm or of posing no threat to their victims. Allen established that professionals absolved female sex offenders of their crimes by restructuring the sexual offense into an event that was more aligned with their view of female behavior. Denov (2001) found similar results in her interviews with law enforcement, social workers, and mental health professionals, including psychiatrists in Canada. Turton (2007) proposes that "female perpetrators are likely to have their behaviors adjusted to fit feminine stereotypes—such as overenthusiastic childcare—to be masculinised or minimized" (p. 43). Tracy Peter (2006) identifies that females committing sexual offenses are labeled "mad, bad or victim" (p. 2) and that when these views are held, a female's agency in committing sexual crimes is lessened and discounts the victim's experience.

Other stereotypes have to do with class distinctions that were identified by Zellman (1992) in a study on what decision-making factors are utilized by individuals in their reporting of child sexual abuse. Family socioeconomic status weighted the judgments of individuals in their reports of child sexual victimization. Zellman identified that people were more likely to report suspected abuse if the case involved poorer families than middle-class or wealthy families. This type of class bias not only skews the public's view of who commits sexual abuse but also camouflages female sex offenders (and male sex offenders) who are employed, are well educated, maintain a certain physical appearance, and present as caring adults toward the children they sexually abuse.

Linda, a victim of sexual abuse by her homeroom teacher and coach, describes her female offender as "someone who attended my church in addition to being my homeroom teacher and coach. No one wanted to believe that she had sexually abused me even though the police records substantiated the abuse. A woman who also attended our church preferred to view me as a 'brat' who made the sexual abuse up rather than admit that someone she viewed as upright and respectable, someone that she knew, was a sex offender." Given the response from others that Linda described, it is easy to understand her anger and frustration at what she terms "ignorance" when it comes to believing (or disbelieving) that females do commit sexual crimes. Linda went onto share "that when I do tell people that the person who sexually abused was a woman, they will at times look at me with disgust, and I tell them 'I agree it is disgusting' that a woman, I trusted as a child, would have done the things to me that she did."[131]

When gender bias occurs in the law enforcement and child protection systems, it is particularly problematic because both are the gatekeepers into the criminal justice system. Law enforcement and child protection determine whether a report is considered valid, an investigation will proceed, an arrest will be made, or a child will be protected as a result of reported sexual abuse.[132] A study by Myriam Denov (2004a) indicated that in Canada, stereotypical beliefs held by police officers about adult female sex offenders and adolescent boys influenced decisions across segments of law enforcement regardless of the fact that the sexual abuse of a minor is a crime. Kay Levine (2006) observes that "to continue to pretend that women are not capable of seducing or manipulating boys to have sex, or to conclude that women who behave this way are too rare to merit attention, will enslave us to the unfortunate habits and stereotypes of the past and cause us to abandon an entire class of victims who deserve better" (p. 3). The words of Levine are also true for women who sexually abuse adolescent girls. Additionally, when this type of double standard exists, it has the unfortunate potential to teach boys that their sexual victimization does not matter to the same extent that it does with girls. It causes girls to feel betrayed by females who stand up for the rights of victims sexually abused by males but ignores the rights of victims sexually abused by females.[133]

Lisa Bunting (2005), in her discussion of the response by criminal justice to female sex offending in England, Wales, and Northern Ireland, asserts that professionals are susceptible to responding to child sexual abuse in the context of sex role stereotypes of male and female aggression and in line with established sexual scripts that culturally define male and female sexual behavior rather than the reality of the behavior presented. Bunting (2007) further contends that "there are more similarities than differences" between male and female sex offenders in terms of "the degree of intrusiveness or use of violence" (p. 235) in the commission of their crimes, yet policies of child protection and law enforcement do not reflect the reality of these similarities. The similarities between male and female sex offenders have been noted by other authors as well (Turner, Miller, & Henderson, 2008), even though a preponderance of studies continue to attempt to identify differences while avoiding the similarities between the two groups, the obvious similarity being that they commit sexual crimes. Bunting (2005) recommends a change in law and public policies that would reflect the reality of female sexual offending and that training for law enforcement should include information on female sex offenders. Michelle Elliott (1993a) suggests that it is important not to suppress discussion and acknowledgment of female sexual abuse "from a fear of going against established opinion" or that "attention paid to female sexual abuse will detract from the problem of abuse by males" (p. 12). These two authors point to the importance of bringing female sexual abuse and the bias that it may engender into the open so that both can be identified and addressed in professional groups, the public, and the media.

Gender bias can also be presented by professionals who provide forensic evaluations of female sexual offenders for judicial sentencing and placement. This level of bias can influence whether a female is considered at low or high risk when eventually released into the community.[134] The level of risk (high-low) assigned a female sex offender will impact the level of supervision she receives from the criminal justice system.[135] Bunting (2005) noted that in England a "lack of a static risk assessment tools was linked to a downgrading of risk when female sex offenders were assessed" (p. 261) and that this downgrading of risk occurred without any reliable method to determine whether females were at lesser or greater risk to reoffend.

Child protection is not immune to the influence of gender stereotypes in their decisions regarding the seriousness of female sexual offending.[136] A dismissal of female sex offenders by some caseworkers can result in abusive mothers being allowed to remain in the home with their victims or engage in unsupervised contact (Faller, 1995). Turton (2007) identifies that there is also an added dilemma for child protection workers, namely, "what to do with the female perpetrators if they do identify them" (p. 63). Turton goes on to explain that an underlying problem is "a lack of any real contingency plans for cases where the sexual abuser is the mother. So it is sometimes considered more beneficial to keep the family together and at best attempt to work through any problems or at worst minimize them, sometimes, perhaps, denying their existence" (p. 63). Given the identification of these issues, it seems it would be of interest to review child protection reports to determine the number of unsubstantiated cases of child sexual abuse involving females. It is also important to remember that simply because the evidence is not available to substantiate a case of child sexual abuse does not mean that the sexual abuse did not take place. Additionally, as pointed out by Circuit Court Judge K. Mark Loyd, "Child protection must be able to substantiate a case of child sexual abuse within a certain period of time which is not always possible with the evidence presented," and "it is not unusual for child protection to keep a case open with the legal time limit while considering additional evidence will be forthcoming."

The question of whether female sex offenders are given differential treatment was addressed by Tardiff, Auclair, Jacob, and Carpenter (2005), who suggest that "women who are thought to be sexual abusers are often treated more leniently and more therapeutically than are male suspected abusers" and that this is true even when the victims of females are their own children. Tardiff et al. found that when the victims are the children of female sex offenders, "the cases are more likely to be diverted from the criminal justice system into the family court, child protective, or mental health systems" than are cases involving male perpetrators. p. 155) Stroud, Martens, and Berker (2000) concluded that cases of child sexual abuse committed by females were less likely to be prosecuted than those committed by males. It is important to remember that law enforcement and child protection are sometimes limited by a lack of sufficient evidence to act on behalf of a child when sexual abuse is reported and that this is one reason that it is important for adults to act on behalf of children and report suspicions of sexual abuse when they occur. It is also important to recognize that for law enforcement and child protection to work on behalf of protecting children, funding at the federal and state levels would most likely need to be increased.

THE IMPORTANCE OF SEXIST-FREE LANGUAGE

The potential for gender bias is not presented as occurring deliberately; rather, that it can occur without a particular awareness. Across societies and cultures, stereotypes abound even though none may be a reflection of a true individual.[137] Research shows that stereotypical beliefs about men and women influence perception about a particular gender and the conclusions that are drawn about an individual.[138] Gender stereotypes are particularly harmful when they inform crucial decisions regarding the protection, health, and well-being of human beings or when they are introduced into information that is meant to be helpful and informative. An example of how gender bias can occur without detection was observed by this author in her review of a study published in the *Journal of Child Sexual Abuse* (2005).[139] When the authors discussed possible reasons for a high level of violence among a group of convicted female sex offenders in their study sample, the authors postulated that female aggression may increase with age and that "younger offenders may be more timid or possibly gentler with their victims" (p. 83). It would indeed be a distinct surprise to find words such as "timid" and "gentler" used in the literature on male sex offenders in the commission of their crimes. The terms "timid" and "gentler" are incongruent with crimes of sexual offending regardless of whether the offender is male or female. That neither the authors nor the editors of this respected journal viewed these descriptive words as sexist or an indication of gender bias is rather surprising yet in some ways is expected given how ingrained the stereotype is that female sexual abuse is "harmless" even when contraindicated by the use of violence. It is also unfortunate because sexism and gender bias, even when unintentional, can be indicative of a displaced level of sensitivity to females who are sexual offenders than perhaps what might be extended and certainly warranted for their victims.

It is also important to point out that researchers can use inappropriate language to describe females who commit sexual offenses that end up promoting stereotypes or give the impression that the behavior of female sex offenders is something other than sexual abuse. For example, Vandiver (2006a), a well-respected researcher, uses the phrase "had an affair" (p. 47) when describing the sexual abuse committed by Mary Kay Letourneau, then a teacher, against her sixth-grade student. The male child was a student of this adult woman when he was eight years old, so she was able to groom him as a potential victim for four years.[140] Describing the sexual abuse of a child by an adult as "having an affair" gives veracity to the stereotype that female sexual abuse is harmless or that females who commit sexual abuse are not committing a crime.

Nancy, a survivor of female sexual abuse, related, "I think what bothers me the most is that so little is known about female predators. I think people need to have more knowledge on how female predators really are and not just what they hear in the news or read in reports." Nancy was sexually abused by the mother of one of her friends who was also the wife of a teacher at her school. The sexual abuse began when she was around 14 years old, and the offender continued to pursue Nancy for several years. Nancy explains, "Even when I tried to keep my distance from her, she soon began a friendship with my mother, who was also a teacher, so she would still see me. I tried to ignore her, but there was a very frightening secret looming over my head." As she related her experience of sexual abuse, Nancy shared, "I really have not spoken about any specifics regarding my abuse to anyone. It is something I have suppressed for so long since there are still those who bring my situation up as 'an affair,' not sexual abuse, so I guess I have still looked at it as something other than sexual abuse."[141]

Sexist or other inappropriate language can negate or confuse the basic understanding that children are not able to give legal consent while failing to recognize that children and teens are not the developmental equals of adults. Words like "affair" imply an adult–adult relationship since "affair" is often used to describe two consenting adults engaging in an illicit sexual relationship, not an adult sexually abusing a child. This style of sexist language is also heard in media reports of sexual abuse, whether the offender is a male or female. It may be that the media are at times mirroring the sexist language sometimes found in the literature on female sexual offenders. Perhaps, in order to screen their language for sexism and gender bias, a question that researchers, the media, and others could ask themselves is, "Would this description of female sexual abuse be used with a male offender in referencing the relationship to his victim or in describing his sexually abusive behavior?" This technique is called reframing, and it is helpful in checking language and attitudes for gender stereotypes.[142]

Language does matter. Language can either obscure the sexual crime and violation of boundaries that females commit against their victims or portray the reality of the crime and the breach of trust. Because language does matter, it becomes important that the media, researchers, authors, and prevention educators be held to a higher standard of language when communicating about sexual offenders and the crimes they commit and not unintentionally misconstrue the crime into something other than what it is or minimize the behavior of the offender through the use of sexist language. It is equally essential for researchers to be aware of their potential for favoring a particular sociopolitical view that may underlie the language employed when describing females who commit sexual offenses or potentially affect how they report the results of their research.[143] Sexist language may also inadvertently reinforce the cognitive distortions exhibited by female sex offenders that in turn further skew the offensive behavior that the sexual offense was somehow "teaching" youth about "love" when in fact the female sex offender was teaching a child about abusive sex and exploitation (Duncan, 2004).

It may also be that an aspect of gender bias is a reflection of a particular generation's beliefs and sociopolitical views reflective of the time period in which the research took place or the limited knowledge of the research regarding sexual offending by females and the consequent harm that occurs to their victims. An example of this possible gender bias can be observed in some of the first typologies proposed for female sex offenders. The "teacher/lover" category suggested by Matthews (1993) is one such typology that is indicative of gender bias. There is not a typology of a male sexual offending that categorizes a male sex offender in the same terms. However, it is true that a prominent cognitive distortion that male sex offenders have used to justify their sexually abuse behavior is that they were "teaching" the child about sex or that the sexual abuse of a child is about "loving a child" and not about abuse, betrayal, and exploitation (Duncan, 2004). Cognitive distortions are considered one of the primary risk factors that increase the likelihood of reoffending.[144] Both adolescent female sex offenders (Kubik & Hecker, 2005) and adult female sex offenders (Strickland, 2008) have been identified as exhibiting cognitive distortions regarding their sexual abuse that are similar to those of adolescent and adult male sex offenders. Both groups of sexual offenders, male and female, strive to exonerate their crimes and deny the harm they cause their victims through the lens of their offending attitudes and beliefs.

When discussing the application of another of her typologies, Matthews (1993) identifies the "male-coerced female offender" without providing clear and objective evidence or specific reliable measures as to how male coercion is substantiated other than through the description of a female offender. A male-coerced female offender described by Matthews was the mother of a 13-year-old female victim. The offending mother was given unsupervised contact with her daughter when the mother moved to an apartment of her own. The offending mother decided to have a party and during the course of the evening is described by Matthews as "giving one of the men permission to have sex with her daughter, who was now 15 years old" (p. 71). In Matthew's description of the mother "giving a man permission to have sex" (i.e., permitting a man to sexually abuse her daughter), there is no indication of male coercion provided. What is of particular concern in the description of this case is how the focus seems to be placed on the maternal sexual offender without purposeful consideration of the impact to the daughter, who was once again betrayed by her mother as well as sexually abused by another male in her mother's social circle. Matthews's depiction of the case also included reunification plans with the offending mother's other four children without seeming to consider that reunification might not be appropriate in light of the fact that the mother re-offended against one of her children while in a treatment program.

The current discussion is not meant to create antagonism or to be critical of another clinician or researcher; rather, it is meant to bring attention to the possible bias that researchers and therapists can have toward viewing female sexual offenders as "victims" rather than as offenders or when concern for the offender is not balanced with a greater concern for the victim.[145] When undetected gender bias occurs, children can be placed at additional risk for sexual victimization by mothers and other females who may or may not have been actually coerced into their sexual offenses or who may continue to sexually offend with or without male coercion (Saradjian, 1996). It is evident that sex role stereotypes regarding gender exist today, as they did in the past, and that these persistent and culturally indoctrinated beliefs can invade and influence professional beliefs, attitudes, and practices when assessing female sexual offending (Allen, 1991; Denov, 2001; Langdon, 1993; Levine, 2006). Therefore, it is essential that, in the identification of and intervention with female sexual offenders—and certainly with their victims—gender stereotypes not determine the seriousness of a crime or the professional response to a victim or offender. Rather, it is the crime committed that makes this important determination and guides rational and judicious response so that protection to victims becomes and remains the priority and female sexual offenders are provided therapeutic support to stop their offending while being held accountable for their crime.

CHAPTER SUMMARY

Michele Elliott (1993a) suggests that female sexual abuse is more threatening because it undermines feelings about how women should relate to children, and this view of female sexual offending may very well be true. However, when sexual victimization by females is not acknowledged as real and female sex offenders are not detected and reported, then victims are left without protection. There is also the impact to females who commit sexual offenses when they are not provided appropriate intervention or held to a personal responsibility for their offending behavior and not provided a judicial accountability to stop their offending. If society is to eradicate sexual victimization, then offenders, whether they are male or female, will need to be held accountable, the harm they cause acknowledged, and their sexual deviance understood to be real.

While it is true that males commit the majority of sexual offenses reported to law enforcement, it is also true that females offend against a substantial number of victims. The sexual crimes that females commit are severe in nature, often perpetrated against their own children or other youth entrusted in their care, and physical violence is not uncommon during the commission of their sexual crimes. Kay Levine (2006), in her article published in the *Fordham Urban Law Journal*, recognizes how "our highly gendered way of thinking about the participants in statutory rape derives, first and foremost, from the statutes that defined the crime for much of its history" and that "statutory rape was traditionally understood as a crime that could happen only to females" (p. 2). This gendered framework has become so intrinsic to how sexual offending and victimization are viewed that it has contributed to the obscurity of female sexual offenders and rendered their victims all but invisible (Denov, 2004b; Vandiver & Walker, 2002). It has also focused the majority of research, treatment, and prevention efforts on male sexual offending even though evidence indicates that a substantial number of female sex offenders do exist, that they are not some new phenomena, and that they engage in a variety of sexual crimes.

Moving beyond the historical framework for viewing sexual offenders and the crimes they commit will challenge basic assumptions about how sexual offending and victimization are thought about and responded to. It will require that stereotypes no longer impede investigations or create barriers to prosecution or prevent full protection to children and teens. For these changes to occur, then, all forms of gender bias will have to be recognized as a prejudice that hinders the rights of all people, not just females. Female sex offenders, like male sex offenders, especially impinge on the right that children and teens have to develop and grow without being sexually abused and exploited an adult. To provide the full protection that children deserve will necessitate assimilating the evidence that some females have the ability and the agency to make choices that harm others and that some females are equally capable of an abuse of power in their intimate relationships, especially their relationships with children and teens.[146] This new perspective requires an acceptance that the sexual crimes committed by females are as real as their victims.

2

Breaking the Silence about Maternal Sexual Abuse

> A mother wounds and violates a sacred bond of trust when she sexually abuses her child.
>
> —Juliann Mitchell and Jill Morse, *From Victims to Survivors*

Human beings as individuals have the capacity to engage in the entire spectrum of human behavior. Aggression, as one type of human behavior, can be enacted by either gender[1] and, by extension, either parent.[2] The literature on domestic violence[3] documents that females engage in physical and psychological aggression equal to that of their male counterparts (Dutton & Nichols, 2005). Physical and sexual violence in same-sex partner relationships is seldom recognized in the literature, and few studies have been conducted to further understand and prevent this type of relationship violence.[4] Children who witness violence between their parents or other intimate partners are equally harmed during these verbal assaults and physical fights.[5] Verbal hostility between parents threatens and undermines a child's sense of safety and security and creates intense feelings of helplessness, fear, and anxiety.[6] The same is true when parents direct their verbal hostilities toward a child. A study by Moore and Pepler (2006) found that a mother's verbal aggression in the form of insults directed toward a child is damaging to a child's health and emotional well-being, reminding us that words do wound and cause considerable harm to vulnerable children.[7] Children and adolescents can also be the direct recipients of family violence by a parent, sibling, or other adult in their home (World Health Organization, 2006).

Studies on domestic violence indicate that women as well as men commit physical violence against each other, and while women may experience more physical injuries, men experience injuries as well; a gender difference is that men do not report their injuries as often because of stereotypes regarding what it means to be masculine, which does not include being a victim of female violence.[8] While it is true that differences in physical size will result in differences in physical injury regardless of the gender of the victim or the offender, it is also true that women will use weapons to bring equality to this physical disparity between men and women.[9] Psychological aggression has been shown to precede sexual and physical aggression in adult partnerships, and this seems to hold true across ethnic groups, especially when alcohol is involved.[10] It is also documented that women's verbal and physical aggression in their intimate relationships is equal to and in some instances can exceed that of men's; this finding is often ignored or minimized in the literature on intimate partner violence where the primary focus of research has been on violence against women and not violence by women.[11] Even though violence committed by females in their intimate relationships has been less recognized, a lack of recognition does not negate its existence, nor does the denial or minimization of female violence help to end the intergenerational cycle of family violence as a significant social and public health problem.[12]

KEY POINTS

There are mothers capable of inflicting great harm to their children. In the United States, in 2007, parents were responsible for 69.9 percent of child abuse or neglect fatalities, and 27.1 percent of child fatalities were perpetrated by the mother acting alone (see Child Welfare Information Gateway, n.d.).

Sexual abuse of a child by the mother often occurs alongside other types of aggression that includes verbal and emotional abuse, physical abuse, and neglect.

Whether male or female, children are adversely affected when sexually abused by their mothers.

Adult children of maternal sexual abuse may question whether they want to be parents or wonder about their ability to be adequate parents to their children. It is important to remember that most of the people who experience sexual abuse in their childhood do not go on to become sexual offenders.

While it is a disturbing reality that in their intimate relationships there are men and women who inflict great harm to each other, it is perhaps even more disturbing that there are parents who inflict considerable harm to their children resulting in long-term emotional and physical injuries and, at times, causing the death of a child.[13] These realities are necessary to face if societies are to address family violence, provide protection to children, and hold parents accountable to stop the harm and instead provide their children with a family legacy that does not include adult violence and child maltreatment (Duncan, 2004).

According to the U.S. Department of Health and Human Services[14] in 2007 an estimated *794,000 children* suffered maltreatment by *859,000 perpetrators.* In 57 percent of the cases where children were harmed, mothers were found to be the primary offenders by Child Protective Services.[15] While child maltreatment by a parent is a particularly sad and pervasive reality for some children, even more disturbing is that in the same year, 70 percent of child deaths were caused by parents, and in 25 percent of child fatalities it was the mother who caused the death of a child.[16] A majority of the children who died while in the care of their parents were six years old and younger.[17] What is certainly becoming apparent is that family violence is not so much a "gender problem" as it is a *human problem* that exacts a particular emotional and physical toll on the developing child and threatens a child's ability to survive these acts of violence.[18]

Among the types of severe maltreatment that children experience in their families is maternal sexual abuse. Sexual abuse committed by mothers is one form of family violence that needs to be understood and acknowledged in order for children to be protected from this group of parental sex offenders.[19] While the present discussion references biological mothers that commit child sexual abuse, the discussion includes other women in caretaking roles with children and teens. Therefore, maternal sexual abuse includes adopted mothers, mothers in foster care, grandmothers, stepmothers, and other women the child considers the woman a "mother substitute" because the child believed she could trust a woman in the same manner that she would trust a parent. What this group of women has in common is the betrayal of a child who had the right to expect protection, guidance, and safety in the mother–child relationship. Rather than meeting these needs of the child, a woman exploited the child's trust, affection, developmental stage, and dependency needs in the context of her relationship with the child.

Amy was sexually abused over a number of years by a woman she thought of as a mother figure. Amy first met this woman when she was entering eighth grade as a new student at a new school. Even though the female offender was a teacher at the school Amy attended, she was not Amy's teacher. She was married with children of her own. As Amy explained, "I began to babysit for her when I was 14 years old, so I was at her house almost daily. At that time in my life she became more of a mother figure to me than my own mother. My mom and I had just moved to town, so she was working most of the time to support us financially." The female offender is described by Amy as "ingratiating herself to my mom, who was a single mom. My mom was new to the community and needed a safe adult for me to spend time with after school." The offender "showed extra attention to me, had me spend time with her after school in her classroom, and even wrote my mom a lengthy letter telling her what a great kid I was and that my mom could depend on her to take care of me." This adult female sex offender exemplifies the opportunistic and predatory sex offender who takes advantage of both the vulnerable child and the vulnerable parent in order to groom both as she prepares to commit sexual abuse. It is a similar offending pattern found with a group of socially skilled male sex offenders who are not necessarily family members but who insinuate themselves into the daily lives of a child's family and over a period of time gains the trust of both the parent and the child in order to commit child sexual abuse.[20] While not Amy's mother, the female offender became a *mother figure* due to the amount of time that Amy spent with her in a family setting, the feelings of affection that Amy came to have for this woman, and the expectation that this woman would provide a safe relationship where Amy would be protected instead of being harmed. Unfortunately, these expectations were betrayed for Amy as well as Amy's mother. The feelings of betrayal that Amy experienced is common to children who experience sexual abuse by a primary caretaker, but is somehow deeper and more confusing when the offender is female, the gender that is "anointed" by societal stereotypes as the guardian of children, not the exploiter of children.[21]

A mother who commits sexual abuse does so in the societal construct that defines what it means to be a mother. The same societal construct that defines for the child what it means to be betrayed by the gender portrayed as the protector of children. It is the essence of this *double betrayal* associated with maternal sexual abuse that is described by sons and daughters as making sexual abuse by a mother more devastating and even more confusing than if the sexual abuse is committed by a father. As one adult daughter shared, "I certainly was brutally penetrated by men at a very young age. Yet the emotional impact of having to perform this sexual act with my mother is just so devastating. The issues just feel so much more complex. There are a lot of similarities but the shame, the stigma, the isolation that come out of being abused by your mother, make it so difficult to talk about" (p. 28).[22] This sense of a deeper betrayal by a female who is "mother" is a common theme, as shared by another adult daughter sexually abused by her mother and father: "When looking at the big picture and the layers of hurt out of all that happened to me, what my mother did was the absolute worst, far worse than what my father had done" (p. 149),[23] and there is a similar sense among men, as indicated by this adult son: "For me to be a victim, and to be a victim of [my mother], I just have so much trouble accepting that" (p. 157).[24] As one son stated, "I'm constantly haunted by [the sexual abuse]. It's not something that just goes away, and I don't know how to put it behind me" (p. 1143).[25] Melinda was in therapy for two years before she disclosed the sexual abuse by her mother. She explains the reason: "I was terrified of the abuse by my brother because he was so violent, but I could at least acknowledge it happened. The abuse by my mother was something I just never wanted to believe. I refused to even think about it for many years" (p. 22).[26] To admit that it was mother who sexually abused you becomes a betrayal of how "mother" is not only felt, needed, and viewed by the child but also portrayed by society. For after all, "Who is safe, if not your mother?"

Understanding society's resistance to acknowledge maternal sexual abuse is explained by one adult survivor: "Because there's nothing else to hold onto. I really don't think there is much else to hold onto. The world isn't perfect and people don't want to face that and if we have to let go of that one about the mother, we may think that's all that's left of humanity" (p. 295).[27] Another woman sexually abused by her mother shares a similar perspective: "There is a deeper sense of betrayal [with a female perpetrator]. It's like there's no safe place" (p. 149). Amy, whose sexual abuse was described previously, brings the discussion back to facing the reality of maternal sexual abuse by sharing, "Yes, it is disturbing to learn that females commit child sexual abuse, but it is an important truth to learn. How else will we prevent sexual abuse by females?"

THE REALITY OF MATERNAL SEXUAL ABUSE

Denial is a primary defense used by human beings in order to avoid accepting that which is found to be unacceptable. Susan Strickland (2008) observes that the sexual abuse of children by women has been denied largely because people believe that women are not capable of committing such acts. Strickland bases her observations on her study of 60 females incarcerated in Georgia for sexual offenses. Karen Duncan (2004), in her book, *Healing from the Trauma of Childhood Sexual Abuse*, observes that "while we accept that there are men who will perpetrate abuse, we do not want to believe that some women, especially mothers, abuse children" (p. 21). Duncan goes on to state that "if we are to prevent child sexual abuse or stop it when it is occurring, we are going to have to accept that female perpetrators do exist and that they abuse both boys and girls" (p. 22).

Beverly Ogilvie (2004), writing on the experience of 60 women who experienced mother–daughter incest, offers a perspective regarding the scarcity of research on mothers who commit child sexual abuse. Ogilvie shares that "incest by a male/father is viewed by our society as more normal and acceptable than similar behaviors perpetrated by a female/mother." It is important to clarify that Ogilvie is suggesting not that paternal incest is normal or acceptable but rather that there is a greater propensity to believe that paternal incest occurs and to disbelieve maternal incest. Ogilvie goes on to explain that, as a society, "we are operating a double standard" where "we take it for granted that men/fathers abuse, yet we refuse to accept that women/mothers sexually abuse as well," so it is not surprising that society "responds to sexual abuse by mothers with extreme discomfort, shock and disbelief" (p. 5). The societal resistance toward acknowledging maternal sexual abuse that Ogilvie is describing is not that different from past societal views regarding sexual abuse committed by some fathers and other males both inside and outside the family.

Olafson, Corwin, and Summit (1993)[28] provide a historical perspective of the social, legal, political, and medical views that have contributed to cycles of awareness, discovery, and the suppression of information about the trauma of child sexual abuse in intermittent cycles of the acceptance of its existence. Anne Banning (1989) identifies that recognition and concern about child sexual abuse is a recent phenomenon in spite of its documented occurrence throughout history. Given these historically ambivalent views of child sexual abuse, the viewpoint that maternal sexual abuse is rare or misunderstood is in some ways to be expected. Sexual violence against children has remained a contentious social problem even as awareness about its existence and the potential long-term impact to the health and well-being of a child have continued to be documented.[29] As shared by Circuit Court Judge K. Mark Loyd, "It took us several years to come to accept that there are men who sexually abuse children, it would not surprise me if it takes a similar amount of time to accept the same about some women."[30]

However, with increasing reports of sexual crimes committed by females and the emerging literature on female sexual offending, ease of access to the Internet and other electronic media, a lessening of gender stereotypes and a public willing to discuss topics once considered outside the purview of "socially acceptable talk" (e.g., same-sex marriage, breast cancer, and erectile dysfunction), it may be that contemporary society is more willing to accept that mothers do in fact have the capacity to commit child sexual abuse. In turn, they become a public willing to understand the considerable harm that results from women who commit sexual crimes against children and teens.[31] From the perspective of the sons and daughters who have experienced sexual abuse by mothers, this would be an affirmation of a society willing to understand what they, as survivors of maternal sexual abuse, consider the last secret of family sexual abuse, better known as maternal incest.[32]

THE MYTH OF THE INCEST TABOO

The suggestion that the incest taboo prevents child sexual abuse from occurring in families is a common assertion in spite of reports that confirm that a significant number of child sexual abuse cases are committed by family members.[33] Therefore, it may be that the idea of an incest taboo is more prevalent than the actual taboo itself, which certainly is one explanation as to the reason that child sexual abuse committed by family members is greater than child sexual abuse committed by strangers. Lloyd DeMause,[34] in his article "The Universality of Incest," contradicts the popular view that a universal taboo against incest exists; rather, DeMause asserts that

> it is incest itself—and not the absence of incest—that has been universal for most people in most places at most times. Furthermore, the earlier in history one searches, the more evidence there is of universal incest, just as there is more evidence of other forms of child abuse. (DeMause, 1991)

DeMause provides compelling evidence from his extensive review of incest as it has existed throughout ancient history, in modern society, and across cultures, citing 600 references to support his assertion that it is incest that has been prevalent and not the taboo of incest. DeMause does not argue that there is a *belief* of an incest taboo; rather, he argues that the taboo itself has not prevented child sexual abuse from occurring. In other words, just because an incest taboo exists does not mean that certain members of a family are adhering to the taboo. What is certain is that less is known about mothers who commit child sexual abuse than what is known about fathers who commit child sexual abuse and that the reason for this discrepancy is that there may be more of a taboo about discussing maternal incest than there is about discussing paternal incest.

DeMause also provides a particular insight regarding Sigmund Freud, who is frequently cited by feminists as contributing to the suppression of father–daughter incest.[35] DeMause contradicts the criticism by some feminists that Freud "lost his courage and denied that any incest had actually taken place"; rather, DeMause states that "Freud reiterated his belief that these clear memories of incestuous attack were real" and that Freud "even called his own memories 'genuine' of having been sexually molested as a little boy by his nurse, who had not only forced him to perform sexually and, he reported 'complained because I was clumsy,' but also, he said, washed him in water that contained her menstrual blood" (p. 2).[36] Therefore, rather than abandoning his patients, it is more likely that Freud identified with them because of his own reported experience of sexual abuse by a woman charged with his care and that both Freud and his patients faced a society not willing to listen to or believe either Freud or the accounts of his patients. It is also interesting that feminists who have complained about Freud's views of incest perhaps never considered that Freud himself was also sexually abused—but by a woman!

Christine Lawson (1993) reiterates that "current cultural bias against recognizing mother-son sexual abuse is reminiscent of Freud's struggle to convince a disbelieving audience in 1896 of the possibility of father-daughter incest among his female patients" (p. 262). Banning (1989) also addresses the issue of the incest taboo and child sexual abuse in a historical context. She shared that "in Freud's time father-daughter incest could not be accepted. Child physical abuse was not recognized or acknowledged until the 1960's and child sexual abuse in the mid 1970's. Not until the 1980's were male victims recognized and studied and their victimization found to be more frequent than previously recognized. Mother-son and mother-daughter incest could well be not as unusual as we had thought or hoped" (p. 569). Lawson's view may very well prove to be true as research continues to document the existence of female sexual offenders and maternal sex offenders in particular. At the same time, denial is a formidable weapon. Saradjian (1996) notes that while there is at least 25 years of knowledge that points to a significant number of women that have engaged in child sexual abuse, it is still not a crime that has been readily accepted. Perhaps the lesson to be learned regarding maternal sexual abuse is not to repeat the historical denial that surrounded paternal sexual abuse, where children were not believed and their reports of incest were silenced by a society unwilling to accept that what children had to tell was indeed true.

The incest taboo is also addressed by Craig Allen (1991) in his study on the prevalence of female sex offending. Allen identifies *three reasons* why female sexual abuse of children has not been addressed. First, professionals have overestimated the strength of the incest taboo, particularly those who adhere to the psychoanalytic tradition that in part denied female sexuality. Second, feminists have overextended their explanations of child sexual abuse where only men and not women sexually abuse children. This view stems from the radical feminist framework that supposes that all sexual violence arises from male-dominant social structure, where men are socialized to be aggressors and women and children to be victims. Allen explains that both psychoanalytic and radical feminist theory are similar in terms of the restrictions in understanding female sexuality and the potential for female sexual deviance as well as in identifying a female's potential to abuse her social power and exert control over another.[37] Finally, it is an overgeneralization to hold the view that the sexual abuse of children by women is rare especially if this view is based on crime statistics. Allen explains that this premise occurs when professionals assume that if child sexual abuse by females is not reported in the literature, it is not occurring, or when prevalence studies are taken to reflect actual incidences of crimes occurring rather than a reflection of the incidences of crimes reported.[38] Given the stigma surrounding sexual victimization in general and the added secrecy of sexual abuse by a mother and the gender bias surrounding female sex offenders, Allen's assertion is not unreasonable.

While belief in the incest taboo may reinforce an existing denial in terms of believing that the incest taboo prevents maternal child sexual abuse, the reality of the situation may be that maternal incest is more common than society would like to believe or is comfortable believing and that mothers who commit sexual abuse and the children they victimize know this all too well.

BARRIERS TO DISCLOSING MATERNAL SEXUAL ABUSE

The fact that sexual crimes are often committed by someone the victim knows decreases the likelihood that victims will report the sexual crime to legal authorities.[39] This is especially true for young victims sexually abused by a parent or other primary caregiver whom they love, care about, and are dependent upon for their daily care (Kasl, 1990). Additionally, there is a general consensus that people who commit sexual crimes seldom if ever report their offending, and females have been found to be even less likely to report their sexual offending[40] and more likely to blame the victim and to minimize the harm they cause (Kubik & Hecker, 2005; Strickland, 2008). Unfortunately, this reality can leave the reporting of sexual abuse as the primary responsibility of the victim, that is, unless the sexual offense is discovered by someone else and a report made. However, given the general lack of information about female sexual offending and a potential bias against recognizing maternal sex offenders, the likelihood of someone identifying sexual abuse by a mother and reporting it is less likely than when it is occurring by a male (Nelson, 1994).

Male sexual assault victims can find it especially difficult to report sexual abuse because of the potential shame, embarrassment, and confusion they experience. In addition, males can experience a great deal of ambivalence about being labeled "victims" given the stereotypes of masculinity that exist in cultures.[41] As one man relates, "I felt like I was a victim, and for a man to be a victim is an embarrassment. A real man is not a victim; a real man is always in charge, always resists, and is always in control. A man who is a victim is a failure. In that respect, I felt like I had to hide the fact that I was a victim"

(p. 1149).[42] As explained by David Lisak (1994) regarding the men in his study sexually abused as children and where seven mothers and three aunts were identified as the offenders,

> These men described, often with remarkable eloquence, their struggle to reconcile the experience of sexual victimization with the demands which their culture placed on them to be "masculine." Masculinity, as defined by cultural norms, rejects vulnerability, passivity and helplessness, psychological states which comprise the very core of the experience of sexual victimization. (p. 545)

What is obvious for men sexually abused as boys is that they have forgotten how young they were, how small in size they were, and, most important, that it was a wrong committed against them, not a wrong that they committed. The cultural stereotypes surrounding what it means to be male combined with the gender bias that views males as potential offenders of sexual abuse and not the victims of this crime, adds to the isolation that boys experience when they have been sexually abused by their mother or another woman.

Another barrier for male victims is the widely held albeit misinformed belief that males are not victims of sexual assault if they experience an erection or ejaculation. Sarrel and Masters (1982) clarify this aspect of the human physiological response during sexual assault by first differentiating sexual assault and sexual abuse. They define sexual assault as "sexual encounters in which a man or boy has been forced to participate in undesired sexual activity under threat or physical violence" and that sexual abuse occurs when a "male has not been overtly threatened physically but rather has been overwhelmed by female psychosocial dominance or sexual seduction" (pp. 117–118). Sarrel and Masters then address the question of erection and ejaculation and sexual assault and abuse:

> In the absence of prior documentation that men or boys can be and are sexually assaulted by women, there has been widespread belief that it would be impossible for a man to achieve or maintain an erection when threatened or attacked by a woman. Widespread acceptance of this sexual myth has had unfortunate implications for medicine, psychology, and law. Its persistence in our culture has meant that male victims of sexual assault have not been identified and that their psychotherapeutic needs have remained unmet. (p. 118)

As a result of this sexual myth regarding physiological arousal by men and boys during sexual assault and sexual abuse, males seldom understand that penile erection and ejaculation are common during rape/sexual assault and that neither should be construed as enjoyment, consent, or willing participation. Alaggia (2005) points out that in societies "sexual exploitation of boys by older women is often mistakenly viewed as desirable, and therefore their victimization is minimized or denied" (p. 457). Society's preconceived ideas about masculinity, a lack of education regarding human sexuality, and being misinformed or not informed about physiology and sexual victimization all contribute to create barriers to males not viewing their sexual victimization as a sexual crime while adding a considerable amount of confusion and shame for boys and men when they do experience sexual crimes. When the sexual offender is your mother, the layers of shame, confusion, secrecy, and denial can be intense and deeply felt.

Another barrier to disclosure of maternal sexual abuse is what Duncan (2004) describes as a "forced sexual pleasurable response" that children sometimes experience during the sexual abuse. This physical response can cause children (and later as adults) to believe that they must have enjoyed the sexual abuse or consented to it rather than recognizing that forcing a sexual response was another way that the offender manipulated and controlled the child's body. It can certainly create a great deal of confusion about an individual's sexuality in terms of wondering if they are normal or not. Children and adults need information regarding sexual response as it might occur during sexual victimization in order to address this aspect of shame and confusion that often surrounds these crimes. This information is needed whether the offender is a male or female. As explained by Val Young (1993b)

> Children are naturally sensual, and pleasurable sexual feelings they may have are their own innocent feelings; they are never connected with any real form of sexual relationship. Abusers exploit these feelings and encourage children to engage in sexual activities long before they are able to understand or explain what they want and what they feel. What abusers refuse to recognize is that sexual excitement in children is a natural physical response that is very different from adult sexual pleasure. (p.199)

Sexual responses that occur during sexual victimization are more common than people realize, and victims are more comfortable talking about it. This discomfort by victims of child sexual abuse holds true for both male and female children. Sarrel and Masters (1982) provide help in separating the myths from the facts about this phase of sexual victimization: "male sexual responsivity in a variety of emotional states are consistent with the research but are not generally known. Interestingly, they also parallel unpublished data that most women lubricate and some women respond at orgasmic levels while they are being sexually molested" (p. 118). What Sarrel and Masters clarify is that physical sexual responses (i.e., vaginal lubrication, penile erection, and ejaculation) during sexual victimization is not uncommon and occurs along with emotional states of embarrassment, humiliation, anxiety, fear, anger, or even terror. Accurate information about the potential and actual occurrence of a sexual response during sexual victimization dispels myths, decreases shame and confusion, and may increase the likelihood of disclosure.

As girls and boys and later as men and women, children sexually abused by their mother or other women they cared about have a difficult time reconciling the intense emotions they feel toward the woman offender, and a continuing desire to be loved and cared for by the person who sexually abused them. Sally was 12 years old when she was sexually abused by her homeroom teacher. Sally recalls, "The sexual abuse was so confusing because it felt good, and she told me that she loved me. I didn't want the abuse. I just wanted her to care about me, but it seemed that to get the attention and caring, I had to go along with the touching. My mom was in prison at the time, and I felt very alone, with no one to talk to or share things with." Erin, a female convicted of sex crimes against a 13-year-old girl, shared, "I knew what I was doing. I could manipulate her because she cared about me. I knew how to make her feel what I wanted to make her feel. She just wasn't old enough to know what I was doing, how I was controlling her."

Maternal offenders might also use drugs and alcohol to incapacitate their victims and gain their compliance. Melinda recalls, "The first time I remember my mother sexually abused me it was at home and everyone was gone. I was probably six or seven years old. She fixed us hot chocolate, and then she started hugging and kissing me, saying, 'This is the way moms show affection. There is nothing wrong with it.' After that, she began to touch me all over my body, and I remember the pain when she put her fingers in my vagina. It got worse from there on in. She would insert all kinds of things into my vagina and rectum. I could never tell my dad, I was too embarrassed, and besides he traveled a lot. My older brothers and sisters were already out of the house and living on their own." A child's young age also prevents disclosure and is another reason that detecting and reporting child sexual abuse is so important. It is also important to remember that children and teens are not familiar with the laws that govern adult sexual behavior. Saradjian (1996) points out that an offender sexually abusing young children, especially her own children, seldom needs to groom a child into complying with the sexual abuse. When children are sexually abused from a very young age, they seldom know any other type of treatment, so they come to view the sexual abuse and other types of maltreatment as "normal" because in their world it is normal (Duncan, 2004). Grooming tactics that female sex offenders are known to use are similar to their male counterparts, and include making a child feel special and set apart from other children, isolating a child and preventing outside contact with others, and normalizing the keeping of secrets and threats to harm herself or the child if the sexual abuse is told about.[43] Sarah related how the aunt who sexually abused her "made it feel normal for her to be where I was, to be a part of my life and a presence in my life. After all she was my aunt, so who would question her? I certainly didn't."

CHARACTERISTICS OF MATERNAL SEXUAL OFFENDERS

The study by Loretta McCarty (1986)[44] is recognized as among the first to identify that mothers do commit sexual abuse. It is presented here as an example that the existence of maternal sexual abuse is not new to the literature; rather, it just has not received the research attention or level of examination that paternal sexual abuse has in the literature on incestuous parents and families. McCarty examined in detail the cases of 23 mothers all of whom were substantiated as sexual offenders through Child Protective Services in Texas. In addition to McCarty's study being the first to present detailed information on the offending process of a group of mothers, it was the first to identify that mothers acting with male offenders but who were not coerced have the capability of committing severe sexual abuse. Four of the mothers who acted with male accomplices were criminally convicted of child sexual abuse. As noted by McCarty, one of these mothers "received a 99-year prison sentence" because of the severity of her offenses (p. 448). When examining the mother–child relationship, McCarty identified that 11 of the mothers had offended against daughters, 8 of the mothers had offended against sons, and 2 of the mothers had offended against both sons and daughters. The McCarty study was the first to identify three categories of maternal sexual offenders: (a) the independent offender who committed sexual abuse on her own, (b) the co-offender who committed sexual abuse with a male offender and on her own, and (c) the accomplice who committed sexual abuse with a male offender but may have been coerced.[45] A summary of the characteristics of maternal sexual offenders that McCarty identified from her study are (a) both sons and daughters were victimized, (b) the needs of the mother took precedence over the safety of the child, (c) male offending did not always occur with maternal sexual offending, (d) offending mothers showed characteristics of pedophilia, and (e) the sexual abuse was severe and extensive.

The findings in McCarty's study regarding mothers sexually abusing both male and female children is similar to current research findings on female sex offenders. Unlike their male counterparts who tend to show a gender preference in their victims, that is, male sexual offenders seem to sexually abuse either male victims or female victims with a majority of their victims reported as female; females who commit child sexual abuse do not seem to show a gender preference. Current studies indicate that females are known to sexually abuse male and female children about equally, placing both boys and girls at equal risk of being sexually abused by a female (Deering & Mellor, 2007). These findings were also indicated in a study by Bader, Scalora, Casady, and Black (2008), in which they found that a majority of mothers in the child protection system had offended against daughters but also sexually abused sons. A study by Faller (1987) found a high degree of multiple incest cases among the children sexually abused by mothers. A Canadian study by Denov (2004a) reported that both adult sons and adult daughters identified maternal sexual abuse as children. A study in England by Elliott (1993a) reported on female sexual abuse across family relationships that included sons, daughters, nieces, and nephews. A study by Tardiff, Auclair, Jacob, and Carpenter (2005) found that the mothers not only sexually abused their children but also engaged in other types of violence toward the children that included physical abuse and lacerations. Some of the mothers in the study showed "homicidal tendencies" toward their children and a jealous rage toward the daughters. The mothers frequently had criminal offenders as male partners, indicating that some mothers have an affiliation with this type of male and a tendency to seek out mutually offending partners that perhaps share their deviant sexual interest in children. There were a total of 13 adult female offenders of whom 92 percent were mothers. The women had offended against 21 child victims. Incestuous relations with daughters occurred among 45 percent of the mothers, and incestuous relations with sons occurred among 39 percent of the mothers. The women progressed from sexual fondling to more intrusive sexual acts that included masturbation of the victim, masturbation of the female offender by the victim, masturbation in front of the victim, fellatio in front of the victim, oral genital abuse of the victim, oral genital abuse forced by the victim, digital penetration of the vagina, sexual intercourse, sadism, child pornography, and child prostitution. The age range of child victims was from 8 months old to 17 years old with the majority of the victims in the age range of 8 months old to 7 years old (62%) followed by 11 to 17 years old (43%). The women indicated paraphilic and atypical sexual behaviors other than child molestation that included bestiality, spying on parents having sex when they were children, sadomasochistic behaviors, and having "sexually initiated" younger brothers. A majority of the woman offenders had a high school education, and some had a university education. Regarding the backgrounds of the mothers, the study found that a majority of the mothers had been victims of incest, that they were victimized at a young age (often six years old or younger), and that penetration had occurred more often than not by a male family member. The women also described that they had experienced rejection by their mothers and that their mothers were nonprotective against sexual abuse. The women also reported that their mothers were physically abusive. The relationship the women offenders described with their fathers was one where the father was distant or absent. The women also described their fathers as controlling and violent toward family members and engaged in alcohol abuse. In general, this group of mothers tended to come from highly violent families where mothers and fathers were violent and nonprotective, death and the murder of family members was not uncommon, and severe maltreatment of children and of each other was a part of the family's daily life. At the time of the study, this group of women sex offenders was being seen on an outpatient basis at a clinic in Montreal, Canada. The authors did not indicate if any of the women were incarcerated prior to the study. This aspect of the study is brought up in order to highlight the severity of sexual abuse that mothers and women are capable of committing and the importance of monitoring women sex offenders living in the community especially if they are not restricted in their access to children. Identifying the offending patterns and characteristics of maternal sexual offenders will improve the detection and investigation of child sexual abuse when reported and most certainly will improve services that are offered to children sexually abused by mothers and other female caregivers (Duncan, 2006). Additionally, extending the principles of prevention education to detect, intervene, and stop mothers who commit child sexual abuse can make the lives of children only safer and more secure (Oliver, 2007) and provide the opportunity to prevent another generation of children from becoming either victims or offenders of family sexual abuse and other forms of family violence (Duncan, 2006).

TYPES OF SEXUAL OFFENSES MOTHERS COMMIT

The type of sexual offenses that mothers[46] commit include genital fondling and masturbation, physical penetration of a child's genitals with objects, forcing a child to engage in sexual intercourse with the mother or other adults, forcing children to engage in sexual activities with other children, and involving children in pornography and prostitution (Denov & Cortoni, 2006; Elliott, 1993a; Faller, 1987, 1989). Vandiver (2006a) suggests that females who engage children in pornography and forced prostitution may do so as part of a well-established criminal pattern where they use children for economic gain. Laura is a female offender convicted and incarcerated on conspiracy to commit child molestation. Laura solicited males to purchase child pornography through a day care center she operated out of her home. During the interview, she shared, "I did not think that what I was doing was child sexual abuse because there was no touching involved. I mean, I never touched the children. I was manipulating men to get money from them but not with the intent to commit child sexual abuse myself." What was evident throughout the interview with Laura is that she minimized the harm she caused to children, did not admit to betraying the trust of parents who paid her to care for their children and not use them in child pornography, and she never owned up to the fact that her motivation in committing this form of child sexual abuse was for money. Another aspect of her sexual offending that came through in the interview was that Laura was also motivated by the status and power that she felt with the men who purchased the child pornography. At one point in the interview, Laura stated, "I had those men right where I wanted them. If they wanted what I had [child pornography], they had to pay for it." Who really paid for this crime were the children Laura used for economic gain and the parents who trusted her.

A particular type of maternal sexual abuse is the frequent insertions of enemas into a child's rectum for no apparent medical or health-related reason (Mitchell & Morse, 1998; Rosencrans, 1997). Mothers who sexually and physically abuse with enemas do so under the guise of medical care, making this type of maternal sexual abuse a possible *reference point in the screening of children for sexual abuse* among health care professionals, especially nurses, pediatricians, and family physicians.[47] Toni was a woman who came to counseling because of chronic depression, hypertension, and muscle pain. Her physician had recently diagnosed her as suffering from fibromyalgia. As therapy progressed, Toni shared that "almost daily my mother would subject me to enemas, usually before I went to school and sometimes even after school. I have never told anyone because I am so ashamed and embarrassed. I have never been able to feel relaxed in my own body, and it seems like I am in a constant state of physical rigidity and tenseness where I am always on guard."[48] Toni had not considered that the enemas were an act of sexual and physical abuse by her mother. A survey of 46 adults (males and females) found that enema abuse was considered one of the most serious forms of maltreatment committed by mothers (cited by Mitchell & Morse, 1998). It is provided here as an example of how sexual abuse by mothers can be different than sexual abuse committed by fathers and that the repeated insertion of objects into a child's vagina or rectum is one of the known types of sexual abuse committed by mothers.

Lawson (1993) categorizes of maternal sexual abuse to help identify the *range of sexual abuse* that mothers commit and proposes that prevalence studies be specifically designed to ask about maternal sexual abuse so that sexual abuse by females and mothers in particular can be identified. This recommendation is supported by Finkelhor, Araji, Baron, Peter, and Wyatt (1986), who state that "sexual abuse surveys that use specific questions yield a higher prevalence rate than those using general, open-ended questions" (pp. 261–262). Given that the historical context of child sexual abuse has been viewed from the perspective of males as offenders and females as victims, and that a significant number of child sexual abuse studies have therefore focused on male sexual offending and have not necessarily included questions about female sexual offending, this recommendation by Lawson holds greater significance in helping to determine a more accurate rate of maternal sexual abuse and female sexual offending as it occurs in the real world.

Lawson proposes that studies categorize maternal sexual abuse along the following five classifications that identify the range of sexual abuse that mothers commit and the level of harm that children experience: (a) subtle abuse, (b) seductive abuse, (c) pervasive abuse, (d) overt abuse, and (e) sadistic abuse. Lawson does not limit her proposed classification only to mothers, suggesting that they can be applied to other female offenders. In doing so, she lends support to the idea that studies on child sexual abuse need to provide more in-depth information in order to be useful in their application to clinical practice in the treatment and prevention of child sexual abuse (Banning, 1989). The five classifications of maternal sexual abuse suggested by Lawson are described here:

1. *Subtle sexual abuse* is defined as behaviors that do not involve coercion and may or may not involve genital contact. Subtle sexual abuse is viewed as overstimulating, erotic, and confusing to the child. While subtle sexual abuse may not be intentional in nature, it serves to meet the parent's emotional and/or sexual needs at the expense of the child's emotional and/or developmental needs. Behaviors include frequently sharing a bed with the child, massaging the child or asking the child to massage the mother, and continuing to bathe a child when this behavior is inappropriate to the age and development stage of the child. In addition, Saradjian (1996) identifies the following behaviors that could be placed in this category: obsessively cleaning and washing a child's genitals and repeatedly giving a child unnecessary enemas.
2. *Seductive sexual abuse* is defined as sexual stimulation that is inappropriate for the child's age and/or is motivated by the parent's sexual needs. Seductive abuse implies conscious awareness and the intent to arouse or stimulate the child sexually, distinguishing it from subtle sexual abuse. Behaviors include exhibitionistic displays of nudity or sexual behavior, exposure to pornographic materials, or exposure to seductive posing, gestures, or verbal messages with a sexual content and the intent to arouse the child. What is problematic about this category is Lawson's term of "sexual stimulation that is inappropriate for the child's age" since it brings into question whether Lawson considers that some types of sexual stimulation by a parent to a child is age appropriate rather than specifically stating that sexual stimulation by a parent to a child regardless of the child's age or development is inappropriate.
3. *Pervasive sexual abuse* is intended to embarrass and humiliate the child regarding his or her developing sexuality. It would include emotional abuse (derogatory labels, remarks, and insults), criticism of the child's body and appearance, and physical abuse. Behaviors could include forcing a child to dress in opposite-sex clothing and criticizing a child's sexual physical development, such as the size of a boy's penis or the shape and size of a girl's breasts. These sexually abusive behaviors are an attempt to disrupt the child's establishment of a healthy sexual identity and may also arise from a pervasive jealousy the mother has toward the child or rage at a particular gender. Behaviors may include examinations where

the child is forced to strip naked in front of the mother and the mother then proceeds to comment on the child's physical and sexual development. Saradjian (1996) identifies pervasive sexual abuse as an attempt to make a child feel that his or her sexuality is something corrupt or to make a child feel afraid or ashamed of their developing sexuality.

4. *Overt sexual abuse* is defined as direct sexual contact between mother and child that would involve coercion, physical force, verbal threats, and manipulation. Behaviors include attempted intercourse, cunnilingus, anilingus, fellatio, genital fondling, digital penetration, clothed or unclothed touching of genitals, lingering sexualized kissing or hugging, intentional genital exposure, and direct exposure to adult sexual activity. The intent is for the mother to gratify her own sexual needs and may or may not be accompanied by other forms of abuse.

   It is unclear why *completed intercourse* is not included by Lawson. Women are capable of coercing, pressuring or forcing a male child or teen to insert his penis into her vagina. A woman is also capable of inserting sexual objects (e.g., a vibrator) or other objects into a child's vagina, anus, or mouth. As discussed previously, the insertion of objects into children appears quite frequently in the literature on maternal sexual offenders.[49] Also, the biological sexual response provides the capacity for spontaneous erection and ejaculation in males during sexual trauma and vaginal lubrication for females, which aids in preventing physical trauma during sexual victimization.[50] Of course, artificial lubricants are also available for use in the sexual penetration of a child or teen by both male and female sex offenders.

5. *Sadistic sexual abuse* is intended to physically hurt the child and may be a part of a general pattern of more severe physical and emotional abuse. Lawson considered this form of maternal sexual abuse the least frequent and the most harmful.

The categories proposed by Lawson (1993) help clarify the characteristics of maternal sexual abuse along a continuum that encompasses the range of sexually abusive acts that have been reported in the literature from victims, from clinical studies on maternal incest, and in the criminal justice records of female offenders (Davin, 1999; Mitchell & Morse, 1998; Saradjian, 1996; Sgroi & Sargent, 1993; Turton, 2007; Vandiver & Walker, 2002). The categories help to improve the understanding of the reality of a child's experience of maternal sexual abuse. Lawson's classifications also has relevance to identifying associated risk factors for reoffending that are essential to the supervision and management of convicted female sex offenders residing in the community and in families.[51] These classifications can help to guide assessment and treatment of female sex offenders and further support the recommendation that typologies specific to maternal sexual abuse are warranted (for an overview of the research on developing typologies for female sex offenders, see Johansson-Love & Fremouw, 2006; Sandler & Freeman, 2007). Bobbie Rosencrans (1997) provided one of the first comprehensive studies on the experiences of adults sexually abused in childhood by their mothers. Like Lawson, Rosencrans (1997) supports the formulation of categories of maternal sexual abuse in order to understand the different forms of sexual abuse that mothers can commit, and this in turn can "help validate the survivor's experience as real and significant" and assist in the "understanding of female-perpetrated child sexual abuse that includes a wide range of behaviors" that are different and yet similar to male sexual offending and that occurs in the context of parental incest (p. 25).

The ability to identify the emotional and psychological harm from child sexual abuse is significant to assessing the emotional injury to victims since physical injury is not often present in sexual abuse cases.[52] A measure of emotional harm to a child victim is also relevant in the judicious sentencing of sexual offenders (male and female) since it would give judges and juries an objective means to evaluate the totality of harm inflicted on and suffered by victims from the trauma of child sexual abuse.[53] As shared by Judge Michael L. Howard, "It is only in the last several years that we, as a court, have educated ourselves about trauma. As a result, we now know that it is important to ask about trauma. Indeed, we often discover a history of trauma that has gone undetected, despite attempts to help the child through traditional counseling services."[54] Among the undetected traumas that children and teens experience is maternal sexual abuse. Ensuring that professionals in the criminal justice system are educated about maternal sexual abuse and female sex offenders is essential in order for law enforcement to provide an appropriate response to victims and ensure the safety and protection of children.[55]

Explicitly defined categories of maternal sexual abuse that provide specific examples of the types of sexual abuse behaviors that mothers commit would also benefit health care professionals in the screening and detecting of child sexual abuse by mothers, investigations of child sexual abuse by child protection staff, prosecution of child sexual abuse cases in the criminal justice system, prevention education programs that are delivered in schools, and community education programs that help to inform the public about child sexual abuse,[56] mental health professionals who work with victims of child sexual abuse, and professionals who might be working with female sex offenders residing in the community.

A VIEW OF THE IMPACT OF MATERNAL SEXUAL ABUSE

While there are an increasing number of studies regarding the sexual victimization of boys by men, there is little systematic research that has been conducted on the sexual victimization of boys offended against by women and even less on sons sexually abused by mothers.[57] What research is available is found in the clinical literature and reported through case studies.[58] The following case studies are from the literature on mother–son incest or from qualitative studies on male sexual victimization by women where mothers are identified as the offenders. Each case is summarized to capture the essence of what was reported and the impact that maternal sexual abuse can have on sons. The reader is referred to Lawson's (1993) categories of maternal sexual abuse cited previously to evaluate how maternal sex offenders carry out their sexual offending against their children. Sarrel and Masters (1982) presented a case of mother–son incest that is an example of how pervasive, long-standing, sexually damaging, and emotionally confusing maternal sexual abuse can be for sons. The man disclosed the sexual abuse by his mother when he was 30 years old while seeking therapeutic intervention because he had been unable to consummate his marriage after three years. As far as the man could remember, he had never seen his father and was told by his mother that his parents had divorced when he quite young. The sexual abuse by his mother began when he was just entering puberty around the age of 13. His mother initiated the sexual abuse with genital fondling. She then progressed to genital manipulation and fellatio and eventually to intercourse. The incestuous behavior by the mother continued at the rate of two or three times a week until the boy left for college. The young man shared that he never approached his mother for sexual contact but that he did respond to her initiations of sexual contact with him. The son describes how he felt strongly devoted to his mother stating that he "enjoyed her obvious pleasure during their sexual encounters far more than his own" (p. 124). The young man had never dated prior to enrolling in college, indicating that he had little social experience with girls his own age. His first attempt at sexual intercourse occurred when he was a college freshman and resulted in his inability to achieve an erection because he was "overwhelmed with guilt at the thought of being unfaithful to his mother." The young man reported that the sexual abuse by his mother continued until she died, which was during his senior year in college. Following his mother's death, he resumed dating. Whenever he attempted sexual intercourse, he could not maintain an erection and consequently was overwhelmed with constant fears of performance. After several negative sexual experiences, he described how he "became nauseated at the prospect of sexual opportunity," and began to feel that his sexual life had ended with the death of his mother (p. 124). The man eventually married in an attempt to combat his sense of loneliness and isolation from others. When he and his wife were seen in therapy, she was fully aware of his impotence while completely unaware of its cause, that is, extensive and repeated sexual abuse by his mother over a number of years. The case captures the profound adverse outcomes that can result when sons experience maternal sexual abuse.

Margolin (1987) describes the case of a 17-year-old who was in treatment for anxiety and confusion about his sexual identity. This son had experienced intrusive maternal sexual abuse that included his mother sharing his bed during vacations and at other times would examine his penis under the guise of wanting to determine if his penis was growing properly. Wahl (1960) presented a case of maternal sexual abuse against a teenage son. Wahl describes the mother as attractive, sexually provocative, rigid, and controlling. At one point during her son's treatment, she threatened the staff with action if her son was not allowed to return home. The mother was observed by a hospital staff member as "extremely physically affectionate toward her son" and was overheard as calling her son "lover." On one particular day the mother was observed lying on the grounds wrapped in a blanket with her son and on another occasion was observed opening his fly and playing with his penis. Wahl shares that during a therapy session the teenager described how his mother would "initiate sexual intercourse and precede each of these experiences by threatening him with fears of homosexuality unless she gave him this special training" (p. 191).

Ronald Krug (1989) reported on eight case histories of sons experiencing sexual abuse by their mothers. A common theme throughout the case histories was the role reversal that the son assumed in terms of becoming the caretaker of his mother emotionally and in some cases financially. This role reversal began at a young age, often during early or middle adolescence, and extended in some cases until the son was in his early adult years. The sexual abuse by the mothers of their sons began in many of the cases with the mother sleeping in the son's bed. Mothers are described as both single and married. When fathers were present, they were often described as distant and unavailable. None of the mothers was reported by the sons to be psychotic, although a few did use alcohol. Krug identified that significant adverse problems were experienced by the men and included an impaired ability to relate to a significant other in an intimate, sustained, and meaningful manner. The men also experienced depression, substance abuse, and sexual identity issues. A majority of the men reported that when they tried to establish independence from their mothers, they were accused of not loving their mothers. The men were observed by Krug as extremely agitated and reluctant to discuss the sexual abuse by their mothers.

Anne Banning (1989) presented the case of a four-year-old boy named Rex. This case is a good example of how important it is for child-care professionals to receive education and training in the recognition of child sexual abuse that includes sexual abuse by mothers (and other females). Education and training on sexual abuse can provide child care professionals the skills and information they need to intervene in cases of suspected child sexual abuse and prevent other children from being injured when children who have been sexually abused act out their abuse experiences on other children. Rex was observed by his preschool kindergarten staff as persistently inserting his finger into the vaginas of girls. Rex eventually inserted a stick into the vagina of one little girl that resulted in injury. Rex described his sexually intrusive behavior as a game that he called "check-a-bum." When his mother was interviewed, she played down the seriousness of Rex's behavior with the other children and referred to his behavior as "games" that Rex was playing with the girls. Rex's mother viewed the staff's inquiries as criticism of her and Rex rather than as concern for the children's safety. When Rex's mother was challenged about her son's sexually provocative behavior, she shared that both she and her mother had kissed Rex's penis when he was a baby and that she had learned this from her mother as a method of giving comfort. Rex's mother described a game she played with Rex that she called "chasing a naked Rex." When she caught Rex, she bit his bare bottom, saying, "I'll eat your bottom," and she again reported that this was a game her mother had played with her. The mother went on to describe the four-year-old Rex as "highly sexed, interested in her body when she was having a bath, liked to fondle her breasts, and give her tongue kisses." When questioned about Rex's inability to show appropriate boundaries,[59] the mother was surprised since she had not viewed her behavior, her mother's behavior, or her son's behavior as indicative of a lack of or the violation of personal boundaries. This case study shows how child sexual abuse is viewed by some mothers as normal behavior especially when sexual abuse beliefs are passed forward into the next generation (Duncan, 2005a).

Traditionally, women in our society are allowed more freedom to touch children more frequently and in more ways than are men because females are viewed as unwilling and less able to cause harm to children and unlikely to become sexually aroused by contact with children. While there is evidence of a growing recognition of the injury that children experience at the hands of their mothers,[60] the stereotype of mother as the protector of children has limited society's ability and willingness to recognize when mothers cross boundaries and violate the physical, sexual, and emotional autonomy of children and teens. Even when a mother's boundary violations are recognized, the violations may not necessarily be acknowledged as causing harm, and therefore action might not be taken to intervene.

Cultural stereotypes about male and female sexual behavior also contribute to a lack of recognition of the harm that arises to sons who are sexually abused by their mothers. Schwartz and Cellini (1995) explain that "by the time a child is old enough to recognize sexual intent, for example, the young male adolescent may already be subscribing to the gender stereotype that males are in control of all sexual encounters or that any sexual contact with a woman is enjoyable." It is unfortunate that boys are at-risk of adhering to the stereotypes about gender roles even in the context of sexual abuse by a mother (p. 55). At the same time there are adolescent boys who are able to recognize a mother's inappropriate behavior and may even discuss it when provided an opportunity to do so and a willingness to understand their experience. After a prevention education program that I had presented for high school students and where I had talked about female sexual offending, I was approached by a 14-year-old boy who asked if he could speak to me in private about his mother's behavior. After I finished with questions from other students, this young boy and I stepped into the hallway in order to offer him some privacy. Other people were close by but not within listening distance of our conversation. He shared, "My mom walks around our house in her bra and underwear and sometimes in just a towel. She flirts with my friends and dresses where you can see her breasts. This makes me really uncomfortable, and it embarrasses me." This boy's disclosure allowed a brief yet timely occasion to discuss how he might approach his mother to discuss his feelings and explain what he needed her to change in terms of her dress, her behavior toward his friends, and her attire around the house. A few days later, he sent an e-mail letting me know that the conversation went better than he expected, that his mother was changing her behavior (she did need some reminders from him), and that he appreciated our conversation. I was glad to hear from this young boy and was certainly happy to hear that things were going better with his mother. I was also grateful that his mother had listened to him, that his high school had sponsored the training for students and staff, that this young boy perceived me as someone willing to listen and offer some guidance. I am reminded now, as I was then, that it sometimes takes only a few moments to make a difference in the lives of young people.

Boys have a great capacity to love and care about others, that goes beyond the stereotypes of masculinity that societies try to place them into. It is unfortunate that boys are at risk of internalizing stereotypes about male identity and may lack information about human sexuality that would help them to understand their emotional and physical responses when sexual victimization happens to them, whether the offender is a female or a male. When the offender is his mother, a boy potentially suffers not only from the betrayal of a parent but also perhaps from the indifference of a society that has historically resisted—and at times refused—to consider that boys can be victimized by the very women they too have the right to trust.[61]

Compared to the abundance of research and literature on daughters who have experienced sexual abuse by their fathers, there is scarce research on daughters sexually abused by their mothers.[62] Mitchell and Morse (1998), in their book *From Victims to Survivors*, present the collective experiences of 80 women who completed comprehensive surveys regarding the sexual abuse they experienced by mothers and other females. The women who participated in this study resided in several countries with the majority being from the United States. This group of women reported that it was a mother or a grandmother who most often sexually abused them and that, unlike the established grooming process of male offenders, the women in their study did not report being groomed by their female abusers. The women reported long-term consequences from the sexual abuse that included an inability to trust and to trust women in particular, self-injury behaviors, problems with their sexuality and sexual relationships, confusion about their female identity, and shame about their bodies.

When daughters have been sexually abused by their mothers, they can feel a sense of double jeopardy in discussing the sexual abuse by their mothers. This double jeopardy arises from a feeling that not only are they betraying their mothers but also that in telling about the sexual abuse, they are somehow betraying the feminist movement. In reflecting on the experience of female victims sexually abused by mothers, Kasl (1990) observes that women experience a reluctance to report female sexual abuse because of a fear of "incurring the anger of other women who may believe that by exploring sexual abuse by females, we are apologists for men" (p. 261). The idea that recognizing female sexual violence will somehow diminish the reality of male violence is frankly not the best of arguments. To ignore violence of any kind by either gender perpetuates violence into the next generation, creates a potential divisiveness among groups of people who have mutual goals of prevention, and endangers the lives of children caught in the cross fire. Val Young (1993) challenges feminists who may discount or disbelieve the reality that female sex offenders exist or who become defensive during discussions regarding female violence to remember that "part of sexism is the belief that women are innocent and somehow sexually dormant until claimed and sexualized by a man. So it is actually sexist, rather than feminist, to disbelieve initiatory female sexual abuse" (p. 107). Young continues with the following caution: "sooner or later, someone will ask if any feminists are abusing their children, and whether this is why they do not like the subject discussed" (p. 107). Tracey Peter (2006) asserts that "unlike mainstream constructions of masculinity (where aggression is often normalized), there is less acceptance that some women have the capacity to sexually abuse children" (p. 283). Child sexual abuse can only be prevented when victims are no longer afraid to speak and offenders (regardless of their gender) are not provided a safe haven to commit their sexual crimes by a society unwilling to acknowledge the existence of child sexual abuse.

While daughters and sons experience an array of effects arising from sexual abuse by their mothers, one of the most anxiety-provoking ones is a fear that they will be like their mothers and sexually abuse their own children. As explained by one man: "I know that my sexual stuff has really warped my ability to parent my daughter. I'm afraid to be alone with my daughter. It's probably one of the most troubling components of my adult life. You know, I'm good with her. But still, I'm afraid [of sexually abusing her]. I'm very afraid. It makes me spend less time with her than I normally would" (p. 1150).[63] Because of this fear, it is not uncommon that adult children sometimes choose not to become parents,[64] while those who do choose to become parents experience a high degree of self-doubt about their ability to be adequate parents (Duncan, 2005a; Ogilvie, 2004).

Understanding the impact of maternal sexual abuse on a daughter's transition into motherhood was explored by Anne Reckling (2004) through in-depth interviews with four women. Following is a brief summary of the women's backgrounds and their childhood experiences of maternal sexual abuse:

1. Kim was in her late forties and had two daughters (ages 9 and 12). She reported that she experienced severe physical beatings and daily enemas by her mother. Kim's mother would also strip naked and masturbate in front of Kim, fondle and penetrate her with her fingers, or make Kim fondle her. While Kim was unclear as to when the sexual abuse began, she shared that it was must have been when she quite young because she could not remember not experiencing the enemas leading her to believe that she was really little when it started. Kim did remember that the sexual and physical abuse continued until late into her teenage years.
2. Suzanne was in her late forties, married, and had one son (age 24). Suzanne reported that the sexual abuse by her mother occurred when she was between the ages of 8 and 14 and included digital (finger) penetration and fondling. She questioned whether her stepfather was involved in some of the sexual abuse but was unsure if he was.
3. Sarah was in her late thirties, married, and had one daughter (age 10) and one son (age 13). Sarah reported that the sexual abuse by her mother occurred when she was between the ages of three and seven and that her mother was verbally abusive and neglectful throughout her childhood. Sarah identified that the sexual abuse by her mother included fondling, digital penetration, exposure to her mother masturbating, and being forced to watch her brother being sexually abused by her mother. Sarah reported that this brother sexually abused her as well when she was between the ages of 9 to 14.
4. Charlene was in her mid-thirties, single, and had one daughter (age 14). Charlene identified her stepmother as the maternal offender. The sexual abuse by her stepmother occurred to Charlene when she was between the ages of 7 and 13 and included fondling, penetration, and oral sex and being forced to have sexual intercourse with two uncles. Charlene reported severe physical abuse that included beatings with a belt and being cut with a machete and being forced to endure enemas when she complained of feeling dirty.

The impact of maternal sexual abuse to the daughters reported by Reckling (2004) is summarized here. These effects are not in any particular order of severity or frequency, nor are they meant to imply that all daughters who experience child sexual abuse and other types of maltreatment by their mothers will experience these particular effects. Rather, they are provided to help understand how a daughter's self-concept as a mother can be impacted when she has experienced maternal sexual abuse. The daughters reported ambivalence about having children, feeling uncomfortable with the role of being a mother and anxious about not knowing what to do or how to feel as a mother. As one woman described it, "I just really felt that I would have no chance to be a good parent because I was afraid that I would be abusive, but my larger fear was how would I possibly know what to do" (p. 55). The women also described fears related to the gender of the child, specifically if they had a girl child and questioned whether they would know how to provide what their daughter would need emotionally. While the women did not report a fear of sexually abusing a daughter, Reckling observed that the women did articulate "a fear of repeating other painful aspects of the relationship with their mothers and feared recreating mother-daughter relationships similar to those of their childhood" (p. 57).

The daughters expressed concerns about not knowing what was appropriate or inappropriate as a mother, lacking confidence in their ability to mother, and feeling unprepared to parent. They also worried about discipline and that they would not be able to make good judgments and thereby do something that would unknowingly hurt their child. Specific to having a daughter was a fear of not being able to meeting a daughter's developmental needs, such as explaining when and how menstruation begins. One woman described facing this developmental milestone with her daughter: "I have had nothing that even remotely resembles an appropriate interaction with this stuff" (Reckling, 2004, p. 58). Another woman feared that her daughter would physically resemble her mother or that by simply having a daughter would "awaken painful childhood feelings" (p. 58). All of the daughters reported needing to recognize and work through feelings of detachment toward their children, which was viewed by Reckling as a way to avoid abusing their children by keeping their children emotionally distant. A sense of detachment from children might also reflect a lack of confidence in knowing how to bond with their child since they themselves did not receive appropriate and nurturing bonding by their mothers.[65] Feelings of detachment can also result from prolonged symptoms of anxiety, depression, and dissociation that arise from repeated and severe sexual abuse (Duncan, 2004). These particular symptoms can increase in severity and frequency for mothers who have experienced child sexual abuse or become exacerbated due to the normal hormonal shifts that occur to women during pregnancy and after childbirth (Duncan, 2005a).

Reckling (2004) also discussed the resilience of the women and the decisions they made to diminish the effects of maternal sexual abuse on their own mothering. The daughters identified seeking out sources of information on mothering, such as books and parenting classes. They also looked to other people to provide guidance and to serve as positive role models (e.g., one woman named her mother-in-law a positive role model). The daughters engaged a network of supportive people by establishing friendships, attending self-help groups, and seeking therapy to work through the more difficult issues of maternal sexual abuse and to support "becoming safe, loving parents" (Reckling, 2004, p. 62). Some of the daughters chose to attend therapy before their child was born, and some returned to therapy after the birth of their child. One woman shared her belief that she could break the cycle of abuse, and another woman admitted that therapy helped her with her struggle to sexually abuse her daughter and to learn how to restructure these impulses and not to act on them.

Supportive husbands were also identified by the women as a source of resilience. One woman identified her husband as being good with children even before she gave birth to their children. Reckling (2004) suggests that "it is possible they watched their husbands to learn about parents" (p. 63) and that the women were positive overall about their relationship with their husbands. Two of the women identified their husbands as the people who encouraged them to seek help or who acted on their behalf to engage supportive help.

A particular aspect of the women's resilience was their eventual ability to embrace their motherhood with joy and enthusiasm and to have a sense of their own agency in making different choices and that they were not destined to repeat the legacy of maternal abuse. The ability of the women to identify and express their fears and insecurities and identify the need for information, support, and guidance about positive parenting is viewed as a particular strength and a measure of their motivation to secure a different future for their children and for themselves as mothers.

Sexual victimization in childhood is known to have long-lasting adverse effects on a child's development (Duncan, 2004). Among the adverse effects that have been identified as a result of maternal sexual abuse are a deeper sense of betrayal, shame and confusion, problems with substance abuse, self-injury, suicidal thoughts and attempts, depression, rage, mistrust of women, identity issues, discomfort with sex, fear of abusing children, and reported victimization of children.[66] Other adverse effects include dissociation, sexual confusion, loss and grief, problems with remembering the abuse, fear of disclosing sexual abuse by a mother, experiencing intrusive memories of the abuse, and problematic relationships in adulthood.[67] The more pervasive and physically intrusive the sexual abuse was, the more problematic the adverse effects.[68] When considering the impact that maternal sexual abuse has on children, the potential for adverse effects is quite similar to when the parental offender is a father (Elliott,

1993a). The difference appears in a deeper sense of betrayal and the intensity of the experience of maternal sexual abuse (Denov, 2004a). Therefore, while all sexual abuse is problematic for a child, there does appear to be a greater overall adverse effect when the offender is a mother or another woman who serves this role for the child.

The stigma that children of female sexual abusers face is similar to what children of sexual abuse by males faced several years back and, at times, still face today. To remove this stigma, society is charged with not repeating the mistakes of the past where children were silenced by a refusal to believe their experiences of sexual abuse. Lifting the silence around maternal sexual abuse allows sons and daughters to be heard and their lives can be reclaimed.

RELINQUISHING THE ICONIC IMAGE OF MOTHER

"The American mother is the greatest source of the country's strength and inspiration," so declared President Woodrow Wilson on May 8, 1914, when he signed a congressional resolution to create Mother's Day as a national holiday in the United States.[69] The words of President Wilson sum up the iconic image[70] of mother that is held across societies and cultures around the world. The bond between a mother and child is considered the quintessential relationship that provides the basis for developing healthy human connections (Bowlby, 1988). In their relationships with children, mothers are expected to be warm, nurturing, supportive, caring, and protective, not abusive, violent, humiliating, and exploitive. It is perhaps because of the discord between the iconic image of mother and the reality that there are mothers who commit acts of aggression against their children that maternal sexual abuse is considered the most hidden form of child sexual abuse (Banning, 1989; Bunting, 2005; Burroughs, 2004; Peter, 2006). As shared by Deborah Burroughs (2004) "sexual abuse of children by women is a crime that seems so unnatural that it offends society's moral instincts." Burroughs goes on to explain that "a growing body of research, however, indicates that the incidence of sexual abuse of children by women, primarily mothers, is occurring in alarming numbers, and the increase in the numbers of occurrence is rapidly rising" (p. 481) indicates that maternal sexual abuse may no longer be as invisible as it once was.

Grandmothers, like mothers, have a special relationship with children that extends from one generation to the next. Emily's grandson, Michael, was sexually abused by his paternal grandmother. Emily shares, "The initial reaction was shock and dismay. Before this situation happened to my grandson, I really did not think much about female sexual abusers. I think the main reason is the fact that a woman's traditional role in the home as mother/grandmother tends to put her above any wrongdoing or suspicion because females are supposed to be the 'nurturer,' and we have a tendency to assume that sexual abuse is a male-perpetrated crime."

Emily is not alone in her views about females, nor is she the first to be shocked to learn that mothers and even grandmothers entrusted with the care of children have the capacity to harm children. Kevin Fagan, an award-winning journalist with the *San Francisco Chronicle*, shared that "it is the stereotype in our society that women are nurturers and that it is females who are the victims of sexual violence, not the other way around. In fact, I have found that people are more shocked when a woman commits a sexual crime than when a woman actually murders a child."[71]

Both Emily and Fagan affirm the importance of moving beyond the mythical image of mother as created by societies. When the iconic image and myth of motherhood are replaced with reality, there is the opportunity to view women as human beings capable of a range of behaviors that include the capacity to nurture children or the capacity to harm children. This shift in perspective also supports the growing belief that it is the parent–child bond that is essential for developing healthy human relationships and not the gender of the parent. This broader perspective expands the capacity for children to be nurtured by parents who have the ability to serve this essential role for children because it is not based on gender, rather it is based on the premise of caring about children. Additionally, maintaining societal stereotypes about what it means to be a female or what it means to be a mother will limit our understanding of the experience of child victims who are sexually abused by their mothers and create barriers to our efforts to identify and prevent maternal sexual abuse.

CHAPTER SUMMARY

Accepting that mothers are human beings and not iconic images is essential in combating child sexual abuse and other forms of child maltreatment that exist in families where violence is the norm. Stopping parental sexual abuse begins when mothers and fathers who commit these crimes admit to the harm they cause their children. Preventing child sexual abuse is furthered by a society willing to admit that there are mothers who do in fact commit child sexual abuse. Including information about maternal sexual abuse and female sex offenders in prevention education programs will assist in these efforts and provide protection to children across age-groups, ethnicity, and economic backgrounds.

For many survivors of maternal sexual abuse, their victimization is made invisible by a persistent denial that some mothers, like some fathers, can and do harm their children. While it is an unfortunate reality that some women are in fact sexually abusive and physically violent, denying this reality will not keep children safe, and it will not allow mothers to create an alternative to their abusive behavior. Denial silences victims and gives their offenders ample opportunity to continue their sexually abusive behavior. As one survivor put it, "A consequence of this attitude in society is that, for people like myself who have survived being sexually abused by a woman, we suffer intolerable alienation and little recognition or support from the public or professionals alike" (p. 284).[72]

While it may be that mothers were at one time victims of the parents from whom they too had a right to expect protection, it is also true that mothers who become offenders have no right to harm their children regardless of what occurred to them. The fact is that mothers are seldom "all victim or all offender," and it is also true that neither mother blaming nor mother excusing will provide the protection that children need and deserve to live a life free of sexual abuse and its effects. There is a call to action emerging in society to end violence against children. Meeting this challenge will require that parents who harm their children are held accountable, and perhaps from this personal and societal accountability will emerge a new reality where sexual victimization is no longer a family legacy or a societal reality.

3

Female Sexual Coercion and Aggression in College Dating Relationships

Knowing my own mind, I also know that a good mind must be flexible and open to change.

—Susan Brownmiller, *Against Our Will: Men, Women and Rape*[1]

MOVING BEYOND GENDER STEREOTYPES

It has been proposed by anthropologists Fry and Gabriel (1994) that a main reason for a lack of attention to female aggression has been the result of Western scholarship that has constructed mostly one-sided theories that explain human aggression as primarily a male phenomenon. Fry and Gabriel contend that one-sided theories are problematic because they create "gender-traps in which the very same act taken on by women and men is differentially represented" (p. 166).[2] An alliance toward one-sided gender theories has promoted the impression that aggression by females does not exist in the natural world or that, if it does, it is only under certain circumstances.[3] For example, when female violence occurs in intimate relationships, it is often explained as occurring as a woman's defense against male violence,[4] and if alternate explanations are offered, these explanations are dismissed as attempts to blame women for male violence. This narrow framework for viewing relationship violence does not necessarily consider that a particular woman may be committing acts of aggression under her own volition; it summarily dismisses female agency (i.e., a woman's ability to act on her own and without being under the influence of a man) and the possibility of mutual violence occurring between couples.[5] A study by Shook, Gerrity, Jurich, and Segrist (2000) on courtship violence identified that among their sample of college-age couples 82 percent of the students across both genders reported using tactics of verbal and physical aggression against a partner within the past year, indicating that both male and female college students engage in and are subjected to acts of partner aggression in their dating relationship.

Rose Medeiros and Murray Straus (2006) challenge gender-based theories of partner violence while providing a judicious, balanced response to this social and family problem in terms of recognizing that violence by either partner should be recognized and prevented. These authors put forth the following for consideration and thought:

> The unstated agenda of authors such as Dobash and Dobash and Nazroo is to excuse violence by women by implying that violence by women is morally courageous because it is assumed to be in self-defense, whereas violence by men is morally indefensible because it is assumed to be an act of domination rather than self-defense. Some violence by women is in self-defense, but, this also applies to some violence by men. The same distortion of the scientific evidence applies to discussion of dominance and con-

KEY POINTS

Sex role stereotypes obscure female sexual coercion and aggression against males on college campuses.

Contrary to popular beliefs young men experience adverse effects when they experience sexual coercion by females.

College women report committing a range of sexually coercive and aggressive behaviors that include physical assault, verbal coercion, psychological manipulation, and sexual stalking.

Sexual harassment and sexual stalking of men by women on college campuses includes the use of social network sites on the Internet.

Alcohol abuse plays a significant role in both male and female college students experience of legally defined sexual assault.

Adversarial beliefs about dating relationships and prior victimization are associated with an increased risk for females to commit sexual offenses defined as sexual coercion and aggression.

> trol. Only studies showing male use of violence to coerce, dominate, and control are cited despite a number of studies showing that this also applies to violence by female partners (Dutton & Nicholls, 2005). We agree that violence by men against a partner is morally indefensible but that this also applies to partner violence by women. (p. 59)

Whether ignoring female violence is due to a hidden political agenda, from a general naïveté regarding female aggression, or because of a lack of interest in preventing female violence is not readily clear. What does seem to be the case is that one-sided gendered theories about violence can contribute to all forms of female violence continuing across cultures and sectors of society, thereby continuing the harm that female aggressors cause to their victims.[6]

Carney, Buttell, and Dutton (2007) assert that studies substantiating female-initiated violence have been "suppressed, unreported, reinterpreted, or denied," beginning with the findings of the first National Family Violence Survey conducted in the United States in 1975, which found women also committed acts of violence and aggression against men at about equal rates. Carney and colleagues are not the only ones who hold the view that information about female-initiated violence is suppressed. Dutton and Nicholls (2005) propose that the silence around female violence and aggression is due to political agendas and is perpetuated by the acceptance of unfounded ideology that alleges that spouse assault is exclusively male perpetrated. When female intimate violence is ignored or reinterpreted to be solely defensive in nature, it risks viewing female aggression as harmless. Furthermore, the act of ignoring female violence appears to occur even when women themselves report that their physical violence against a male partner is not motivated by self-defense.[7] Referring back to Medeiros and Straus (2006) they make the case that:

> Those who believe that male dominance and male degradation of women is almost always at the root of partner violence tend to focus on asserting or implying that, when women physically assault a partner, the causes or motives are different than when men attack their partners. Unfortunately, much of what has been written on differences in causes and motives is based on the beliefs and values of the authors rather than on empirical comparisons of men and women. (p. 59)

The susceptibility for female acts of aggression in their intimate relationships to be ignored, dismissed, or discounted is similar to the findings of Allen (1991), Anderson (1998), Denov (2001), Duncan (2006), Hetherton and Beardsall (1998), Nelson (1994), Peluso and Putnam (1996), Rentoul and Appleboom (1997), and Sarrel and Masters (1982), who found that sexual crimes committed by women tended to be ignored, dismissed, negated, and reinterpreted to align with cultural stereotypes about females in general and female sexual behavior in particular, and that these actions have occurred in spite of the evidence on female sexual offending (see Chapter 1).

That female aggression exists is known by any person, male or female, who has been on the receiving end of a controlling, aggressive, rageful or predatory female. Three young men share their experience of being on the receiving end of female sexual violence. As one young man explained, "This girl who was I was at a party talking to offered me drink after drink. Once alone with her and 'making out' she pulled down my pants and hers and put my erection in her vagina. She had sex with me for about 5 minutes when a friend saved me and came into the room and helped me get away" (p. 133).[8] Another young man shared, "She got me drunk and tied me up and then had sex with me 6 times in one night. She was an ex-girlfriend and was getting back at me for dumping her. She was psycho" (p. 134).[9] A young man related this experience: "I visited my girlfriend after drinking with guy friends. She was horny and I wasn't. We had sex once, but I was hit and yelled at when I wanted to leave without doing it again. I made her happy, waited for her to pass out and fall asleep and then left" (p. 135).[10] What is familiar about these young men's descriptions of female sexual aggression is that they are similar to what some young women have reported in their accounts of male sexual aggression where they were pressured or forced into sexual behavior and that physical aggression occurred with the sexual aggression and that alcohol had a role in the aggressive acts that they experienced. For the purpose of the present discussion, *sexual aggression* is defined as any form of behavior directed toward the goal of making another person engage in sexual contact against that person's will or capacity to provide informed consent (adapted from Krahe, Waizenhofer, & Moller, 2003). *Verbal sexual coercion* is defined as insisting, pressuring, or threatening an individual to engage in sexual contact, and *forced sexual coercion* is defined as the use of physical force to make an individual engage in sexual contact (adapted from Hines, 2007).

PROMOTING AN HONEST AND RESPECTFUL DIALOGUE

Sexual aggression is viewed as a significant social and public health problem on college campuses. However, it may come as a surprise that not all victims of sexual aggression on college campuses are females and not all offenders are males and that female sexual coercion on college campuses may be more prevalent than previously recognized.[11] Evidence that male sexual victimization occurs in college-age dating relationships is cited as beginning with Charlene Muehlenhard's study published in 1988 that found college men also experienced unwanted sexual activity in their heterosexual dating relationships. Hines and Saudino (2003) reported that in a sample of 481 college students, in which 179 men and 302 women responded to questions on the revised Conflicts Tactics Scale, 29 percent of men and 35 percent of women reported perpetrating forms of sexual, psychological, and physical aggression in their relationships.

As noted by Russell and Oswald (2002), sexual coercion is "a complex social problem and includes a variety of behaviors, typically ranging from verbal manipulation (insistent arguing, false pretenses, threats to terminate a relationship, or threats of physical force) to forced physical aggression and rape" and that studies suggest "that verbal coercion is the predominant form of sexual coercion used by men and women in relationships" (p. 273). Russell and Oswald identify that verbal coercion, rather than physical force, is the type of sexual aggression that occurs most often between heterosexual men and women in their college dating relationships. The research on male sexual victimization by college females has been consistently reported for a number of years even though it is seldom talked about in college-based prevention education programs where the focus is on sexual coercion and aggression committed by males against females.[12] This accumulating body of research has consistently identified that while using physical force to gain sex (rape) is still the predominant domain of males, college-age females engage in a wide range of sexually aggressive and coercive behaviors in their heterosexual dating relationships and that their offending patterns and coercive strategies are quite similar to that of their male counterparts.[13]

However, given how contentious it is to challenge gender stereotypes about sexual aggression and coercion and the prevailing acceptance of one-sided theories about relational aggression, it is understandable that acknowledging and discussing sexual aggression by females against males in their college dating relationships may not be considered in some circles a politically correct topic. This may be in part due to a fear that an open discussion of female sexual aggression will threaten the established movement to end sexual violence against women on college campuses rather than considering the possibility that by acknowledging that both males and females commit sexual aggression, this dual acknowledgment may actually improve the overarching goal of ending sexual violence on college campuses.[14] As suggested by Diane Oswald and Brenda Russell (2006), it may be that to understand the problem of sexual aggression in dating relationships, it will be important to acknowledge that both men and women can be sexually coercive.

John Macchietto (1998) shares his experience as a clinician working in this controversial and potentially volatile political climate of addressing male victims of female sexual aggression. Macchietto explains that, as a clinician,

> Dealing with men who have been sexually victimized by women is considered to be a politically incorrect topic. This makes it very difficult to have an open and healthy

dialogue, both from the mental health community, and the general public. My own experience is that discussing or writing about this topic professionally has resulted in a great amount of hostility from several of my peers and other critics who would disagree with me. It has also alienated me from some of my peers, who agree with me, but only privately because they fear being put in a situation where they might become disenfranchised from mainstream thought. (p. 188)

Similar to what researchers in the field of domestic violence have experienced, researchers in the field of female sexual aggression have experienced an analogous sense of hostility. Peter Anderson (1998) addresses the negative politics of studying sexually aggressive women he faced by recalling that when he chose to study women's sexual aggression toward adolescent and adult men as his dissertation topic, some colleagues suggested that his research was potentially damaging to women's causes, while others warned that his work would never be published. Anderson and Struckman-Johnson (1998) encourage people not to take sides since polarized opinions will not advance the understanding of sexual aggression between the sexes.

Admittedly, research regarding female sexual aggression in college dating relationships challenges the long-held assumptions that have been a part of the traditional landscape of sexual violence analysis, prevention education curriculums, and community advocacy on behalf of females.[15] The idea, let alone the reality, of women acting in a predatory and aggressive manner toward men contradicts the long-standing societal stereotypes about gender and violence, power and dominance, and victim and aggressor as they have been constructed and presented in the social structure of Western society.[16] Moving beyond these entrenched beliefs will require that gender stereotypes be deconstructed, sexist beliefs about female sexuality be abandoned; knowledge about female sexual aggression will need to replace gender politics and personal bias; and the idea that males cannot be sexually victimized by females will need to be reevaluated.[17]

The belief that men cannot be sexually victimized by women is in part derived from what Sarrel and Masters (1982) refer to as the "myth of sexual invulnerability," which views men as not capable of being aggressed against because they are "more sexually assertive, more sexually preoccupied and more interested in engaging in sex than are women." The male stereotypes that are reflected in the myth of male sexual invulnerability are also reflected in traditional sexual script (TSS) theory, which expects males to initiate and pursue sexual activity, dominate females, and rarely if ever refuse sexual advances by females.[18] On the other hand, TSS theory expects females to be less interested in sex, acquiesce to male sexual demands, practice chastity, and invested in resisting male sexual advances.[19] It is in these sex role stereotypes that TSS theory identifies males as the offenders of sexual assault and females as the victims,[20] thereby ignoring the potential of female sexual aggression and the victimization of males by females in the real world.[21] TSS theory offers a narrow framework for understanding the range of sexual behavior between the sexes and does not consider that other "scripts" may be operating in young women's sexual relationships as they exist in contemporary society.

Because of its inherent limitations, TSS theory is subject to criticism as being outdated and having less relevance in contemporary society.[22] These criticisms stem from the failure of TSS theory to incorporate research over the past 25 years that indicate that (a) females do in fact act as sexual initiators and are more likely than men to begin sexual encounters, (b) females willingly engage in casual sex outside committed relationships, and (c) when asked, females admit to committing sexual aggression and violence against males (Gannon & Rose, 2008; Greene & Faulkner, 2005; Muehlenhard & Cook, 1988; O'Sullivan & Byers, 1993; Russell & Oswald, 2001; Sisco & Figueredo, 2008; Struckman-Johnson & Anderson, 1998). Additionally, TSS theory is at-risk of promoting gender stereotypes rather than diminishing them.[23]

Since TSS theory has been a primary model for studying sexual aggression, it may also be a contributing factor to less attention being paid to sexual aggression by females.[24] Byers and O'Sullivan (1998) point out that "researchers have been affected by the stereotypic expectations within the traditional sexual script" (p. 147), which is evidenced by a majority of research that only examines females as victims of sexual aggression and not as offenders. Researchers and theorists who hold to the *stereotype of sexual aggression* as the sole domain of males[25] rather than viewing sexual aggression as a human behavior available to both males and females may be less inclined to view female sexual aggression as a social and public health problem that results in negative consequences to both the male victim and the female offender.[26] Anderson and Struckman-Johnson (1998) have suggested that among the reasons for less research on female sexual aggression on college campuses and reasons that the research that does exist may be discounted are three factors: (a) the acceptance of the myth that women can do no harm, (b) the failure of investigators to ask women and men about female sexual aggression, and (c) the existence of a *double standard* in defining male and female sexual aggression. Sisco and Figueredo (2008) propose that the nature and strategies of sexual violence have shifted over the years and that research has not kept abreast of these changing norms in terms of the instruments used to measure sexual aggression or the theories to explain its occurrence by both genders.

Indeed, denying the sexual aggression of one group of people (females) while magnifying the sexual aggression of another group of people (males) will not put an end to sexual aggression.[27] Adversarial beliefs held by either gender can promote antagonism between the genders and thereby sustain the risk factors for males and females to engage in adversarial sexual behavior rather than consensual and mutually satisfying sexual relationships.[28] It is also important to consider that trivializing or ignoring the male experience of being on the receiving end of unwanted sexual behavior by females may inadvertently give men permission to trivialize or ignore the female experience of unwanted sexual behavior and give females permission to continue their sexually coercive behavior.[29] Oswald and Russell (2006) remind us of the reason that it is important to study both men and women with regard to sexual dating violence stating that "coercion from any person in a relationship, regardless of his or her gender, is problematic for the relationship and the people involved" (p. 93).

Acknowledging female sexual aggression on college campuses or in the general community does not need to detract from the seriousness of female victimization, nor does it have to create a backlash to feminist causes. However, feminist advocates and researchers alike are reminded that equality between the sexes is sustained by equality among the sexes and that the women's movement and feminist scholarship were founded on the rights of all human beings to live a life free of the worry or threat of violence.[30] By acknowledging female sexual aggression, the opportunity is provided to understand the entire spectrum of sexual aggression as a complex human problem that exacts a serious toll on individuals, couples, families, and society. The reality is that all genders will experience meaningful gains when sexual violence, as an expression of human violence, is ended.

FEMALE SEXUAL AGGRESSION AND MALE VICTIMIZATION

> "We were alone together and he didn't want to have sex because he wanted it to be special. I felt rejected, telling him 'what it's not special enough that's it's just you and me.' I started crying and basically guilted him into having sex." (Struckman-Johnson and Struckman-Johnson, 2003)

In a summary of their review on female sexual aggression and male victimization in college dating relationships, Larimer, Lydum, Anderson, and Turner (1999) point out the following:

- While a majority of states have by now adopted gender-neutral laws, the essential definition of rape has remained in the institutionalized construct of females as victims and males as offenders.
- The majority of past research on unwanted sexual contact used survey instruments that excluded the female experience of committing sexual aggression and coercion.

- Males either have been excluded from victimization studies or are included only as an offender; this has limited the information on male victimization and female offending.
- In recent years, researchers have expanded their assessment of sexual aggression to include men as potential victims and females as potential offenders.
- With the use of more gender-neutral survey instruments, male victimization by females is no longer excluded as it once was in research.
- Despite recent reports suggesting few gender differences in the prevalence of unwanted sexual contact, there continues to be relatively little attention focused on the phenomenon of male victimization as compared to the research on female victimization.

Unfortunately, it is not unusual that male victimization can be scoffed at and ridiculed, contributing to males not admitting to acts of sexual aggression when they are committed against them and thereby diminishing the willingness of males to seek personal support or legal interventions when they experience sexual victimization.[31] A college coed describes her *sexually aggressive* behavior toward a male partner: "I told him how sexy he was and that he turned me on. I asked for sex. He refused. I retreated for a while but then continued to ask and say erotic things to him [putting ideas into his head] and every chance I could I would touch his genitals or buttocks."[32] Another young woman shared, "I locked the room door that we were in. I kissed and touched him. I removed his shirt and unzipped his pants. He asked me stop. I didn't. Then, I sat on top of him. He had two beers but wasn't drunk" (p. 84).[33] What is striking about these examples is that the behavior the young women describe could result in legal charges of sexual assault and expulsion from college if committed by a male. *Questions to ponder:* Would legal action or expulsion from college occur against a female if her sexual aggression were reported? What would be the response to the male victim? What would be the response of the college student's parents if no action were taken against the female on behalf of their son? What policies and actions are needed by colleges and universities to prevent and respond to sexual aggression among college students? What types of education would benefit college students regarding consent and the value of respecting personal boundaries?

Among the types of sexually coercive tactics that college-age females report using against males include *psychological coercion* and *emotional abuse*, such as threats of self-harm and suicide, spreading rumors about males that include sexual impotency or references to homosexuality when the male is heterosexual, and threatening to tell a girlfriend that a young man had sex outside a committed relationship, whether he did or not, in order to gain his compliance to sexual demands.[34] For example, one young man reported, "She entered my apartment to discuss a recent break-up, began to get real 'handsy.' Stated that if I did not stop the pain by having sex with her, she would find a way to 'end it all.' I could only assume she meant herself." Females also report using or threatening to use physical force and weapons, such as a knife or a gun, to gain control and force sex with a male.[35] Alcohol and drugs are readily available to females, just as they are to males, to gain control over an unwilling partner.[36] The use of weapons and physical force, and inducement through drugs and alcohol are defined as a form of date rape and physical assault when committed by a male against a female (Sisco & Figueredo, 2008; Struckman-Johnson & Struckman-Johnson, 2003).

While the prevalence of male victimization by females varies across studies because of varying methods used by researchers to measure and define sexual aggression, research does indicate that between 4 and 44 percent of males on college campuses have experienced some form of female sexual aggression. A study by Muehlenhard and Cook (1988) was among the first to ask males about their experience of sexual victimization. What they found surprised them. Among 507 male and 486 female college students, 94 percent of the males and 98 percent of the females reported experiencing unwanted kissing, petting, or intercourse sometime in their lives, and *more men* (63%) *than women* (46%) reported unwanted intercourse. In their review of 13 studies that occurred between 1982 and 1996 and that compared college-age men's and women's participation in sexual aggression Byers and O'Sullivan (1998) found that across the studies, college males consistently reported females who would not stop their behavior when asked, got them drunk or stoned and then had sex with them, and verbally pressured them into sexual behavior even when they refused. The types of sexual behaviors that the young men reported included kissing, fondling, and sexual intercourse. While a minority, males also reported being threatened by physical force or having a knife or a gun used against them to make them engage in unwanted sexual behavior. In these same 13 studies, *females reported using coercive techniques* that included the use of weapons, getting a partner drunk or stoned, threatening self-harm and suicide if a male did not comply with their sexual demands, verbally pressuring a partner with arguments, and both threatening and using physical force.

Sisco and Figueredo (2008), in their study of sexual aggression among college-age males and females, identified the following behaviors that both males and females engage in: knowingly exposing a person to sexually transmitted infections, verbally pressuring partners for sex, posting intimate images to the Internet or sharing sexual images with friends without permission, technological and social network sexual stalking, forcing victims to engage in sex with more than one person, forcing a victim to disrobe or flash, nonconsensual oral or manual contact of the penis or vagina, and forcing a victim to self-masturbate while being watched. Fiebert and Tucci (1998) found that approximately 70 percent of the college males in their study reported experiencing some type of sexual harassment, verbal pressure, or physical coercion by a woman, while Hannon, Kuntz, Van Laar, and Williams (1996) found that 10 percent of males in their study had experienced a completed sexual assault by a heterosexual partner during college. Struckman-Johnson and Struckman-Johnson (1994) found that 34 percent of the 204 college men in their study reported experiencing sexual aggression where women were responsible for 24 percent of the sexual aggression, males were responsible for 4 percent, and both males and females were responsible for 6 percent of the sexual aggression reported.

Anderson and Aymani (1993) reported that about half of the 212 women in their study *reported initiating sex with a man while he was drunk*, and 6 percent of the females reported using *physical force*. Lottes (1991) discovered that 24 percent of males in a classroom sample of 300 college students reported that they had been coerced into sexual intercourse. Larimer et al. (1999) found that when using a gender-neutral (not biased toward males as offenders) survey instrument with 296 college students in Greek organizations, a similar percentage of men and women reported having unwanted sexual intercourse because they were verbally pressured while drinking or using drugs at the time. Russell and Oswald (2001) found that in their college sample, 18 percent of females reported engaging in sexually aggressive behaviors, ranging from verbal coercion to the use of physical aggression.

Cross-cultural studies outside the United States have also found that females sexually aggress against males. Hines (2007) provided analysis on female sexual aggression from 38 sites across seven countries[37] participating in the International Dating Violence Study. The majority of study participants consisted of female college students. Hines reported that across different cultures, females engaged in a wide range of sexually aggressive behaviors toward males. Specifically, Hines found that the greater the hostility that females reported against males, the more victimization the men reported. A study in Poland (2008)[38] compared rates of psychological and physical aggression, sexual coercion, and resulting injury across college-age women and men that included 100 women and 101 men. The researchers found that all three types of interpersonal violence were high among both Polish men and women in this college sample. For women the rates for each type of violence were 89 percent for psychological aggression (men: 77%), 48 percent for physical aggression (men: 36%), and 40 percent for sexual coercion (men: 42%). Relative to the International Dating Violence Study, this group of *college women—but not the college men—had high levels of causing injury* to their male partner and using threats or actual physical force to obtain oral, anal, or vaginal intercourse.

In Germany, Krahe et al. (2003) found that 9 percent of 248 women between the ages of 15 and 24 reported having completed sex with a man against his will and that 5.4 percent reported attempting to have sex with a man against his will. In responding to the Women's Sexual Aggression Survey, the females indicated that they had sexually exploited a man while he was incapacitated. The young women also admitted to using verbal coercion and physical force to gain sexual compliance from males. The males who were identified as the target of the young women's sexual aggression were frequently an ex-partner, friend, or acquaintance, although a few of the men were strangers. A study in Sweden (1996)[39] found that an equal number of men and women (approximately 8% of the study sample) reported that someone had gotten them "drunk or stoned" in order to have sex with them. A Canadian study[40] found that 24 percent of males reported being pressured or forced into sexual contact in a heterosexual dating context during the year the study was conducted. Wilcox and Francis (1997) concluded from their survey of 236 adolescent and young adult women in England between the ages 16 and 19 that females no longer held to the traditional gender roles as measured by the Bem Sex-Role Inventory prevalent in the United States in the 1970s. Wilcox and Francis suggest that females are no longer assimilating cultural stereotypes about what it means to be female, and this may very well include no longer adhering to stereotypes about female sexual behavior.

The question arises as to whether some college-age females begin their sexual offending and aggression early in their dating relationships? In New Zealand,[41] a survey of 221 high school seniors revealed that 67 percent of the boys reported that they had engaged in unwanted sexual activity because of pressure from teen girls. One finding of the study that was particularly troubling was the level of acceptance (i.e., "no big deal") that the teen boys had in terms of being sexually coerced by females. That boys would so readily dismiss their sexual victimization by a female substantiates the disregard of male victimization that occurs so readily in our society and the dismissal of the potential harm to a boy's development when he is victimized by a female (Duncan & Williams, 1998). Results of the survey indicated that it was not unusual to find that among students 16 to 18 years old, both teen girls and boys coerced their dating partners into sexual activity, something that has been substantiated in other studies on teen dating behavior (Centers for Disease Control, 2008). It is a problematic trend when studies indicate that sexual coercion among males and females may well become established in the early stages of dating which indicates that educational programs and public campaigns to reverse this trend is sorely needed for our youth.

What is a concern in reviewing the research on female sexual coercion and aggression occurring by young women is that there has been no remarkable attention given to it in national studies on college campuses[42] and programs funded to prevent sexual violence on college campuses[43] despite what 25 years of evidence indicates. Given what studies substantiate about the sexual norms on college campuses regarding male and female sexual aggression, it is evident that both college men and women would benefit from resources, personal support, and education regarding how to approach, develop, and maintain positive affiliation in their relationships with each other.[44] Questions for college-based prevention education programs that would include young women might include the following:

1. What screening, support services and educational programs would benefit young women entering college to assist them in navigating their intimate relationships that would include information about the difference between sexual aggression and sexual assertiveness?
2. What stereotypes about male sexual behavior might be contributing to female aggression against males?
3. Have some females assimilated the stereotype of the TSS theory for male sexual behavior and adapted it as their own?
4. Are young adult females aware of what defines sexual assertiveness and consent in terms of open discussion, verbal agreement, and genuine respect for another modeled through words and behavior?

Studies do not appear to address these basic questions in order to help determine what is motivating and sustaining female sexual aggression. Additionally, perhaps the time has come to change the direction of research to become less about identifying gender stereotypes about sexual violence and more about paying greater attention to educating both males and females on the adversarial beliefs inherent in committing sexual violence and to teaching about how to have healthy, genuine relationships that are mutually respectful and satisfying. This approach will require an inclusive view where sexual aggression and gender stereotypes that sustain sexual aggression by males and females are recognized and the universal causes remedied.

Two of the male stereotypes embedded in TSS theory that could promote female sexual aggression is that (a) males do not refuse sexual advances by females because (b) males are constantly seeking sex. It may be that there is a group of females who engage in sexual aggression, who have internalized stereotypes about male sexual behavior, and adhere to the myth of male sexual invulnerability, and while holding adversarial beliefs about men. As stated by Muehlenhard (1998) in her discussion regarding research that perpetuates gender stereotypes,

> Limiting research to studying only sexually aggressive men and the women they victimize implicitly perpetuates gender stereotypes, such as the stereotypes of men as active and women as passive, men as victimizers and women as victims, and men as always seeking sex and women as either resisting or acquiescing to male pursuit. (p. 29)

The stereotype that men are always willing to engage in sex prevents the recognition that (a) men are capable of making other choices about their sexual behavior, such as deciding not to engage in casual sex because of preferring a committed partner; (b) men are not always thinking about sex; and (c) men do not always act on their thoughts about sex.

Another example of a stereotype in the traditional sexual script is that males seek to dominate females, including sexual dominance. This stereotype was refuted in a study by Renaud and Byers (2005), who found that when males did think about engaging in sexual dominance, they reported a greater frequency of *negative reactions* to these thoughts and sought ways to disrupt these thoughts from occurring. In addition, young men reported that they did not find thoughts of sexually dominating a female acceptable or pleasant. However, *females in the study* indicated that they found thoughts of *sexually dominating a male partner* pleasant, not aversive and not something to avoid. The authors concluded that *contrary to the traditional sexual script*, it was the women who were more likely to find thoughts of sexual domination of a male as pleasant, while the men were more likely to find the thoughts of sexual dominance of a female unpleasant. Of course, the good news might be that these young men were raised in a value system of respecting individual boundaries that includes sexual boundaries and that these men are reflecting the reality that not all males are out to rape, sexually dominate, and sexually coerce females as proposed by "many theories of rape that implicitly assume that the capacity to rape can be found in most if not all men" (Schewe, Adam, & Ryan, 2009, p. 219).

A study by Schewe et al. (2009) on the temptation to use force among college-age males further dispels the stereotype of the ever-aggressive, sexual-seeking, dominant male. Schewe et al. found that out a total of 83 male participants, 57 men indicated "that they were never tempted to use force to obtain sexual contact" (p. 228). Among the reasons that young men cited for not being tempted to use force were that they did not need to use force to obtain sex, moral reasons, respect or empathy for the other person, and a desire for future opportunities for consensual sex. Additionally, there were 22 college males in the study who reported the temptation to use force; however, only four acted on their temptation to gain sexual intercourse. The other 18 males who acted on their temptation to use force engaged in fondling genitals and breasts, kissing, and holding hands. These 18 males *stopped* their behavior because of reporting feelings of "feeling like an ass, guilt, and being selfish" (p. 227). The 22 young men who endorsed the temptation to use force also indicated adversarial beliefs in their relationships with females and characteristics of hypermasculinity. While a minority of young men acted on their temptation to use force, the majority of young men reported not experiencing the temptation to use force, indicating that the stereotype of males seeking sex, forcing sex, and dominating females to have sex is just that: a stereotype. Similar studies are needed with college-age females regarding their temptation to use sexual aggression, actual use of sexual aggression, adversarial beliefs held toward males, an equivalent measurement of the "hypermasculinity" scale for females, and acceptance of the male rape myth. The good news is that the study indicates that college-age males are not always driven by thoughts of sexual dominance and coercion in their goal of having a relationship with college-age females and that males are capable of being more than what stereotypes have proposed. What is important to determine is whether college-age females have achieved similar goals (i.e., not using sexual coercion) in their relationships with young males and whether society as a whole has moved beyond acceptance of the traditional sexual script and the male–female stereotypes that it engenders.[45]

Struckman-Johnson and Anderson (1998) identify that while both men and women judge a range of coercive sexual strategies as unacceptable by either sex, adherence to sex role and gender stereotypes suggests that "sexual violations by a woman are seen as romantic and motivated by intimacy, whereas the identical behaviors by men are viewed as threatening, aggressive, and motivated by power and control" (p. 15). Struckman-Johnson and Anderson give the following examples of how female sexual aggression is redefined by audiences in public and professional forums when they present their findings on female sexual aggression:

> To paraphrase the actual reactions of some people in our audiences, a woman who persistently demands sex from a reluctant man is viewed as expressing her "sexuality"; a woman who persistently kisses, touches, and removes clothing from a reluctant man is being "seductive"; a woman who uses physical restraint to sit on a man or lock him in a room is being "playful"; and a woman who initiates sex with a drunken man is "way too horny for her own good." Some of these same actions by a man could potentially result in criminal prosecution. (p. 15)

It appears that there may be a shifting of the *double standard* when it comes to sexual coercion by females whereby women are now given social approval to sexually aggress against a reluctant male partner when in reality neither males nor females should receive approval for sexual aggression.

John Macchietto (1991) makes the point that cultural stereotypes and biases in the shaping of the male gender make it less likely for victimized men to receive recognition. Macchietto offers three explanations into the reluctance by males to defend themselves against female aggressors. One explanation is that most males are socialized never to hit a woman and that most men often fear that their physical force would be more damaging to a woman because of their size. As an outcome, males are reluctant to respond to a woman's aggression with physical force. A second explanation is that men are injured but seldom report their injuries, or they minimize and discount the emotional aspects of the traumatic experience as shared by this man: "All the scenes in college where girls would seduce me, and I'd just kind of let them do whatever they wanted to do. Or I would do for them whatever they wanted me to do. And then just get out" (p. 534).[46] The apathy as expressed in the young man's lack of emotional response is apparent in his statement "whatever they wanted to do." Another man shared this perspective about societal denial of male victimization: "It's like, men aren't abused? You know, who ever heard of that? Who talks about that? If men aren't abused how could I have been abused?" (p. 536).[47] A third explanation has to do with stereotypes about masculinity and sexual behavior where young men feel social pressure to comply with the male stereotypes as explained by this young man: "Me and a friend went out and we ended up making out. She wanted to have intercourse but I didn't feel that attracted to her at the time. I ended up having sex just because she was so persistent and I didn't want to feel like a wimp" (p. 134).[48]

Gender stereotypes harm men and women alike by perpetuating myths and misinformation that in turn maintain unnecessary antagonism between the sexes that can perpetuate a cycle of violence and personal harm.[49] Countering sex role stereotypes in an open forum where discussion of the experiences of unwanted, nonconsensual sexual behavior is defined and understood to have meaning for both genders makes it possible for college men and women to view their coercive behaviors and the beliefs that sustain them as damaging to self, other people, and society at large. Most assuredly, it expands the opportunities available to young adults to interact in a mutually respectful, forthright and honest and manner with each other.

ALCOHOL AND THE RISK FOR SEXUAL COERCION[50]

> "Alcohol was involved. She undressed me, tried to arouse me by touching my genitals, oral sex, and trying to force me inside of her."[51]

College is a time that provides opportunities for further independence in the development of an adult identity that includes forming decisions about future life directions; acquiring knowledge and content of a particular academic subject; meeting new people with similar interests; intellectual discussions;

establishing values, attitudes, and beliefs that guide personal decisions; developing critical thinking skills; enhanced learning opportunities; and the management of time and money. College is also a time that provides increased opportunities for underage drinking and illicit drug use, engaging in unprotected sex, acquiring a sexually transmitted infection, experiencing an unplanned pregnancy, experiencing alcohol- and drug-induced sexual behavior. Because of these diverse and conflicting opportunities, college students can find it difficult to navigate this stage of their lives. Consequently, they end up living with and through the outcomes of their decisions, some of which are not so pleasant and will potentially have lasting effects on their lives.

Over a 14-year period, the Harvard School of Public Health's College Alcohol Study (2008) demonstrated that alcohol-related problems for college students do not begin at the level of drinking, legally defined as intoxication. Rather, reduced cognitive and psychomotor functions are found at lower levels of alcohol consumption. College-age *binge drinkers* consume 91 percent of all the alcohol that students consume, and 68 percent of alcohol consumed is consumed by *frequent* binge drinkers.[52] Unfortunately, parents (23%) and college students who are of a legal age to drink (72%) are the primary source of alcohol for underage college drinkers.[53] A majority of college students who drink alcohol (65%) began their alcohol consumption in high school and even in junior high, and middle school (8.3%).[54] College students who begin this early stage of alcohol consumption are more likely to drink more often and in greater amounts, with a younger age of beginning to drink increasing the likelihood of this pattern of alcohol consumption. Regrettably, few students who are binge drinkers consider themselves to be heavy or problem drinkers.

Virtually the same percentage of male and female college students binge drink; however, studies indicate that *females are more likely than males* to frequently binge drink and females admit to being drunk three or more times and drinking on 10 or more occasions in the past 30 days.[55] Given the amount and frequency of alcohol use by college students, it is perhaps no coincidence that students report that, while intoxicated, they are more likely to be sexually active and to have sex with someone they just met.[56] A report by the National Center on Addiction and Substance Abuse at Columbia University (2007) indicated that more than 78 percent of college students who have used illicit drugs have had sexual intercourse. In fact, the report indicated that in 2001, 21.3 percent of college students reported engaging in *alcohol-related unplanned, unprotected sexual activity* up from 19.2 percent in 1993. The relationship between alcohol-related unprotected sexual activity increases the likelihood of being exposed to a sexually transmitted infection and creating an unplanned pregnancy. A study conducted by the Centers for Disease Control and Injury Prevention indicates that college students and teens are more likely to contract a sexually transmitted infection than any other age group.[57] According to the study, out of the 12 million new cases of sexually transmitted infections in the United States each year, two-thirds of these infections occur in people under the age of 25. The relationship between alcohol consumption and experiencing sexual aggression is reported by Columbia University as occurring most often at colleges with high rates of binge drinking. Finally, in spite of the attention given to "date rape drugs," such as Rohypnol and GHB, these account for less than 1 percent of reported rape.[58]

When college students, both male and female, report committing and being on the receiving end of sexual coercion, studies consistently indicate that a significant number of both male and female students were drinking at the time.[59] The relationship between alcohol consumption and engaging in sex might explain the low frequency with which college-age sexual assaults are reported to authorities and the confusion surrounding the question of whether sex under the influence of alcohol constitutes rape, sexual assault, sexual coercion, or none of these categories. For example, if both males and females are consuming alcohol at the time of engaging in nonconsensual sex, the individuals may be inclined to accept mutual responsibility for the lack of consent because both were intoxicated at the time, or the individuals do not view alcohol-related sex as nonconsensual sex even though intoxication prevents giving consent according to the legal standard of consensual sex (Underwood, 2010). Consequently, college students may not define sex that occurs during alcohol use and after intoxication as sexual assault.[60]

Another contentious dilemma is the confusion inherent in the attitude, interpretation, and enactment of state laws and college policies regarding consent and sexual assault on campuses (Underwood, 2010), and whether laws and policies apply equally to both males and females and whether there is even a recognition that they should (Levine, 2006). An article by opinion columnist Alex Knepper (2010), a student at American University, spawned an intense reaction from opponents and supporters alike about the intersections between rape, alcohol, sex, personal responsibility, and consent on college campuses. In response to Knepper's article, there were student protests against the article and vandalism of the student newspaper, the *Eagle*, that published Knepper's column (Hess, 2010). The negative reactions to Knepper's column eventually lead to an apology from the editorial board of the *Eagle* (Editorial Board & Calantone, 2010). Remarkably, all of these reactions took place in a relatively short period of time—from March 28, 2010, to April 9, 2010, on the eve of National Sexual Assault Awareness month, which is in April. However, what does not seem to have occurred is whether the intense responses to Knepper's article ever included a discussion about female sexual coercion and aggression as it occurs on college campuses versus focusing the debate on the potential for female victimization by college males and what some opponents called

Knepper's "rape apologist" attitude. The outcome of these actions resulted in American University taking steps to revise its student code of conduct to include among other items definitions to differentiate between sexual assault, sexual harassment, and harassment and intimidation, and a clarification of what constitutes consent: "Sexual contact will be considered without consent if no clear consent, verbal or nonverbal, is given; if inflicted through force, threat of force, or coercion; or if inflicted upon a person who is unconscious or who otherwise reasonably appears to be without the mental or physical capacity to consent" and that this amendment will describe "different scenarios that are often mistaken for implied consent" (Fowler, 2010). However, there appeared to be a potential for gender bias as evidenced in the example of what would not constitute consent that was given by Julie Mills, Deputy Director of the Student Advocacy Center and a member of the Sexual Assault Working Group at American University. She said, "Whatever you're wearing does not imply consent" (Fowler, 2010). Consider whether Ms. Mill's example applies to which gender or what type of example might be given that would be meaningful for men. Perhaps, "just because you have an erection does not imply a willingness to engage in sex with a woman" or "simply because you have been drinking in a social setting does not give permission to be groped on the buttocks or penis by a female or rubbed against by a woman's breasts."

It is commendable that American University is taking steps to educate students about the difference between sexual consent and sexual coercion and under what circumstances consent and coercion occur; however, it would be equally commendable to assure that examples of female sexual coercion are also included in the revisions of the student conduct code at American University. Finally, while Knepper's article certainly garnered opponents and supporters alike, the article also brought about a needed dialogue regarding the sexual behavior of college students, and the views college students have about their sexual behavior, and the role of alcohol in diffusing and confusing consent. Such discussions are key to defining what consensual sex means in the social realm of college students and what universities can do to address a culture that risks promoting and sustaining acts of sexual coercion. College students would benefit from an open and honest dialogue regarding what it means to give and receive consent within the context of how they and their contemporaries actually practice sexual behavior and finding out what their views are for addressing and resolving these contentious issues and the problem of mutually harmful sexual behavior and attitudes on college campuses.

The views of college students regarding sexual coercion was addressed in a study by Oswald and Russell (2006), who found that a majority of the 426 college students in their study did not view the strategies that the researchers had defined as coercive (i.e., verbal pressure where the aggressor threatened to end the relationship unless sex occurred, purposeful intoxication of a partner, and physical force). The students also did not view the person who used coercive strategies to gain sex as particularly aggressive, or the target of the coercive strategies as particularly victimized. These results held true whether the offender/victim was male or female and even held true for the vignette that Oswald and Russell used to depict the classical script of date rape. However, Oswald and Russell did find that there was a trivialization of the woman's sexual aggression against the man, and this is consistent with other findings when females are the aggressors.

In addition, the study by Oswald and Russell (2006) *did not find evidence* of the sexual double standard, since both the male and the female in the vignettes that depicted either a male or female initiating sex were viewed in essentially the same positive manner by both men and women—once again giving support to the idea that the traditional sexual script is outdated, has less relevance in contemporary society on college campuses, and may have outlived its usefulness in terms of understanding sexual behavior as it is practiced by young adults today. Therefore, it would be advisable that researchers re-evaluate their use of TSS theory and the measures that derive from it as their dominant approach in future research and that prevention education programs operating on college campuses not form their program goals or outcomes measures for preventing sexual aggression on college campuses based on TSS since there is evidence that traditional sexual scripts have changed on college campuses. Following this line of reasoning, it may be that research studies, entrenched in TSS theory, are not accurately measuring contemporary social norms on college campuses where there is a culture that supports *sexual coercion and aggression by both males and females,*[61] and where nonconsensual sex is occurring in the context of consuming alcohol. Therefore, if researchers are not assessing contemporary social norms,[62] are ignoring research that substantiates female sexual coercion and aggression,[63] and are leaving out alcohol consumption[64] in their studies, they are missing three central variables to fully understanding what contributes to and sustains sexual aggression among female students.

Oswald and Russell (2006) explain that their findings about how college students view behaviors that define sexual coercion suggest "that in college dating relationships these behaviors might be considered to be socially normal" and that if sexual aggression is the norm, this is "troublesome because behaviors seen as normal or 'expected' in college dating relationships are likely to continue" (p. 10). Sisco and Figueredo (2008) also propose that "in modern society, sexual aggression seems to be the norm rather than the exception," lending support to Oswald and Russell's observations. Cook (1995), in her survey of 546 college students, found that while a majority of the young men and women rejected the use of violence and coercive behavior, this same group of young adults also reported *expecting the use of coercion to obtain sex*, especially in dating situations involving the use of *drugs or alcohol.* These findings certainly provide direction for future research in terms of what might be contemporary values, experiences and beliefs that are supporting an acceptance of sexual aggression among groups of male and female college students. Additionally, research might also consider the following question with college students: How might prevention education programs (a) effectively address the specific practices and beliefs among male and female college students who participate in these contemporary norms, and (b) assist college students to understand and view norms that promote sexual coercion as problematic in their social relationships with each other?

The findings on alcohol-related sexual aggression patterns on college campuses suggest that alcohol has a similar if not equal effect on the behavior and attitudes of both male and female college students when it comes to the expectation, expression, and acceptance of sexual aggression as the norm. The findings certainly bring to light questions about alcohol and sexual aggression on college campuses that go beyond the one-dimensional theories of sexual aggression and victimization discussed earlier in this chapter. These findings also bring to light the need to understand the specific interaction between the expectation of sex and the consumption of alcohol during social situations on college campuses, and the question of what contributes to the double standard that males cannot be aggressed against by college-age females, especially when a male is intoxicated and the female is not? Additionally, there is the question of whether the expectation for sex is constructed by the college female aggressor as not violating a male's personal boundaries regardless of whether the female uses direct aggression such as physical force or indirect aggression such as manipulating a man with threats of self-harm or by crying or by taking advantage of an intoxicated male. Finally, there have been few studies on female sexual violence in same-sex relationships (Girshick, 2001). Also whether females who commit sexual coercion in college began their sexual offending behaviors at an earlier age has not been readily explored.[65]

Expectations mirror the beliefs that individuals develop their behavior in a particular social environment. Therefore, behavior is likely to be influenced by the expectations and beliefs of the social norms of the culture as these norms are assimilated by the individual in a particular social environement.[66] If the individuals that determine the social norms in the environment of college campuses establish and reinforce the expectation that alcohol consumption and sexual aggression is acceptable during social events, then it is probable that male and female students alike are acting with agency when they make the decision to engage in these behaviors rather than transgress the social norms as they exist.[67] Additionally, the quantity of alcohol consumed and the context in which drinking alcohol occurs by a female college student will also be influenced by such factors as personal values, prior history of alcohol consumption, peer group influences, and their individual beliefs about alcohol and sexual behavior.[68] The same holds true regarding the personal choice to engage in nonconsensual or consensual sex—personal values, prior history of sexual aggression or sexual victimization, acceptance of interpersonal violence, beliefs about a particular gender group, peer group influences, and individual beliefs about nonconsensual and consensual sex will exert their influence on the individual.

Extending this premise to the pursuit of sex while consuming alcohol as an acceptable social norm, college-age females may be distinctly at risk of behaving in a manner consistent with this assumptive social norm, that is, to consume alcohol and actively pursue and engage in sex, regardless of whether direct consent is asked for or provided by the person being pursued. Therefore, it is possible that there are a group of college females who aggressively pursue sex partners while intoxicated or who engage in sex with an intoxicated partner and who view their behavior through the socially constructed norms established on college campuses. Consequently, there may be a group of young adult female aggressors who does not view their coercive, aggressive behavior as transgressing legal definitions of sexual assault. Put another way, given the inherent and pervasive stereotypes surrounding female sexual offending (see Chapter 1), young adult females who engage in sexual coercion and aggression may not be "socialized" to view their behavior as illegal or coercive. This framework is not presented as excusing sexual offending by females anymore than it would be offered to excuse male sexual offending; rather, it is presented to clarify that female sexual coercion and aggression is no more acceptable than is male sexual coercion and aggression. This framework broadens approaches to sexual assault prevention education programs on college campuses and advocates for awareness of female sexual aggression so that females who engage in sexual coercion are not left out of the opportunity to change their attitudes, beliefs, and behaviors.

GREEK MEMBERSHIP: A HIGH-RISK ENVIRONMENT FOR SEXUAL COERCION

> "I liked this guy and I thought the only way we'd every hook up is if we got drunk and fooled around"
>
> —A female describing her motive for getting a man drunk.[69]

The consumption of alcohol is found to be especially prevalent among Greek members,[70] placing this particular group of college students at a higher risk for engaging in sexual aggression while consuming alcohol. These factors combine to make college students in fraternities/sororities a specific target for college-based prevention programs aimed at decreasing alcohol consumption and preventing sexual aggression (Moynihan & Baynard, 2008). A factor in the Greek structure that has made it difficult to provide meaningful intervention in this specific college environment is the isolation of the Greek community. These organizations often act as an "island unto themselves" where they are socially isolated out of choice in the university setting. Similar to families where abuse occurs, Greek membership has its secretive language and rituals, long-standing traditions that maintain the status quo rather than promoting openness to change, and adhere to a social structure where new members are expected to pledge an oath of loyalty to protect the "brothers and sisters" and the Greek organization or "family structure."[71]

Studies clearly indicate that fraternity and sorority members view the consumption of alcohol as positive and accept higher levels of drinking as normal and use alcohol as a conduit for forming friendships among their peers.[72] Living at a sorority or fraternity was found by Wechsler and Nelson (2008) to contribute to binge drinking, as was living in other off-campus housing. However, Wechsler and Nelson (2008) identified fraternities and sororities as being the college environment for heaviest drinking, especially among underage college students. Greek membership is identified as one of the most pervasive environmental risk factors that contribute to college students who did not drink alcohol prior to college to begin binge drinking when they arrive.[73]

Larimer et al. (1999) found in their study of 165 male and 131 female college students inducted as new pledge members in Greek organizations that the men and women who had been the recipients of unwanted sexual contact reported heavier alcohol consumption than peers who had not had these sexual experiences. Sex while under the influence of a drug or alcohol was the most common type of sex reported by both males and females, while physical force was the least common type of unwanted sexual behavior reported for both groups. Gender differences in this study were not found to be significant in terms of the occurrence of unwanted sexual intercourse across coercive measures or while under the influence of a drug or alcohol. Larimer and colleagues also found that the young men who had been the recipient of *unwanted sexual contact by females while intoxicated* (i.e., intoxication prohibits consent) reported more symptoms of depression, along with reporting shame, sadness, and other negative emotions in addition to their feelings of victimization. The importance of these findings regarding the adverse effects this group of college males experienced from intoxicated, nonconsensual sex contradicts the common view that sexual coercion by females has little to no effect on males.[74] These findings certainly contradict the myth of male sexual invulnerability and confirm that *men are harmed* by sexual aggression directed toward them by women just as women are harmed when they are aggressed against.[75]

The peer influence of Greek membership, alcohol consumption, and sexual aggression is summed up by Antonia Abbey (2002):

> The peer group norms in some college social environments, including many sororities and fraternities, accept getting drunk as a justification for engaging in behaviors that would usually be embarrassing. The peer norms for most fraternity parties are to drink heavily, to act in an uninhibited manner and to engage in casual sex. (p. 119)

While perhaps unintentional, what is unfortunate is that while Abbey succinctly describes what research has found among some groups of fraternity members, she does not balance her observation with the research that indicates that sorority members also condone excessive drinking and casual sex.[76] Additionally, while the majority of research has focused on alcohol and the sexual behavior of males that includes sexual aggression (Greek members and non-Greek members), there has been little research on the impact of alcohol on female sexual behavior that would include *sexual aggression* and membership in sororities.[77] Indeed, while Abbey states that "men are legally and morally responsible for acts of sexual assault they commit, regardless of whether or not they were intoxicated" (p. 119), she does not include the statement that females are legally and morally responsible for acts of sexual assault they commit, regardless of whether or not they were intoxicated. Additionally, there is little recognition that female sorority members who attend Greek parties—and indeed host Greek parties—can have similar motives and personal agendas as some of their male counterparts, that being to socialize, consume alcohol, become intoxicated, supply alcohol to men, and engage in sexual behavior that is either *planned with a specifically targeted male* or *not planned with an available male*. To what degree female sorority members admit to similar motives and agendas has not been readily determined by researchers who hold these assumptions. Consequently, Abbey's article appears to imply gender bias that applies *intoxicated responsibility for sexual aggression* to only one gender, that gender being male, which may be an indication of male prejudice.[78] Abbey's assumption is of course in direct contradiction to the findings in the Larimer et al. (1999) study.

While the "rape culture" is widely accepted as part of the social fabric of college males, especially among fraternities, this same rape culture is not widely accepted as part of the social fabric of college females, especially among sororities, where females are viewed as the victims of the college "rape culture" and not also as potential offenders (Papon, 2010). It is perhaps this double standard of sexual coercion within the culture on college campuses that confuses students, adds to the tensions between the genders, allows female coercion and male victimization to go unchecked, and unwittingly promotes a general view of hypocrisy toward rape and sexual assault prevention advocates on college campuses and the feminists that appear to engage in this undisguised gender bias (Knepper, 2010). Perhaps the various groups who are concerned about this particular social and public health problem on college campuses could begin to have a sensible dialogue, absent of gender prejudice and framed within the reality of the contemporary norms and adversarial beliefs that exists between the genders.

Nurius, Norris, Dimeff, and Graham (1996), in their study on what reduces the risk of sexual aggression among fraternity and sorority members, were surprised to find that the majority of males in the study reported that they would *stop pursuing* sex with an unwilling woman and that this was especially true when a woman was assertive and nonambivalent in her indication that she did not want to engage with the man sexually. Unfortunately, the females in the study who indicated less self-assurance in their ability to communicate assertively and who were found to be ambivalent in speaking up about their desire to not engage in sexual behavior were found to be at risk of unwanted sexual behavior. Nurius et al. suggest that a nonassertive, ambivalent communication style regarding sexual consent has a role in increasing the likelihood of college males engaging females in unwanted sexual behavior and of females being less able to resist male engagement. It is presumed that the same would hold true in the case of a nonassertive male who is ambivalent about his intention to not engage in unwanted sexual behavior. In other words, direct and honest communication between men and women protects against unwanted sexual behavior. When alcohol is factored into fraternity/sorority members' communications, it may be that alcohol is a mediating factor for *misinterpreting* ambivalent or nonassertive communication and a factor that *magnifies* nonassertive, ambivalent communication.[79] Studies highlight the greater risk for some type of unwanted sexual contact along a continuum of sexually aggressive behavior among Greek-affiliated college students who maintain a nonassertive or ambivalent communication style while consuming alcohol in these particular social environments.[80] Testa and Dermen (1999), in response to their findings that (a) low assertiveness and high sex-related alcohol consumption were associated with sexual coercion experiences but not with rape or attempted rape and that (b) *higher levels of casual sexual behavior and alcohol consumption* were associated with sexual coercion and rape/attempted rape, suggest that "sexual coercion may be prevented by improving sexual assertiveness and weakening alcohol consumption to emphasize personal control" (p. 548)—important information for prevention education programs where reducing the risk of sexual coercion includes a comprehensive approach in high-risk social environments.

It is important to keep in mind that the research on college-age sexual aggression indicates that the majority of unwanted sexual contact is not rape—physically forcible sexual assault; rather, it is the less intrusive forms of nonconsensual sexual behavior ranging from kissing, holding hands, and hugging, to more moderate forms of sexual intrusiveness, such as rubbing a person's body or rubbing up against another's body, to more intrusive sexual acts of fondling breasts, buttocks, and genitals.[81] This clarification is not meant to minimize any of these forms of intrusive, unwanted behavior or to trivialize even one person's experience of physically forced sexual intercourse (rape); rather, it is meant to bring a sense of clarity and balance to perceptions of college-age sexual coercion and aggression as occurring across a continuum of sexual behaviors that includes sexual aggression and that from this continuum the injury to the victim is better understood (Russell & Oswald, 2002). As stated from the beginning, progress will come through an open dialogue that is free of gender bias and informed in its approach about female offenders, and that includes information about the risk factors for sexual coercion that prevail in contemporary college life. To prevent female sexual coercion and aggression on college campuses, there must be a commitment to preserving the safety and well-being of *all* college students.

Strikingly it has been found that Greek-affiliated college-age women consume on average 5.5 drinks per week, more than twice the amount used per week for non-Greek female students. Studies indicate that college females living in a sorority house are three times more likely to be the victim of sexual assault and that a common thread for interpersonal violence among this group of women is alcohol use, social norms that promote risk taking, and women not assuming responsibility for their choices and behavior (Wuthrich, 2009). While sororities are promoted to young women as being protective, caring, and supportive and many young women would confirm this type of experience, there is also the reality that a callous attitude and nonprotective stance toward other "sisters" in a sorority does exist. As noted in a quantitative study by Wuthrich (2009) of 1,264 sorority members sanctioned over a period of time because of alcohol-related interpersonal violence during Greek functions, this previously mentioned reality was a theme among the reflection papers written by this group of sorority women. Wuthrich found that a majority of the sorority women expressed little support to prevent alcohol consumption among underage members/sisters; older members of a sorority failed to show leadership by taking on the status quo to reduce harm to their members, promoted and knowingly engaged in high-risk behaviors, resisted taking responsibility for decisions and behavior, seldom assumed a collective responsibility for the sorority, readily conformed to the social norms of the sorority, acknowledged knowing that sorority social practices were problematic while they continued unabated, and even though these sorority women had attended educational programs in the prevention of alcohol abuse, underage drinking, and interpersonal aggression, they persisted in these behaviors nonetheless. Interestingly enough and echoing a familiarity in the literature, sorority women tended to blame fraternity members for problems even though there was consensus that sorority members knew the risk behaviors among fraternities, chose to socialize with their male counterparts nonetheless, and engaged in similar if not the same problematic behaviors that they blamed fraternity members for causing.

Wuthrich (2009) identified that unsafe sorority events did not happen by chance. As one sorority president wrote, "Many people in college drink underage. That is what most people describe as a 'benefit' of higher education. You finally are living on your own and free of your parents' rules. To many, this means drinking until belligerent, blacked out, and independent" (p. 240). The overriding themes among this group of sorority women were identified by Wuthrich as (a) minimizing interpersonal violence by blaming others or excusing behaviors as simple unintentional mistakes; (b) women in leadership roles failing to provide leadership and having poorly developed concepts of risk management; (c) ignoring risks that they knew were occurring; (d) minimized harmful behavior; (e) reinstating members who engaged in "lewd behavior" and who were "completely disrespectful toward others" in terms of their sexual behavior, intoxication and belligerence; and (f) viewing incidences of violence and intoxication as a "rite of passage"; as one sorority member stated, "any organization without some members who cause a little drama would be boring" and even "it builds character" (p. 239). Wuthrich also found that sorority members viewed each other as looking for a good time; interested in getting, not giving; seeking opportunities to find a date and do their own thing; and having a general lack of acceptance and respect for authority in the chapter. Overall, Wuthrich suggests that results of the study "call into question the efficacy of harm reduction education among these two groups of sorority members to combat alcohol abuse and associated interpersonal violence" (p. 246) and that the sorority women in the study typify a generation of "rule dodgers who master rule systems and quickly identify ways to work around them, or comply with the technical letter of the rules while evading the spirit" (p. 249). As suggested by Linda Kalof (1993), "Some campus sororities have developed subtle ways to combine the sorority image of 'good girls' with contemporary sexual liberation. A sorority woman described the unofficial rules to achieving "successful sorority sex": "no public display of sex (take it upstairs), use discretion when staying at a fraternity (don't make a scene as you go upstairs, don't roam the halls half-naked), don't stay for breakfast with the brothers, avoid riding on campus transportation the morning after your fraternal slumber party, and never participate in group sex (it will make you as well as everyone else in the house extremely famous)." (citing Moffatt, 1989, pp. 262–263). By any indication, these "rules" are not so subtle but rather alarming especially if they represent the behavior of some sorority members and if such rules are sanctioned among some sorority houses on certain campuses. This set of rules may also encourage a manipulative, deceptive, and gamey relationship style that align with tactics of female sexual coercion.[82]

Wuthrich's (1999) study, along with the other studies cited throughout this chapter, and in the existing literature, certainly suggests that research into whether sorority membership and the social norms in these specific college environments act as a risk factor for *female sexual aggression* is warranted and would assist the development of meaningful prevention education programs for college women.[83] The degree to which sorority membership supports alcohol abuse, sexual victimization, and sexual aggression is certainly needed as well; however, it is hoped that studies would be inclusive, meaning that sorority members would be evaluated as to whether the social structure of sororities condone or perpetuate sexual aggression by females, whether the social norms in sororities pressure women to become sexually active or participate in nonconsensual sex, and how often alcohol is involved in mutual sexual aggression by either men or women in the Greek system. Sororities are known for their easy access to alcohol and the social norms that promote frequent binge drinking; therefore, it is possible that intoxication may be "sexually coercive tactic" for some Greek college students and a conduit to a range of sexual behaviors that includes sexual coercion. It is also possible that alcohol consumption is the *primary motive* for engaging in Greek social activities rather than sex serving as the primary motive. It is even probable that both alcohol consumption and nonconsensual sex are equal motivators for the men and women who participate in sexual coercion while intoxicated or sober during Greek functions. In addition, determining whether the consensual consumption of alcohol and the acceptance of sexual harassment and sexual exploitation during Greek social functions serve as mediators for conceptualizing the acceptance of sexually coercive behavior is certainly warranted. For example, while Struckman-Johnson and Struckman-Johnson (2003) found that 40 percent of the college students in their study were sexually exploited during intoxication, the study did not identify whether the sexual exploitation was planned alongside the intoxication, whether sexual exploitation occurred as a result of intoxication, or whether the willing consumption of alcohol occurred alongside the acceptance of the risk for sexual exploitation.[84]

ADVERSARIAL BELIEFS, LOVE STYLES, AND SEXUAL COERCION

Alcohol consumption among college students and affiliation with college Greek organizations are but two factors that are known to contribute to sexual coercion on college campuses. Endorsement of adversarial beliefs has also been found to contribute to male[85] and female sexual aggression.[86] Adversarial beliefs are defined as the degree to which a person believes that sexual relationships are exploitive and adversarial in nature (see Appendix A for an example of an Adversarial Beliefs Inventory for Heterosexual Females).[87] Peter Anderson (1998), in his study of 461 adult female college students from New Orleans, New Jersey, and New York, found that "college women who have been sexually abused in the past and/or those who hold adversarial beliefs about relationships are more likely than their nonabused, nonadversarial counterparts to engage in sexually aggressive behavior" (p. 90). Anderson's study of adversarial beliefs and previous sexual victimization provided one of the first frameworks for understanding sexual aggression among college-age females. This framework has also been cited as helping to explain sexual coercion by males where previous victimization by females and adversarial beliefs toward dating relationships were correlated with a group of college-age men committing a range of sexually coercive acts toward their female partner (Gamez-Guadix & Strauss, 2009; Russell & Oswald, 2002). Anderson's framework also aligns with understanding adolescent girls who commit sexual offenses against same-age peers or young children.[88]

Therefore, a pathway from sexual victimization to sexual offending for a group of college-age women is potentially indicated by the relationship between (a) adversarial beliefs, (b) past experience of sexual victimization, (c) recent revictimization, and (d) other types of interpersonal traumas that are enacted in the context of social norms that promote or sustain sexual aggression for a particular individual. The context of the social norms would be college environments and Greek organizations that provide little protection against social norms that promote sexual coercion and aggression by college females in terms of not taking action to either (a) directly address sexual coercion or (b) directly promote and sustain social norms for sexual health, personal responsibility, mutual respect, and sexual assertiveness among college female's social relationships. These topics could comprise a viable educational course that all college students would be required to take and would need to be taught by experienced and skilled faculty who could also serve as mentors and advisors to college students. This level of commitment to a comprehensive and long-term approach to promote healthy relationships and sexual health education, and the prevention of sexual coercion and other forms of sexual aggression, is more than likely what is required to address this social and public health problem effecting such a significant number of young adults (Centers for Disease Control and Prevention, 2004).

Adversarial beliefs among college-age students in other countries and cultures were also found by Hines (2007) in her multinational analysis of

7,667 university students from 38 sites around the world. Hines found that adversarial beliefs across these 36 international sites significantly predicted sexual coercion for both males and females. In addition, Hines also found that greater levels of hostility towards men predicted higher levels of sexual coercion against men by women and that greater levels of hostility toward women predicted higher levels of sexual coercion against women, once again supporting the contention that sexual aggression is a human behavior, not a gender behavior. Hines also found that the greater the status of women at each site the higher the level of forced sex against men occurred by females. Adversarial beliefs, whether held by males or by females, appear to contribute to a higher level of hostility and sexual aggression by both males and females against each other, and this finding is similar in studies that investigated dating aggression across cultures and countries (Doroszewicz & Forbes, 2008; Hines & Saudino, 2003).

Shea (1998) sheds light on a group of college women who justify sexual aggression and the use of coercive tactics in their relationships with males. Shea explains that these women tend to begin having sex with their partners early in the relationship and that aggression and game playing have been longstanding attitudes in their intimate relationships, beginning with their parental relationships, and extending into their dating and romantic relationships. Their attitudes toward equality are marked by believing that the traditional roles for women are restricting, and so they dismiss these roles as not acceptable or rewarding for them. Similar belief holds true for sexual equality where they find it both acceptable and appropriate for a woman to have sexual thoughts and desires and to act on her desires directly; if directness does not achieve the desired results, then it is acceptable to resort to emotional manipulation or other types of coercion. These women do not view their coercive behavior and attitudes as necessarily wrong, and they believe that even forcing someone to have sexual relations against their will is acceptable. Thus, Shea asserts, for this group of college women, they simply expect and accept coercion and force as a natural part of relationships. The women are described as "socially flexible, able to put others at ease, dramatic in their style and like to be the center of attention" (p. 101). Their first dates with a partner are likely to be attending a party or other social event with friends and where alcohol is consumed. These women are more likely to be goal directed in their pursuit of sex, and they describe being "very sexually attracted to the man, 'horny' and feeling powerful" (p. 102). They view men as conquests, and their sexual behavior is an indication of "lust and suggests less concern about the relationship itself. Sex is the goal, not romance. When fantasizing about forcing a man to have sex, they are also aroused by the elements of raw sex and power" (p. 102). Shea points out that this view of sex held by a particular group of females supports the "feminist view of sexual aggression as being driven by power and control rather than sex" (p. 102). However, it is also possible that all three are motivators for this group of women, that is, sexual arousal, power, and control, and that sexual arousal derives from the motivations for power and control. Shea points out that "verbal coercion, for this group of women, has aspects of both rape and seduction, and therefore seems to lie near the center of the continuum between consensual sexual expression and rape" (p. 102).

As previously suggested, it is more than likely that there have been new and emerging sexual scripts that have been occurring and have not necessarily been identified by the research that has followed TSS theory.[89] These more contemporary sexual scripts are less likely to follow the traditional gender stereotypes and one-sided gender constructs that explain human aggression in general and sexual aggression in particular. It may also be that new and emerging sexual scripts are in part contextualized in the modern beliefs about relationships and human sexuality practiced by contemporary young adults that has yet to be fully understood.

Lee (1973) describes six styles of love that reflect an individual's attitudes and orientation toward romantic relationships. For the present discussion it is the person with a ludic love style, described as a person who is uninhibited and detached with a preference for uncommitted relationships and who holds an attitude and view of love as a game, that correlates with the attitudes and behaviors indicative of a person likely to commit acts of sexual coercion and aggression.[90] Based on Lee's love styles, Hendrick and Hendrick (2003), developed the Love Attitude Scale to measure Lee's six love styles. Researchers have utilized the Love Attitude Scale developed by Hendrick and Hendrick to investigate sexual coercion. For example, Russell and Oswald (2002) used the Love Attitude Scale in their study on behavior that would be predictive of individuals who perpetuate sexual coercion. Russell and Oswald reported that sexually coercive females exhibited a higher tolerance for sexual harassment and were significantly higher in femininity than noncoercive females. They also found that sexually coercive women were found to "embrace a ludic (manipulative, game-playing approach toward love) love style significantly more than noncoercive women, while the love style pragma (a logical approach toward love) was negatively, associated with coercion" (p. 103). Russell and Oswald also found that 81 percent of women who reported using coercive strategies also reported previous sexual victimization. Within the same study, similar findings were found by Russell and Oswald when reporting love styles and men's perpetration of sexual coercion against their female partners and men's experience of sexual victimization by their female partners. Russeli and Oswald found that men who reported engaging in coercive strategies were more likely to report a Ludic love style while men who reported sexual victimization were more likely to identify with two other love styles, storge (a friendship attitude toward love) and pragma (a practical approach to love). Russell and Oswald also found that men reported higher rates of verbal and sexual victimization (45%) by females when compared to their reported coercion of females (35.4%). The study also indicated that "there is a close link between being sexually victimized and sexually coercive in a relationship. Males who had been victimized were far more likely to use sexually coercive strategies in their relationships. This could indicate that sexual violence is a pattern within a relationship where both individuals act coercively" (p. 282–283). Russell and Oswald identified two primary categories and subcategories for their study: (a) *perpetrator* (inexperienced, consensual, or coercive) and (b) *victim* (never victimized, verbally victimized, physically victimized, or both verbally and physically). What Oswald found was that love styles predicted both offending and victimization for males. Males who reported *engaging in coercive strategies* with females were more likely to endorse a ludic love style (a game-playing and manipulative attitude toward relationships) and less likely to endorse an agape love style (an attitude of unconditional love) when compared to noncoercive men. Men who reported emulating the love styles of storge (a friendship-first attitude toward love) and pragma (a practical approach toward love) were more likely to report being victims of female sexual coercion. Russell and Oswald's findings of females who reported using coercive strategies also reported previous sexual victimization is similar to the study by Anderson (1998), who reported adversarial beliefs and sexual victimization as a predictor of female sexual aggression. Adversarial beliefs contain the attitudes found in the ludus/ludic love style described by Lee (1973) and measured by the scale developed by Hendrick and Hendrick (2003).

In an earlier study, Sarwer, Kalichman, Johnson, Early, and Akram Ali (1993) also explored sexual aggression and love styles in an attempt to link sexually coercive behaviors to a theoretical model of intimate relationships. On the basis of self-reports, they grouped college men as either having *consensual sexual experiences* or having *verbally coercive sexual experiences*. The authors then analyzed constructs that measured the likelihood to rape, likelihood to use sexual force, masculinity, and sociopathy and compared the results to the six love style measurements developed by Hendrick and Hendrick (2003). The results of the study indicated that a ludic love style was the consistent predictor of sexual coercion among the six love styles measured. Additionally, the authors found that the ludic love style was as effective at classifying men as coercive or noncoercive as were the other measures.

Together, these studies support the findings by Anderson (1998) regarding the suggested predictive value of the relationship between adversarial beliefs and previous victimization and college females who are at risk of committing sexual coercion. These studies also suggest support of the findings by Shea (1998) that indicated college women who commit acts of sexual coercion have a manipulative, emotionally detached, and gamey style in their dating and romantic relationships, where a female seeks excitement and values having power and control in her heterosexual dating relationships. Collectively, studies substantiate that there are college women capable, and willing, of committing acts of sexual coercion and aggression in their dating relationships with men, and that further research is needed to understand and prevent sexual coercion and aggression on college campuses by females, but first must come the willingness to admit to its existence.

CHAPTER SUMMARY

Research into sexual coercion and aggression on college campuses has focused primarily on heterosexual males and their offending patterns against heterosexual females, resulting in considerably less information about college women who commit acts of sexual coercion and aggression against college men. However, more recent studies regarding female sexual coercion are appearing in the literature that may indicate a lessening of the gender bias that has been inherent in the research on sexual coercion and aggression on college campuses. Perhaps this shift in research is indicating a growing recognition of the essential value in identifying, understanding, and preventing sexual coercion and aggression by women on college campuses and in the community at large. While there may be a concern that studies on female sexual aggression as it occurs on college campuses will distract from the victimization of females that occurs in this environment, it is equally important to recognize that it is possible—and actually necessary—to address the reality of sexual aggression as a human problem that requires comprehensive, bias-free strategies in order to prevent this form of relationship violence that exacts such a heavy toll on young men and women. It is also important to realize that within dating relationships where sexual victimization takes place, physical and psychological aggression frequently occur as well. As pointed out by Sabina and Straus (2008) multiple types of victimization that occur in dating relationships are associated with heightened health consequences for both male and female victims. This finding has also been substantiated in the literature on children for whom multiple forms of family violence have been experienced along with sexual abuse and literature on belief systems that sustain multiple forms of abuse directed at children and other family members (Duncan, 2004).

Research findings also suggest that the propensity to commit adult relationship violence has its roots in the experience of early childhood victimization (Gil-Gonzalez et al., 2007). While the pathway from sexual victimization to sexual offending is not yet clearly understood for women who commit sexual crimes, early childhood vicitimization is reported throughout the literature on female sexual offending (Strickland, 2008). In addition, when considering that a significant number of adolescent girls are reported to commit sexual offenses against children (Kubik & Hecker, 2005), that adult women commit sexual crimes against teens, including statutory rape (Levine, 2006), that beliefs and experiences related to perpetrating sexual offenses may be established early in life (Prescott, 2004), and that women who commit sexual offenses have been invisible within a sociopolitical culture that has denied their existence (Allgier & Lamping, 1998; Gannon & Rose, 2006; Hunt, 2006), it is clear that the prevention of female sexual offenses is as important of a social and public health imperative as that of preventing sexual offenses by males. Additionally, it is important to consider whether college women who commit sexual offenses began their sexually coercive behavior during adolescence and have continued these behaviors into young adulthood (Allen, 1991; Anderson, 1996, 1998).

Given that alcohol abuse on college campuses is considered a social norm and has been found to increase the risk of adverse behaviors that include sexual coercion and aggression, unplanned pregnancies, and sexually transmitted infections,[91] understanding the role of alcohol abuse is particularly relevant to preventing sexually aggressive attitudes, beliefs, and behaviors in the social environments on college campuses[92] and in college-age dating relationships.[93] These mutual goals would improve the well-being and certainly the sexual health of college students as well as have a positive impact on academic performance. Additionally, it is integral to prevention efforts to acknowledge the saliency that males both report being victims and females report being perpetrators of coercive sexual behavior.[94] The reality is that males and females on college campuses are committing sexual acts that are legally defined as date rape, sexual assault, and sexual harassment whether they commit these acts while intoxicated or sober. It also appears that theories of sexual coercion and aggression need to be updated to reflect the contemporary behavior of young adults within the context of decreasing gender bias. Rather than using sex role stereotypes that date back to the 1970s as the presumed standard by which today's young adults make and practice sexual decisions in their dating relationships, perhaps it is time to simply sit down, ask some questions, and listen to what they have to tell us. There is also the need to clarify the confusion about what it means to be "aggressive, coercive, and violent" and what it means to be "assertive, consensual, and mutual" in college dating relationships. How college-age young adults continue to be influenced by peer expectations, the media, contemporary social standards, and the pressures of navigating this stage of adulthood are all integral to providing the support, understanding, accountability, and responsibility that young adult men and women need during this time of their lives, whether they are in college or working in their communities. It is for these reasons that providing information about what it means to have an emotionally healthy and mutually satisfying adult relationship will certainly be an important part of ending sexual violence and promoting sexual health.

What the overall findings suggest is that when developing and implementing prevention education programs on college campuses, the greatest benefit will come from assessing and addressing multiple types of relationship violence together with alcohol and drug abuse so that program funding is directed toward comprehensive and sustained education to prevent campus-based dating violence. Addressing both male and female violence is what will ultimately support the overarching goal of ending the types of violence that occurs on our college campuses and in the absence of gender bias.

Additionally, research on the sexual offense patterns of college-age females is included in the overall identification and discussion of female sexual offenders because they represent a group of young adult females who commit acts of sexual coercion against males and yet their behavior is not readily identified in the research literature on college-based sexual violence as sexual offenses or crimes. Considering that there is not much that is actually known about the offending patterns of adult female sex offenders (Gannon, Rose & Ward, 2008) it seems important to include a more comprehensive understanding of the types of sexual offending behavior that females exhibit across the communities in which they reside. For example, it is not yet known whether some females who begin a pattern of sexual offending in adolescence (Kubik & Hecker, 2005) continue to commit sexual offenses into early adulthood and beyond or whether some females begin a pattern of sexual offending in early adulthood that then extends into later years (Ferguson & Meehan, 2005). Also, there are very few recidivism studies on adult female sex offenders (Sandler & Freeman, 2009) and it is not clear whether there are any recidivism studies on adolescent females (Center for Sex Offender Management, 2007a). Therefore, it is important to recognize that in reviewing the variety of research on female sexual offending it is appears that there are females who commit different types of sexual offenses at different stages of their development and that they commit sexual offenses against various age groups and against both males and females (see Chapter 1).

4

Sexual Exploitation and Sexual Harassment in Schools

> A teacher in high school found out I slept with a different teacher. She threatened to expose the situation if I didn't sleep with her.[1]

Along with parents, schools are primary partners in the social and moral development of young people. After all, schools are where students spend an average of six hours a day, five days a week, on academics and where they participate in social and athletic events. Through daily interactions with others in the school environment, students begin to form opinions, attitudes, and values that serve to guide their choices over the course of their adolescent development. It is through these daily exchanges with adults that students are expected to receive the guidance required to cooperate effectively with each other and the adults around them. Parents expect their children to be educated in a place where healthy boundaries between people will be not only taught but also modeled by the adults responsible for the daily care of students. It is this sacrosanct relationship that in part makes it difficult to comprehend, let alone accept, that students can experience sexual exploitation, harassment, and abuse by the very people responsible for their education, safety, and well-being. It is bad enough when students experience these offensive attitudes and behaviors from each other, but when the sexual misconduct comes from the adults they are meant to trust, it is even more disturbing. As one parent said, "Educators are expected to prevent students from getting abused, not be the ones abusing them."

KEY POINTS

At the core of educator sexual misconduct is the exploitation of a student's age and stage of development and the inherent trust that students have for teachers, school counselors, and other adults in their school environment.

Sex offenders in schools exploit and take advantage of the natural curiosity that students have about their developing bodies and emerging sexuality.

Adults in educational settings are not granted license to take advantage of students simply because they can.

Unions and schools are equally responsible for the protection of students from predatory adults in schools. Teacher unions need to become proactive in their investment to prevent child sexual abuse in educational settings. They could take this action by requiring that all teachers complete an annual course in the recognition and prevention of sexual misconduct by teachers as a condition of their union membership and regardless of teacher tenure.

Reports of sexual misconduct should be made directly to law enforcement so that reports of suspected sexual abuse can be investigated by law enforcement and child protection services and not by school officials who do not have the specialized training to conduct investigations.

The reality is that there are women and men in schools that take advantage of students. These adults abuse the trust and goodwill they receive from parents, their adult peers, and the students they abuse. These adults willingly manipulate and take advantage of a student by exploiting the positive feelings that a student may have toward them as a doorway into sexual abuse. They are good at camouflaging their sexual intentions, and they use deceptive tactics to groom and convince the student to keep the sexual behavior a secret.[2] They are also quite good at grooming other adults either to ignore their behavior or by convincing adults who question them that what was observed or reported was "misinterpreted" "mistaken," or "unintentional."[3] Adults who cross boundaries with students know that their behavior is both illegal and ethically wrong.[4] They have the ability and the wherewithal to control the student and the situation that stems from their positions of status, power, authority, and trust.

When the offender is a well-liked teacher or someone who is considered attractive, an athletic coach, or other popular adult in the school, students may not be willing to tell and adults may not be willing to question, let alone report, this person. It is important to remember that "asking" someone about his or her behavior or expressing concern for a student's safety and well-being is not the same as accusing someone of sexual abuse. Speaking with another adult about their behavior may also provide the opportunity for that person to consider another way of interacting with students and most importantly, that having this conversation might give the person a reason to pause and consider seeking professional help to examine their behavior and beliefs and stop the potential exploitation or abuse of students and prevent future problems from occurring. Manipulative and deceptive adults can use their position of authority, likability, and access to students in order to commit an array of behaviors that, for the purpose of this discussion, are defined as educator sexual misconduct.

A REVIEW OF FINDINGS FROM THE U.S. DEPARTMENT OF EDUCATION (2004) STUDY ON EDUCATOR SEXUAL MISCONDUCT IN SCHOOLS

In the comprehensive report issued by the U.S. Department of Education (2004), educator sexual misconduct is defined as "any behavior of a sexual nature which may constitute professional misconduct" (p. 2).[5] Therefore, educator sexual misconduct includes sexual crimes against minors as they are defined by state laws and behaviors that are outside established laws but are considered ethically prohibitive because of the inherent relationship between an adult affiliated with the school and the student attending the school. This definition of sexual misconduct in schools broadens the scope of the types of sexual misconduct that adults who have access to students are known to commit. This broader scope of sexual misconduct in schools includes offensive behaviors that may not be specifically defined in state law because a student has reached the age of legal consent but where the adult continues to take advantage and exploit the student relationship.

It is also important to remember that labels like pedophile and hebephile are not legal terms; rather, they are clinical terms used in the mental health profession that have no bearing on identifying or reporting educators or other adults who commit the various crimes that constitute child sexual abuse. As clarified in the report by the U.S. Department of Education (2004), the sexual disorders of pedophilia (i.e., a sexual disorder characterized by a sexual preference for prepubescent children) and hebephilia (i.e., a sexual preference for adolescents) limit rather than expand the recognition and reporting of the array of motives and sexual behaviors that correlate with educator sexual misconduct because "not all sexual contact with children is delivered by a pedophile or hebephile" (p. 22). Among the cases of educator sexual misconduct that was reported by Shakeshaft and Cohan (1995) were adults who were (a) exclusively interested in children or adolescents and (b) adults who were more likely to be exploiters of any sexual situation, whether the victim was a child, a teen,or an adult.This broader definition is also more inclusive of female sex offenders.

The U.S. Department of Education's (2004) study[6] is considered one of the only reports on educator sexual misconduct, as well as one of the most comprehensive. The study was conducted to respond to the mandate in Section 5414 of the Elementary and Secondary Education Act of 1965 (ESEA) to conduct a study of sexual abuse in U.S. schools (as cited on page 1 of the report). The study defined a student as "any person, whatever age, in an educational institution up through 12th grade" and an educator as "any person older than 18 who works with or for a school or other educational or learning organization" where the service they provided was "paid or unpaid, professional, classified or volunteer" (p. 1), in other words, any adult in the school. Adults covered in the study were defined as including "teachers, counselors, school administrators, secretaries, bus drivers, coaches, parent volunteers for student activities, lunchroom attendants, tutors, music teachers, special-education aides or any other adult in contact in a school-related relationship with a student" (p. 1). The study found the following:

- Teachers whose job description includes time with individual students, such as music teachers or coaches, are more likely to sexually abuse students than other teachers. Other job groups included substitute teachers, bus drivers, teacher aides, other school employees, security guards, principals, and counselors. Indicating that supervision and monitoring of adults by administration and other adults in the school system should be a priority in the detection and prevention of sexual misconduct against students. Please note that the emphasis in the report was not on a particular occupation in the school, rather it was on the propensity of sexually abusive adults to purposefully seek out alone time with students and the higher risk for educator sexual misconduct to occur and to go unobserved in this type of situation with this type of person when monitoring and supervision is absent.
- In contrast to other studies on child sexual abuse, the American Association of University Women Educational Foundation (2001) study, which was one of the studies cited in the report, found that 57.2 percent of the students in the study indicated that *adult males composed 57.2 percent of the offenders*, while *adult females composed 42.8 percent of the offenders*, indicating that students are at about equal risk of having a sexual crime committed against them by both women and men within their schools. This finding *challenges the sexual double standard* that it is only men who commit sexual offenses against students.
- Across analyses of studies on sexual misconduct in schools committed by adults is the consensus that female child sexual abusers are underreported if the

target is male because males are socialized to believe that "they should be flattered or appreciative of sexual interest from a female" (p. 25). Unfortunately, this sexual double standard toward boys appears to hold true even though the female is an adult who is supposed to be looking out for a boy's welfare, not sexually exploiting him. This sexual double standard also implies that adult women who sexually abuse boys are not "really" sex offenders.

- Same-sex offenders, male and female, ranged from 18 to 28 percent of the reported cases across studies. It was noted that a majority of same-sex offenders identify themselves as heterosexual, with most living in married or heterosexual relationship.
- Both boys and girls are targeted in schools by adult offenders. Sexual victimization of girls ranged from 56 to 76 percent of students and sexual victimization of boys ranged from 23 to 46 percent of students. It is also important to remember that in schools boys and girls are targeted by adults of the opposite gender and same-sex gender. Given the uncertainty that some students have about their sexual orientation and their fear of being labeled gay or lesbian,[7] it is easy to understand how adult same-sex offenders are able to gain the silence of a student, and in turn, are less likely to be reported.
- While white students report being the target of educator sexual misconduct most often, African American, Latino, American Indian, and Asian students also reported experiencing educator sexual misconduct.
- Students with behavior disorders are more than five times as likely as nondisabled students to be sexually abused, with students identified as having a diagnosis of some level of mental retardation more than three times as likely to be the targets of sexual abuse by adults in their schools.
- Like other sexual predators, sex offenders in schools use a variety of strategies to coerce, manipulate, and gain control of a student in order to commit sexual offenses. They lie to students, isolate students, grant favors and give special attention, give students alcohol or drugs, and entice them to meet on school grounds and off school grounds.
- The report notes that the abusers who target children in elementary grades are "often professionally accomplished and even celebrated" (p. 31) and that this is particularly true when compared to their nonabusing counterparts. "This popularity confounds district officials and community members and prompts them to ignore allegations on the belief that 'outstanding teachers' cannot be abusers" (p. 32).
- At the middle and high school levels, the sexual crime may not necessarily be premeditated (i.e., where the student is groomed over a period of time with the goal to commit sexual abuse), as it can also result from being "opportunistic or as a result of bad judgment or a misplaced sense of privilege" (p. 32).
- What is pervasive throughout the report is that educators who commit sexual crimes against students do so in the context of "helping a student" and use the opportunities to groom students while sensitizing students to increased amounts of touch and gain a student's compliance for secrecy. Offenders are deliberate

in their efforts to keep students from telling. Debra Lafave was a middle school reading teacher when she was arrested and later convicted of several counts of sexual abuse against a 14-year-old male student. Her sexual crimes were committed at her home, at a portable classroom at the middle school where she taught, and in the back seat of a moving vehicle that the male victim's young cousin, age 15, was driving. Lafave was never charged for exposing a minor to a sexual crime (i.e., the cousin would be the child exposed to the crime). Lafave was described by witnesses as being flirtatious with the boy, and she was known to initiate contact with her student during the summer by way of cell phone. She was reported for the sexual abuse when the boy's mother asked her son about it, and he disclosed what was going on. News reports indicated that Lafave had encouraged the boy to lie to keep the sexual abuse a secret (Krause, 2005). Lafave's behavior is similar to the common manipulations by school offenders cited in the report such as: "if you tell, no one will believe you"; "if you tell, I'll get in trouble"; and "if you tell, I won't be able to be your friend" (p. 33).

- While almost all students respond to positive attention from a teacher, coach, counselor, or other adult at their school, students who are estranged from their parents, unsure of themselves, or engaged in risky behavior are often at higher risk. It is important to remember that all students, of all ages, are usually unsure of themselves at some point in their young lives and may on any given day "feel estranged" from their parents or peers. What is at issue is that it is the adult in the school environment that sexually exploits a student and may succeed in doing so regardless of a student's background or family status, especially if other adults are not paying attention and acting on their behalf.

The study also found that while a majority of students (71%) indicated that they would report educator sexual misconduct, only a minority of students (23%) actually reported the sexual misconduct they experienced, and when they did report, it was most often to another teacher or another school employee. The question then becomes did these adults take action? The most common reason that students gave for not reporting was a fear of not being believed. As cited by the U.S. Department of Education (2004), there was the case of a teacher, Kenneth DeLuca, convicted of sexually abusing 13 students between the ages of 10 and 18 over a period of 21 years, and while nearly all the students reported this teacher's abuse, school officials did not take the accusations seriously. Additionally, the report goes on to explain that not only were the students not believed, but some were told to leave school, and in some cases the parents of the students were threatened with lawsuits (as cited by the U.S. Department of Education, 2004, p. 35).

What also needs to be considered is that school officials will choose to conduct their own investigations, without any qualifications to do so and from the possible motive of protecting their school's reputation, rather than provide protection to students. More often than not, it was a parent who finally reported to law enforcement and not the school official (principal, school counselor, other teacher, administrator, and so on) to whom the student or parent told about the sexual behavior by the teacher or other adult in the school. This finding emphasizes that school officials were not reliable in their responsibility to report sexual misconduct in their schools to law enforcement, nor were they reliable in bringing appropriate action against the adult found to have committed sexual abuse or harassment against a student or students.

Rubin and Biggs (1999) describe the case of a female teacher who sexually abused a male student. While the sexual crimes had occurred away from the school, there was inappropriate behavior that had occurred at the school that raised concerns for the assistant principal. Rubin and Briggs report that the assistant principal had become very concerned about this teacher's behavior when she was observed as "spending a great deal of time" with him after school in her room and had been observed "dancing a slow dance with Carl with her arms around his neck and his arms around her waist." The assistant principal met with the teacher to "discuss her professional behavior" (notice her behavior is not described as unprofessional) and was cautioned (not disciplined) by the assistant principal "not to put herself in a position that could be misinterpreted" (notice the assistant principal did not say than the teacher had put the student in a position that was inappropriate for him or that her behavior was inappropriate and unethical). The teacher was not disciplined at this point with a suspension for crossing professional boundaries nor was she sanctioned due to a pattern of behavior that the authors summarize as "the dances, having students in her room, and giving students rides home" and which would be considered as blatant unethical behavior in terms of "slow dancing" with a student at a school dance, which the authors state "had immediately preceded the first sexual contacts" (see Rubin & Briggs, 1987, pp. 80–85). In their discussion of the above case, Rubin and Briggs bring several points to the forefront about female sexual offenders in schools which are summarized below,

- Our society is struggling with the question as to whether women are equally culpable and responsible for their behavior when compared to men?
- Not only should this teacher have lost her certificate, she should have been prosecuted for statutory rape.
- The teacher was fully aware of what she was doing and that she was taking advantage of a student.
- Her colleagues should have done more to prevent the exploitation of a student.
- Our laws require that the treatment of culpable adults be gender neutral.

- Female sexual offenders in schools are not the exception but they can be among the most difficult to investigate.
- Administrators must learn to challenge suspicious events and behavior by asking "What is the educational purpose?" and when that purpose is not apparent, actions must be taken to prevent it.
- A student's right to an educational environment free of sexual exploitation should always take precedence over employment rights of the teacher. This right of students should be rigidly applied whether the offending adult is a man or a woman (pp. 85–86).

Reports regarding suspected sexual abuse in schools against students need to be acted upon immediately and reported to law enforcement in order for a formal investigation to occur outside the school system where impartiality is more assured. A final aspect of the Department of Education's 2004 report has to do with the protection of teachers through their union contract taking precedence over the rights of students to an educational environment that is safe and nurturing and where their well-being is assured. Often the union will act to protect the teacher rather than students, an unacceptable aspect of teacher union contracts, and while it understandable to want to protect teachers from potentially false accusations, unions should not protect offending teachers or move them to another school system in order to abide a union contract.[8] It is certainly time for unions and school administrators together to become equally involved and equally accountable for the safety, protection, and well-being of students. After all, without students, what would be the need for the school or the union?

FEMALE SEXUAL PREDATORS IN SCHOOLS: IT HAPPENS TO GIRLS TOO

The sexual double standard that females are only victims and not sexual offenders has been shown to be false, as crime reports indicate that in contemporary society more females are being reported and convicted for sexual crimes.[9] As discussed in previous chapters, it is generally viewed that female sexual crimes have been underreported (Allen, 1990); therefore, the true prevalence of sexual crimes committed by females remains unknown but is considered higher than what is reported to law enforcement.[10] However, simply because stereotypes and gender bias have been barriers in the recognition of female-perpetrated sexual crimes does not negate the existence of female sexual offenders, nor does it negate the fact they are known to sexually abuse both male and female victims.[11] While it has been documented that fear of being labeled homosexual is among the reasons that boys, molested by males, seldom disclose sexual abuse by men,[12] there has been less documented about the effects that teen girls experience when they are sexually abused by a woman. Similar to boys sexually abused by a man, girls are confused by the woman's behavior, experience a sense of betrayal, and question their sexuality when sexually exploited and abused by a woman. Girls can also blame themselves for trusting an adult whom they thought was safe and fear that they will be blamed or that their sexual abuse by a woman will be minimized. Girls struggle to fully accept that it is the woman offender who needs to take responsibility for the betrayal of trust and the sexual crimes they commit against girls.

The following reports depict the sexual abuse of teen girls by adult women who gained access to them through their schools and who also attended their churches. The impact of how teachers, female and male, who sexually exploit and otherwise commit sexual crimes against students are in the communities where students live. This point may be overlooked in terms of understanding how students might also come across their offenders when they are away from school at restaurants, grocery stores, and other places that students and their parents frequent as they go about their daily lives. What this means is that offending women are a constant presence in the lives of students whom they sexually abuse both at school and in the communities where they live.

Laura's story is how a young girl was victimized by an adult woman who gained access to her through her school. Joanna's story depicts sexual abuse by a female minister that began when she was 15 years old. Laura and Joanna generously agreed to share what happened to them, how they were manipulated by the women who sexually abused them, and how they were affected by the sexual abuse. They share their experiences with a sense of purpose that sexual abuse by female sexual predators will be recognized as a reality that can happen to students and that, when it does, it is harmful. Most important, Laura and Joanna hope that in telling what happened to them by two women they thought they could trust, sexual abuse by a woman can be prevented from ever happening to other children and teens.

LAURA'S STORY

Laura was 12 years old when she was sexually abused by a woman who was her homeroom teacher and coach. Laura was active in track, volleyball, and basketball, and the teacher/coach was forever present in Laura's life as a student athlete. The sexual abuse occurred over a period of time and was eventually disclosed by Laura when her brother found out that she was missing from home one night and the police were called. Laura recalls how her teacher/coach would "take me out of classes for 'counseling sessions' where she would have me discuss issues that I was having with my parents." This grooming process with Laura occurred over a three-month period. While other adults were aware of this behavior by the teacher/coach, Laura does not recall that any of the other adults questioned this woman's behavior. As these "counseling sessions" progressed, they changed from telling Laura what wonderful parents she had and that she should listen to them to telling Laura that she had horrible parents until Laura was convinced that she wanted "to run away." Instead, her teacher/coach suggested to Laura that "she would come and pick me up at night so that I would be safe." Laura shared that "I started sneaking out of my window at night, and she would be waiting and we would go to the park." Eventually, the woman offender started taking Laura to her apartment and once even took Laura to her parents' house in another city. Not every excursion involved molesting. Some nights when she would take Laura to the park, she would bring pizza, which they shared while they talked. Laura recalls that "she would also give me gifts like tanning products and other things she knew I liked." Laura can remember how this female predator would give her just enough attention to make her believe that she cared about her while never stopping the sexual abuse. She manipulated Laura by making Laura think that "she could be my mother." Laura stated, "As an abuser, she was really smart. We would write notes back and forth during school, but she would always make sure she got the notes back from me." When asked what the sexual abuse involved, Laura responded, "Use your imagination, anything you can probably imagine, happened. There was oral sex, digital penetration, and she even had me shower with her." When the sexual abuse finally came out, the offender denied the sexual abuse to the police. Laura's parents believed Laura and supported her. However, "the offender was not prosecuted," and according to the police file that Laura was allowed to look at as an adult, this teacher was "the first report in the county of a female sex offender." Laura recalls that because "I chose to go with this woman, I blamed myself for years." Laura also had questions about her sexual identity and "wondered if this experience made me a lesbian." Laura shared, "I did not know what gay was, but I knew that I had this new awareness that my friends did not have." Laura views herself as heterosexual but admits that she still has questions. The sexual abuse left an indelible impression on Laura's development as a young girl. As she matured and with the help of a therapist, Laura came to realize that "I was a child. This was not a relationship, it was child sexual abuse. I might have thought I was making adult decisions, but in reality, this adult had poor boundaries and should have known better. I was not to blame." Even though it is years later, Laura shared that "I still struggle with female relationships. I do a pretty good job of putting on a good front, but I'd much rather be friends with a male than a female any day."

JOANNA'S STORY

Joanna contacted me out of a desire to share her experience of being sexually abused by a youth minister at her church and from a realization that while much is written about men who commit sexual abuse, very little is written about women who commit sexual crimes against children and teens. Joanna was 15 years old when the sexual abuse began and was 18 when it ended. Throughout the interview, Joanna described the sexual violence perpetrated by the female offender and how the sadistic acts of sexual abuse by the woman offender would cause Joanna to dissociate.[13] The woman who sexually abused Joanna was a youth minister, and although the church was well aware of the sexual offenses this female minister committed against Joanna, the woman has never been removed from contact with other children. Joanna shared how this woman "picked me up on her radar" and how as a young girl she felt "bedazzled" to be singled out by someone whom she looked up to. As Joanna explained, "I had just found God at age 14, and she was my youth minister who took an interest in me. I felt special to her because she told me how special I was. She knew more about the Bible than anyone I knew at the time and would often quote from it." Joanna was interested in becoming a social worker, and the youth minister had a college degree in social work. Joanna did not know many people who had graduated from college, so she thought this woman was extraordinary, some one that "knew everything." Joanna recalls how the female offender "paid attention to me, nurtured me, gave me gifts and special favors. She even gave me the nickname 'Joey.' Her attention felt like rain on a dry plant." The female offender was a constant intrusive presence in Joanna's life, showing up whenever Joanna was at school or church and making it seem that "it was normal for her to be where I was all the time." She would show up at "church youth meetings, come to school and eat lunch, walk along beside me during marching band practice, and joined the singing group I was in at church." At the same time, the offender discouraged Joanna from dating and spending time with her friends. Joanna recalls that "no one, not even the adults around me, questioned this woman's behavior."

The first act of sexual abuse occurred when the female offender invited Joanna to her apartment, which was located next to the church. The woman lived in an apartment above the church office. Joanna related, "She came over and sat next to me and hugged me and then kissed me, stating, 'This is the way people show affection. It is okay. We have a special relationship that God has given us.'" After this first incident, the offender began to invite Joanna to her apartment on a regular basis and eventually asked Joanna's parents permission for Joanna to spend the night. What Joanna recalls is not clearly remembered because of the possibility that the offender gave Joanna drugs in the hot chocolate that she served to her. What Joanna does remember is that "she played music, wave music, it was soft. She served me hot chocolate and toast, and I remember feeling very mellow, calm, kind of floating. She started hugging me, and then her tongue was thrust down my throat, and the next thing I knew I was in the bedroom with no clothes. I do not know how I got out of my clothes." There were many incidents of sexual abuse after this one. Joanna shared, "I can remember how she would leave welts on my breasts from sucking them and penetrate my vagina with her fingers and then her whole hand. I remember how my head would bump up against the headboard. I mostly remember how I had nowhere to go. I couldn't get out or get away. I remember how her face would change, and she would look so angry. Even though I felt so much pain, I never said anything." What Joanna remembers thinking at times was "Does she [the offender] like this?" and "Will she be finished soon?" "She was so out of control, so different, nothing like the charismatic Christian leader I knew at other times." Throughout the interview, Joanna described the sexual violence perpetrated by the female offender. Years later, when Joanna was an adult and had become a mother she confronted her offender, she vividly recalls the woman saying, "I am glad to hear you could have children, that I didn't do too much damage." This woman certainly challenges the belief, and perhaps most importantly the myth, that sexual abuse by a woman is somehow a misguided attempt at "love" or that women sexually offend from "desiring an emotional connection" that is often written about in explaining, excusing, and romanticizing the female who sexually abuses an adolescent.[14] It is critical to children's safety and well-being that people remember that what they read in media reports is seldom what occurs in the reality of sexual crimes committed by females[15] and that media personas (i.e., talk show hosts and hosts of "news programs") seldom have the expertise to interview a female sex offender, especially when the interviewer may personify beliefs that reflect a sexual double standard that dismisses the harm that women sex offenders cause to children and teens.[16]

The youth minister gained the trust of Joanna's parents as well. Joanna shared, "She ate pickled herring with my dad and drank beer, a big deal in a German family. My parents did not attend church at the time, so they thought having a youth minister pay attention to me and visit with my family was a big deal, a type of status." The depth of the betrayal and intrusiveness into Joanna's life included joining Joanna's family on vacation where "she sexually abused me while my parents were out fishing," and "she put her hand up my shirt and on my breast while riding in the backseat of a car while my sister and her friend were in the front seat."

The religious abuse by the woman did not escape Joanna either. She vividly remembers the altar that the offender had in her bedroom and how she would pray there after sexually abusing Joanna, but Joanna never recalls that the offender asked for forgiveness. Joanna also remembers how "I could see the top of the church roof next door during the sexual abuse and how the offender's clerical black robe, with sash and symbol, hung from a coat rack in the bedroom." Joanna shares an important perspective of a young teenage girl: "I never thought of what she was doing as something sexual or as sexual abuse. This was in the mid-1970s, and I had little to no information about sexuality, sexual abuse, or lesbian sex acts or about female sex offenders."

Joanna describes episodes of dissociation where she was physically present but would feel emotionally disconnected from what was happening to her.[17] The dissociation and the drugs (i.e., Joanna recalls seeing valium in the offender's medicine cabinet) that were most likely given to Joanna by the offender, would explain the fragmentation of memories and the immobilization that Joanna experienced during the sexual abuse.[18] As another woman shared when describing her experience of dissociation connected with child sexual abuse, "My throat tightens and I find it difficult to speak. I also cannot breathe and I feel every muscle in my body tighten. There is also the feeling of leaving the present and of just not being there" (p. 55).[19]

THE CELEBRITY COACH

Tanda Rucker[20] was 32 years old at the time she was sentenced to one year at a minimum-security correctional facility near Los Angeles for the sexual abuse of three teen girls whom she had coached at Encinal High School. Rucker was formerly a member of Stanford's 1992 college champion team and was named by *USA Today* as California's top high school player of the year in 1991 when she played for Berkeley High School. Rucker was convicted of 18 felony counts of sexual crimes that occurred over a two-year period between 2000 and 2002. Rucker's sexual offending included acts of penetration with a foreign object and oral sex. Rucker could have received a prison sentence of up to 14 years and four months for the crimes she committed; instead, she was sentenced to one year at a minimum-security correctional facility near Los Angeles, given five years' probation, and required to register as a sex offender. However, as a part of her sentencing, Rucker was also allowed to leave the correctional facility during the day and return in the evening so that she could continue to work for her sister, an executive producer of films in Los Angeles. The parents of the three girls were quoted in a news article as "outraged that Judge Thomas Reardon disregarded prosecutor Delia Trevino's request that Rucker be sentenced to three years in state prison for her conviction on 18 felony counts."[21] One mother described the courage it took for her daughter to testify. In the article, the parents were quoted as stating that their daughters were suffering from "long-term psychological damage," that their daughters' lives had been "turned upside down," and that the girls had "lost their innocence, lost their friends, and were ridiculed and gossiped about at school." One of the mothers noted that "Rucker hasn't shown any remorse and has never apologized to her or her daughter." Another of the mothers described Rucker as "a highly intelligent young lady" who singled out the best basketball players on the team with a "charm campaign that included taking them to lunch." In justifying his sentencing decision, the judge in the case was quoted as stating that "he didn't think it would be appropriate to send Rucker to state prison because she has the ability to make something of her life because she has a college education, a steady job, and the support of her family." The judge neglected to realize that all these attributes were in place when Rucker was committing her sexual offenses. However, after the hearing, the victims' parents questioned how helpful Rucker's parents had been to her, stating that "most of the sexual activity charged in the case occurred at her parents' home in Berkeley" since Rucker lived with them during the time of her sexual offending. Michael Kinane, the attorney who represented the teen victims in a civil lawsuit, said that in addition to naming Rucker, the suit named Rucker's parents and the Alameda Unified School District as defendants for allegedly not doing enough to stop the sexual activity. Kinane shared that he thought Rucker was benefiting from being a woman because he believed that "a male coach who had engaged in multiple sex acts with either male or female players would have been sentenced to a lengthy state prison term." The mother of one of the victims said, "Parents should be aware of the fact that female-on-female pedophiles are becoming more common in society." It is not so much that female pedophilia and other types of female sexual offending are necessarily more or less common today as it is that it is starting to be recognized and, reported.[22]

The previous reports of women sexual offenders who gained access to female students exemplify the types of women who manipulate and deceive students and parents alike in order to commit their sexual offenses while keeping their sexual crimes and unethical behavior a secret.[23] Women who commit sexual offenses against both male and female students are quite similar to men[24] except that females tend to use objects to penetrate their victims[25] and are less likely to be recognized as sexual offenders or as exploiters of children and teens.[26] The two female offenders described fit the category of a female offender that Duncan (2006) regards as a child exploiter offender and described as "an adult female who is a non-family member who has a history of exploiting her dominant relationship or authority status with a child or adolescent." Duncan states that this typology of an adult female sex offender (defined as a woman 18 years or older) is recognized by the "cognitive distortions that may be distinct to this category of female sexual offender in terms of rationalizing her sexual abuse of a child or teen as being based on mutual attraction and love interests rather than on the planned manipulation and sexual exploitation of a minor for her own sexual and emotional gratification."[27] This typology of adult female sex offender includes women who sexually offend against both boys and girls, making it important for adults and students alike to realize that students can be at equal risk of sexual exploitation and abuse by a female sex offender in their school as they are by a male. The main difference is whether stereotypes that prevail in the judicial system, gender bias, school officials' denial and lack of action, and social stereotypes about female sexuality will prevent female predators from being noticed, reported, and held legally accountable for their crimes.

Studies in South Africa[28] and Australia[29] have focused on sexual offenses committed in schools where females have been found to be primary perpetrators of sexual crimes against students, both boys and girls. In Australia, Deering and Mellor (2007) documented how even as recently as "1998 the judicial system seemed surprised by the appearance of a female sex offender when, in sentencing one Western Australia female teacher who had engaged in sexual intercourse and performed oral sex with an underage male student, Justice Wisbey justified his suspended sentence in terms of the novelty of the crime" (p. 218). The authors then turn to the media attention that female teachers have gleaned over the past few years regarding sexual offenses against male students and one female student. They refer to Karen Ellis of Victoria, convicted in 2004, whose initial sentence of 22 months was overturned, and a 32-month sentence, with a minimum period of six months' jail time, was applied. Cindy Howell of Melbourne was convicted and sentenced to five years' imprisonment with a two-and-a-half-year minimum after sexually abusing a 15-year-old student who was her daughter's boyfriend. Heidi Choat was convicted of five counts of indecency that included intercourse and oral sex with a 12-year-old student and sentenced to two years' imprisonment. All these cases are noted by the authors as involving "sexual intercourse and/or oral sex, and the courts have related the seriousness of the offences to the fact that the victims were in some way under the care, supervision or authority of the perpetrator at the time of the offences" (p. 219). The authors remind us that the sexual abuse of students by teachers or other persons in schools are but one avenue of sexual offending available to females.

SEXUAL HARASSMENT IN SCHOOLS

Sexual harassment can take many forms that include words, gestures, and writings; through Internet sites; and, of course, through cell phones.[30] Paludi, DeFour, Attah, and Batts (1999) give examples that include covert physical contact, such as brushing against someone's body, blatant propositions, and sexual assaults. There are five categories of sexual harassment that coincide with the legal definitions of sexual harassment and that encompass the range of behaviors that would define sexual harassment:

1. Gender harassment—generalized sexist remarks and behavior designed not to elicit sexual cooperation but rather to convey insulting, degrading, or sexist attitudes.
2. Seductive behavior—inappropriate or offensive sexual advances.
3. Sexual bribery—the solicitation of sexual activity or other sex-linked behavior by promise of reward, such as a higher grade or a letter of recommendation.
4. Sexual coercion—the coercion of sexual activity by threat of punishment (e.g., failure to give the grade earned).
5. Sexual imposition—including gross sexual imposition, assault, and rape (cited by Paludi et al. 1999).

For students at the secondary and elementary levels of school, there are the differences in, power and position, and age and maturity between the adolescent, prepubescent youth or child, and the adult educator or staff person. This power differential, age, and maturity difference is what enables the adult offender to take advantage of a young person's curiosity about all things sexual; the likability that a student may have for the teacher, coach, or counselor; the special status that the student may gain from complying with the sexual intentions of the adult; and the sexual arousal that is felt when sexualized behavior occurs.[31] At the same time, given the highly sexualized culture surrounding youth today[32] and the rapid sexual development occurring during adolescence,[33] it is important to recognize that students may also indicate a sexual interest in an adult at their school. When this happens, it is up to the adult to know and communicate teacher–student boundaries and to practice these appropriate and ethical boundaries with students as a role model and as someone entrusted with the well-being of students.[34]

The American Association of University Women Educational Foundation (AAUW) has conducted some of the most comprehensive studies of sexual harassment occurring in secondary schools. Studies by the AAUW were conducted in 1993[35] and then again in 2000.[36] A major finding of the studies was that students report witnessing (a) sexual harassment of students by teachers and other school employees, (b) students sexually harassing teachers and other school employees, and (c) teachers and other school employees sexually harassing each other. The AAUW studies reported that among the students participating in the study, "almost 40 percent of students report that teachers and other school employees sexually harass students in their schools" (p. 2).[37] The AAUW defined sexual harassment as encompassing *hands-on* offenses

ACTION STEPS

Training adults about sexual harassment and how to address it should come before student education on sexual harassment prevention.

Ensure that all employees have received training about sexual harassment before they enter the school building.

Establish primary prevention councils to review the status of complaints and what action has been taken.

Mandate that all suspicions of sexual contact with students be reported to law enforcement.

Monitor student behavior through peer group councils that promote prevention, early intervention by responding promptly to reports of inappropriate behavior, breaches in policy, and crossing of boundaries between students while at school.

(i.e., physically touching a student in a sexual manner) as well as *hands-off* offenses (i.e., behavior other than touching, such as sexual comments, leering at a student, and sexual gestures) of sexual harassment. Both of the AAUW studies found that hands-off sexual harassment was the most prevalent type of sexual harassment that students experienced by educators, other adults, and peers.

The overall findings of the 2001[38] report regarding *student-to-student sexual harassment* indicate that both girls and boys engage in sexual harassment of their peers and that it is not boys alone who are committing sexual harassment; girls are committing sexual harassment as well. The results of the study are summarized here:

- Sexual harassment is widespread in schools. Boys are even more likely today (as compared to 1993) to experience sexual harassment. In comparison, 79 percent of the boys reported experiencing sexual harassment, while 83 percent of girls reported sexual harassment, indicating that the experience of sexual harassment is about equal for boys and girls.
- Students attempt to deal with sexual harassment by avoiding the person who harassed them, talking less in class, avoiding going to school, and changing their seats in class to get farther away from the person. These findings indicate that victims of sexual harassment are more likely to change their behavior rather than the offender changing theirs.

- Boys today are less likely to report being a perpetrator of sexual harassment (57% of boys reported committing offenses in 2001 compared to 66% in 1993).
- While boys and girls report that they know what sexual harassment is, sexual harassment continues to be a widespread problem.
- The most common forms of sexual harassment that students reported committing were making sexual comments, jokes, gestures, or looks; spreading sexual rumors; pulling clothing down or off; and the most common forms of sexual harassment that students reported experiencing were receiving sexual and nude pictures, photographs, and messages; intentionally being brushed up against in a sexual way; being spied on while they showered or dressed; having their clothing pulled in a sexual way; having their way blocked or being cornered in a sexual way; and being calling gay or lesbian.
- Boys are less likely than girls to consider themselves as victims of sexual harassment and exploitation due to gender stereotypes[39] and prevention education programs that primarily focus on boys as offenders. Conversely, girls are less likely to consider themselves as perpetrators of sexual harassment even when they commit the same or similar behaviors as boys because prevention education programs focus primarily on girls as victims and not also as aggressors of sexual harassment.
- Students admit to being both offenders and victims of sexual harassment; 57 percent of the boys and 50 percent of the girls admitted to sexually harassing their same-sex and opposite-sex peers.

SEXUALIZED SCHOOL ENVIRONMENTS

The 2001 report by the AAUW[40] substantiates that the environment of schools in contemporary society continue to be sexualized cultures where sexual harassment and exploitation occur alongside the academic learning that students are undertaking. What is discouraging is that reported incidences of sexual harassment remain high even though students claim to know what sexual harassment involves. This fact remains true even for those schools where students report policies against sexual harassment. While students report mutual sexual harassment between students, they also report that teachers and other school personnel sexually harass students while also reporting that students sexually harass teachers and other school personnel. Students also report witnessing teachers and school personnel sexually harassing each other. Therefore, what becomes clear is that school administrators, principals, teachers, counselors, coaches, and school staff either may not themselves care about sexual harassment and the sexualization of school environments or may not know what sexual harassment is in a school environment, how to prevent it, how to set and enforce standards in schools for adult and student behavior, and, most important, how to address sexual harassment when it occurs regardless of whether the offender/victim relationship is adult–adult, student–adult, adult–student, or student–student. It may also be that schools are overwhelmed by the behavior of so many students who accept sexual harassment and exploitation as a social norm for their generation. Clearly, schools officials and parents together need to bring a concerted effort to addressing this widespread form of sexual aggression in schools.

The findings from the 2001 AAUW report support the recommendation that adults and students in school environments would benefit from education on what sexual harassment involves that includes specific examples that are free of gender bias. Educators and students would also benefit from information on how sexual harassment creates and sustains antagonistic and hostile school environments, what the personal effects are on students and adults who either experience sexual harassment or witness sexual harassment, and identifying what specifically needs to change in the social environment and social norms that sustain sexual harassment and exploitation and the impact that a sexualized school environments has on the developing values and social relationships of youth. It is also evident that parents need to be more involved and supportive of what schools need to do and are doing to reduce the sexualized cultures in schools. Parents and schools must be equally involved in addressing their role and responsibility regarding the social problem of sexual harassment occurring in schools.[41]

One of the most consistent recommendations that students made who participated in the 2001 AAUW study was for schools to talk less and actually do something about sexual harassment. What students may not realize is that reasonable dress codes, limitations on the use of cell phones in schools or restrictions of cell phone use, and student accountability for sexualized messages and photos on social network sites would be among the actions that schools need to take to "do something" about the problem of sexual harassment and sexually hostile school environments. Additionally, studies continue to show that sexual harassment in teen relationships is correlated with the acceptance of violence and sexual coercion in students' dating relationships.[42] In fact, the AAUW study points to the matrix of sexual coercion, bullying, sexual harassment, and a general lack of respect for boundaries that typifies the hostile environments of schools today and teens' social relationships.[43] The attitudes, beliefs, behaviors, and values established at this stage of a young person's development can result in these same or similar patterns of attitudes, beliefs, and behaviors continuing into college, the workplace, and eventually into intimate relationships in adulthood.[44]

TEACHERS' PARTICIPATION IN SEXUAL HARASSMENT

Regarding sexual harassment by teachers, 40 percent of the students in the 2001 AAUW study reported experiencing sexual harassment by a teacher, with boys and girls equally likely to have this experience.[45] Interesting enough, 8 percent of the boys compared to 6 percent of the girls reported physical (touch) sexual harassment. Boys also indicated that they were less likely to report sexual harassment because of gender stereotypes that indicate that "boys should be able to handle it on their own" (p. 27). This aspect of gender stereotyping can leave boys unprotected when it comes to adult-level sexual harassment in schools. This finding about boys is particularly concerning since both boys and girls report finding physical sexual harassment the most upsetting. Additionally, because of gender stereotypes and sexual bias against boys as victims of sexual harassment and exploitation, boys are more likely to confuse sexual harassment with positive sexual attention.[46] Through male socialization, boys are given the message to accept sexual harassment as something they should expect and receive in a positive manner, even if that is not how they feel.

It is also important to remember that the majority of educators and school personnel do not commit sexual harassment, nor do the majority of educators sexually exploit students or otherwise sexually abuse the youth in their care. It is also important to remember that one person can harm a number of students over a period of months to years when they are not recognized or reported or when an offender does not make the choice to stop her behavior but rather continues the choice to commit illegal and unethical acts toward children and teens. Additionally, there is the question of how many educators and school staff are aware of this kind of behavior by the women and men around them and take on the persona of the "three little monkeys" who "see no evil, speak no evil, and hear no evil" while evil (i.e., sexual exploitation, harassment, and abuse) continues unabated and unchecked. Finally, it is never the fault of the student when sexual misconduct by an educator or other adult in the school environment occurs. This is because it is taken for granted—and rightfully so—that adults know the boundaries in their relationships with youth and that adults are there to teach the difference between right and wrong and are responsible for modeling positive social values and behavior. On the other hand, adolescents are not at the same maturity level or governed by the same laws as adults, so they are not viewed as capable of willingly consenting to sexual relationships with adults and therefore are not culpable for the sexual crime committed by an adult. The idea or proposition of a "consensual relationship" between the adult female sex offender and the student is often used as an excuse by females committing sexual abuse against teens or by a public that attempts to excuse the sexual offending or exploitation of a teen by a female offender by citing that the youth consented. What this faulty thinking fails to acknowledge is "youthful consent" is never a valid reason or an excuse for illegal or unethical behavior by the adult.

Consent is less an issue with younger children (under the age of 12), but child compliance can be misconstrued as consent when the victim is a boy because of the gender stereotypes about boys and sexuality.[47] Adults are expected to know the boundaries with students and to practice these boundaries on a daily basis. When adults are having a problem in understanding or practicing appropriate boundaries, it is their responsibility to ask for help and to seek assistance before a crime is committed and a student is harmed. On the other hand, when students are engaging in sexual harassment and attempting to exploit their relationship with an adult, it is up to the adult to address the student's behavior in the presence of another adult so that boundaries are clarified, expectations for student behavior are clearly defined and stated, and the relationship with the student remains on an adult-student footing. Responding to inappropriate behavior by a student provides the opportunity to model how boundary violations are addressed in a firm, respectable, and straightforward manner. Students should be reminded as to what will occur if their behavior continues. Adults who are engaging in the very behaviors that students are held accountable for set the stage for teaching a lesson about adult hypocrisy rather than teaching a lesson about personal character.

AMY'S STORY

Amy's story was partially shared in Chapter 2 on maternal sex offenders because of the type of maternal/child bond that Amy developed for the woman who sexually offended against her. More of Amy's story is shared here because the woman was a teacher at Amy's school and even though she was only Amy's teacher for a short period of time, it was through her initial relationship as Amy's teacher that she was able to gain access to Amy and begin to groom her for the sexual abuse. Amy recalled how the offender "made an extra effort to ingratiate herself with my mom, who worked constantly at her new job, and was grateful that a teacher took an interest in me." It was during the summer after her eighth-grade year that Amy began to babysit for the woman's children at the request of the offender. Amy enjoyed the time she spent at the teacher's home, being a part of a family. Amy recalls how "she preyed upon my emotions and the loneliness that I felt with my mom working. I wanted so much to be in a family, I really liked kids, and I enjoyed being around her children and being at her house. It was the closest thing I had to a family at that time. There was just a tremendous amount of psychological abuse. She would give me attention and then withdraw. When she withdrew the attention, she also withdrew the affection. I just never knew what was coming from one day to the next. There was also this aspect of the abuse that was not sexual, but I think it was meant to hurt me and control me. When she was cold and indifferent toward me is when she would treat her children like gold, and it was always in front of me, I think to purposely hurt me and let me know that she was in charge." Amy shared that the female offender "skewed reality, she completely distorted her responsibility for the sexual abuse by turning the abuse back on me. She would say things like 'I just don't understand this, I've never done this before, and I can't resist you.' These kinds of comments made me feel like I was causing her pain." The manipulation of this female predator was relentless toward Amy throughout her adolescence and as she entered young adulthood. Amy shared how the woman offender would say, "Are you sure you have not done this before?" and "Do you know what this is?" The female offender made Amy feel sorry for her and that Amy should protect her from the sexual abuse ever being discovered with words like "This will devastate my life, I would lose my job, my family" while never admitting that Amy was underage and that she, the offender, was committing crimes against Amy. Amy has no memory of the female offender ever showing any remorse for the sexual abuse. Amy looks back and realizes that this female predator never considered and had no regard for how she was devastating Amy's life. Rather than remorse, Amy views this woman offender as manipulating her by "withdrawing and being really cold towards me which devastated me at the time. She would just cut off all communications, and then I would suddenly get a letter from her." Amy believed that there was no one she could tell about what was being done to her by this woman, who was a teacher at her school and therefore had access to other children. The sexual abuse continued even after Amy graduated high school and attempted to move on with her life. Between the ages of 19 and 22, Amy shared how she distanced herself from this woman, but the female offender would pull her back in by calling and saying, "After all that we have done for you, and now you can't make time for us?" The final incident of sexual abuse occurred when Amy was 22 years old, and it was then that Amy ended contact with the offender. It was during this stage of her life that Amy felt a "compulsion of wanting to be normal" that resulted in her being "sexual with men right away, I would just jump into sex." Looking back on the sexual abuse, Amy has insights that she could not have developed when she was a teenager. She shared that "the offender sexualized things that should not have been sexualized. She took away from me the natural opportunity to learn and explore sexual interests with boys; she disrupted that for me. I was too young to be sexual and certainly with an adult." Amy continues to struggle with her sexuality in terms of avoiding sex, sharing that "sex was a means to an end; it was not something I found pleasure in or viewed as romantic. I am not comfortable sexually, and I really have no desire to be sexual." It was Amy's avoidance of all things sexual that her husband noticed and what brought Amy to a point of telling him about the sexual abuse. Amy describes her husband "as always loving, affectionate, supportive; we have always had a good relationship. I can talk to him, but telling him about the sexual abuse by this woman was the most difficult thing I have ever done." After her husband found out is when Amy faced the decision to confront the female perpetrator because for her husband it became about protecting other children since this woman had continued to teach at the school. Amy's husband confronted the woman by going to her classroom and then later meeting her at a public park. Amy shared that when her husband met with the female offender, "He got to experience how forceful this woman can be. When he came back from meeting with her, he said to me, 'I am a grown man, and I was intimidated by her.'" From Amy's perspective, what was most important to the female offender was that no one find out about her sexual offending. Amy has found some closure in terms of the offender resigning from her teaching position, but she is unsure whether the offender's husband knows about his wife's offending. Even though the statute of limitations would have allowed Amy to pursue legal charges, she chose not to because of the embarrassment of a trial for her family. One of the distinctions that Amy has observed when listening to women who have been sexually abused by men and comparing her experience of being sexually abused by a woman is that "males are more direct in their sexual offending, whereas females are more manipulative and cunning and tend to coerce in a subtle way at first and then become more emotionally abusive in maintaining control over a child or teen." At the present time, Amy has returned to therapy in an effort to heal from the long-term devastation of child sexual abuse by a teacher at her school.

CHAPTER SUMMARY

Schools are second only to home when it comes to the development of positive social values among our youth. It is in these two critical environments that young people are exposed to the social values and personal morals that will guide them throughout their lifetime and across their stages of development. Adolescence entails entering a time of heightened sexual development, awareness, and interest. It is because of this aspect of adolescence that teens are particularly vulnerable to sexual exploitation and the negative influences of adults and peers alike. It is no secret that girls and boys want to learn about sex and experiment, experience, and engage in the spectrum of sexuality as it emerges as a part of their development and in their relationships with each other. The context of sexual development for today's youth is the reality of a society where they are confronted with a number of conflicting messages. On the one hand, they are surrounded by and immersed in a highly sexualized culture that is full of sexual images, themes, and provocative choices.[48] Music, clothing, advertisements, billboard, Internet ads, and contemporary role models in film and other media seem to condone and promote the sexual exploitation of the very youth who afford them the lifestyles they enjoy.[49]

As stated by Rapsey and Murachver (2006), "Especially in North America, adolescents are often told that they are not ready to, or should not, engage in many sexual behaviors. They are like drivers with traffic lights where both the green and the red lights are on. And, of course, their bodies are becoming more and more ready for green" (p. 64). Adolescents require and deserve the guidance, understanding, and open-mindedness of adults willing to listen to their challenges so that they make thoughtful choices regarding their promising sexuality while protecting their sexual health so that they can emerge from adolescence with a core set of personal ethics and sexual values that will guide them into healthy, loving, consensual, and mutually desirable relationships. It is because of the collective need that children and teens have for real talk about a variety of topics including human sexuality that it is important for parents and educators to come together and find a way to provide students with accurate information about their emerging sexuality in a context of mutual respect and caring. Our students need and deserve informed education on human sexuality so that they are more likely, rather than less likely to make healthy choices and not be exploited by predatory adults.

When females sexually intrude on adolescents and children, they disrupt the normal process of sexual development that is a youth's right to experience absent of adult abuse and exploitation and emotional neediness. One of the first teachers I encountered as a clinician was a 26-year-old who was developing an attraction to a 15-year-old student stemming from the anger she was feeling toward her husband for giving her herpes. She openly talked about retaliating against her husband with "another man" while never openly admitting that she was targeting the student as the "other man." This teacher had not considered the possibility that she was exploiting the student's trust in her as his teacher and therefore had not thought about the harm her actions would cause him or the dire consequences to herself and her family (her mother was also a school teacher in the same community). What she knew at the same that she came for help was that she wanted to seek revenge against her husband, and she saw the student who liked and admired her, as a means to accomplish her goal of punishing her husband. Incidentally, she had experienced a similar situation with a previous student during another crisis with her husband. The teacher eventually resigned her position and sought employment where she did not have contact with young people. She continued in therapy and eventually was seen with her husband as well.

Schools have a responsibility for ensuring that students receive their education in a community of adults who are safe and protective and where they are not exploited or taken advantage of by female sexual offenders. All students have the right to attend school, to enjoy and participate in athletic events, and to socialize in an educational environment where their right to be safe is a promise that is kept by the adults around them.

5

Future Directions

> No matter how sexually aggressive the acts the women perpetrate are, attempts are made, unfortunately often by a professional, to reinterpret them as being "a misguided extension of love."
>
> —Jackie Saradjian, *Women Who Sexually Abuse Children*[1]

FEMALE SEXUAL DEVIANCE

Information regarding the identification and understanding of sexual motivations, sexual arousal, and sexual fantasies of women who commit sexual crimes is not readily addressed or examined in the literature on female sexual offenders, where the majority of the research has focused on social factors, mental health variables, prior victimization, and developing typologies without a concerted effort to also examine the sexual factors involved with female sexual crimes (Johansson-Love & Fremouw, 2006). Gannon and Rose (2008) reviewed the literature regarding male child sexual offenders in the context of research that evaluates the sexual interests, deviant sexual arousal, and deviant sexual fantasies experienced by males committing child sexual offenses. They note the absence of considering these same sexual factors within the literature on female child sexual offenders:

The MCSO (male child sexual offenders) literature is replete with references to sexual interests, deviant sexual arousal, and deviant sexual fantasies (Hanson, 2006; Serin,

Mailloux, & Malcolm, 2001) which, according to severity, are key criteria used by consulting professionals to diagnose pedophilia. A core feature for a diagnosis of pedophilia, according to *DSM IV-TR* (American Psychological Association, 2000), is recurrent and intense sexual urges and fantasies involving pre-pubescent child-related sexual activity of at least six months duration that have been acted upon or cause significant distress to the person experiencing them. Marshall (1997) has reported that

KEY POINTS

Female sexual deviance has been absent in the research on female sexual offending.

Overlooking or ignoring deviant sexual arousal patterns experienced by women sexual offenders contributes to the continuation of child sexual abuse by female offenders.

Development of typologies for female sexual offenders is still in the early stages, limiting the usefulness of these typologies at this point in time; however, continuing research into female sexual offenders is essential and a greater interest in this group of sexual offenders appears to be occurring within the literature on sexual offending.

Treatment components for female sexual offenders are more similar than different to those that are included with male sex offenders; however, the development of sex-offender specific treatment for women lags behind that which exists for men.

Evaluation studies that help to determine what type of sex-offender specific treatment is effective in the prevention of future sexual crimes is needed for both male and female sexual offenders.

Prevention of child sexual abuse by women will occur as society becomes aware that women do in fact commit sexual crimes and becomes willing to acknowledge that female sexual abuse is harmful to children and teens.

Law enforcement, child protective services, health care professionals, researchers, and the mental health system also need to be willing to replace myths about women sex offenders with education about the reality of women sex offenders, because of their active role in the identification, investigation, and treatment of sexual offenders and the crimes they commit, and most importantly because of their role in the protection of children and teens.

60% of extrafamilial MCSO's admit experiencing recurrent sexual urges and fantasies outlined under the DSM criteria. Further, research investigating male sexual offending has shown that inappropriate sexual interests are related significantly to future recidivism (Hanson & Morton-Bourgon, 2004). By comparison, the empirical evidence investigating the existence of pedophilic-related criteria within FCSO [female child sexual offenders] populations is negligible (Grayston & DeLuca, 1999; Nathan & Ward, 2001). (p. 451)

It is as if the idea that a woman who commits sexual crimes and who experiences sexual arousal as an aspect of her motivation to commit or continue her sexual crimes has either not been considered in the research or has been summarily ignored as a possibility (Kaplan and Green, 1995). Another possible explanation for this absence of evaluating female sexual arousal within the context of the sexual crimes committed by women is due to a discomfort by researchers to examine female sexuality in general, and deviant sexual arousal specifically, since neither of these potential aspects of female sexual offending fits the stereotypical sexual scripts of females found within a particular cultural view of female sexuality or behavior (Denov, 2003b).

However, in order to adequately identify, understand, and address female sexual crimes, it is necessary to examine female sexual arousal, as it is experienced and acted on by women who commit sexual offenses. This is especially true for women who commit sexual crimes against children and teens so that these particular types of sexual crimes against this particularly vulnerable group of victims is acknowledged, assessed, and addressed in the criminal justice system and in treatment programs with female sex offenders where the focus is on preventing future sexual offenses. The reality is that if the role of sexuality is kept out of research that supports the identification and reporting of female sexual offending and the development of effective treatment programs with female sexual offenders, then the possibility of preventing sexual crimes, especially those committed against children, is diminished (Gannon & Rose, 2008).

The consequences of ignoring or overlooking sexual deviance in women who commit sexual crimes is that this topic of a woman's sexual offending is not brought up in treatment programs with women to be addressed in a straightforward manner, which in turn can inadvertently allow sexually deviant thoughts and behavior to continue. As observed by Saradjian (1996) in her discussion of female sexual offenders against children and the potential for sexual deviance, "particularly those who have experienced sexual assault, whether as a child or as an adult, have deviant sexual thoughts that they find intrusive but which lead to sexual arousal," and it is important "to enable women perpetrators to talk about these thoughts without fear of censure. Thus they can be helped to learn to stop the thoughts and/or manipulate them to become aversive rather than arousing" (p. 233). Not only is it important to allow sexual deviance experienced by women who commit sexual crimes to be discussed by the women themselves, it is important that the professionals working with the women are informed and capable of hearing such disclosures and responding to them appropriately. Deviant sexual behavior as it is directed toward children and teens can occur along a continuum that includes sexual thoughts and interests that can sustain an arousal pattern toward children and teens and include sexual fantasies or images of children and teens that include masturbation to these deviant sexual fantasies and eventually acting on these deviant sexual fantasies. Deviant sexual thoughts and fantasies reinforced through masturbation can result in deviant sexual behavior when an at-risk woman is in close proximity to children and teens. This example of deviant sexual interests, arousal fantasies, masturbatory behavior, and offending behavior are recognized as core components that are targeted in the treatment of male sexual offenders with the goal of disrupting these deviant sexual patterns in order to decrease the likelihood of their continuance and help to appropriately manage male sexual offenders within the community (i.e., treatment) to prevent future sexual offending.[2] However, information on these core sexual components of sexual offending is conspicuously absent in the majority of research on female sexual offending without an explanation as to the reason for the absence or the importance of being included.[3] In their literature review, Gannon and Rose (2008) identify that while some case studies document female sexual deviance, empirical studies, such as those attempting to develop typologies of female sexual offenders, tend to lack examination of female sexual deviance, which does seem rather odd given that these are sexual crimes being committed.

As noted by Fedoroff, Fishel, and Fedoroff (1999), the literature on paraphilias (i.e., atypical sexual behaviors that can include a definition of sexual deviance), including pedophilia, has been almost exclusively focused on men, suggesting a bias against the study of paraphilias in women. This bias is even evident in the American Psychiatric Association's (1994) *Diagnostic and Statistical Manual of Mental Disorders* (4th ed., *DSM-IV*) as cited by Fedoroff et al. that "except for sexual masochism, where the sex ratio is estimated to be 20 males for each female, the other paraphilias are almost never diagnosed in females, although some cases have been reported" (p. 127). Fedoroff et al. suggest that the *DSM-IV* "reinforces the widespread acceptance in sexology that paraphilias in women are rare to nonexistent" (p. 128). Thus, it appears that even the psychiatric community is susceptible to following the stereotypes of female sexual behavior that negates female sexual deviance as it exists in the real world (Denov, 2003b; Nelson, 1994). Fedoroff et al. (1999) presented 14 case studies of females referred to an outpatient clinic who met the *DSM-IV* criteria for paraphilic disorder. They compared the female group to a group of males who had also met the *DSM-IV* criteria for paraphilic disorders. What Fedoroff et al. found was that the most common diagnoses for the female group was "pedophilia (36%), sexual sadism (29%) and exhibitionism (29%)" (p. 129). A review of the sexual behaviors reported for the females included sexual fondling of boys, sexual assault of boys and girls, fantasies of sex with children, rape of a boy and rape of a girl, public masturbation, sadistic sex acts, and in one case sadistic murder and sex with animals (p. 129). The women who sexually abused children were found to both deny and admit to the sexual offending while also minimizing their behavior as a sexual offense, which is similar to the findings by Allen (1991). Additionally, sexual arousal in response to the pedophilic behavior was found among the women, including sexual fantasies about children. The relationship of the women to their child victims was identified as a caretaker (i.e., babysitter) or as a family member (i.e., aunt or mother). In addressing the question as to the reason that female sexual deviance (i.e., paraphilias) has received such little attention in the literature, Fedoroff et al. suggest that,

> most paraphilia research is conducted on people who have been convicted of sex crimes. . . . Men far outnumber women in criminal populations either because women commit fewer crimes, are caught less frequently, and/or are dealt with differently by the judicial system. If sex crimes are associated with paraphilic sexual disorders and if more men than women are convicted of sex crimes, it would follow that more men than women would appear in the paraphilia literature. (p. 136)

To further the discussion on the potential bias against recognizing female sexual deviance or the potential to overlook female sexual deviance, Fedoroff et al. state that "since the majority of academics, physicians, judges and indeed women themselves do not consider the possibility that females can harbour paraphilic interests, they are highly unlikely to recognize women with paraphilias" (p. 136). Therefore, the lack of research into female sexual deviance may reflect a bias against acknowledging that females, similar to their male counterparts, can exhibit deviant sexual interests, arousal and fantasies before, during, and after the sexual offense that they commit and that sex crimes against children are most likely not the only category of paraphilic disorders that women experience. Fedoroff et al. observe that "what researchers find is strongly influenced by what they are looking for and how they go about the search" and that "the history of sex research has often shown that men and women have more similarities than was previously supposed" (p. 137), and this would include similarities in the experience of deviant sexual behavior. Researchers, as individual members of society, risk overlooking the possibility of female sexual deviance because of the influence of societal stereotypes regarding female sexual behavior. Therefore, researchers need to be aware of how they may inadvertently contribute to the continuation of child sexual abuse by females when they do not explore or evaluate sexual deviance as an essential component of female sexual offending.[4] The same potential holds true for researchers that examine sexual crimes on college campuses and who fail to examine women offenders because they fall into the trap of traditional sexual scripts where males are prescribed the role of offenders and females are prescribed the role of victims. As noted by Denov (2003a), "sexual scripts also exclude the images of women as sexual aggressors, as initiating sex with men, as indicating their sexual interests, and as, at times, coercing their reluctant partners to engage in unwanted sexual activities" (p. 306). Coercion is included in the definition of a sexual crime against an adult (male or female), and deviant sexual arousal serves as a motivator to commit the crime (Shea, 1998).

Turton (2007) explores the narratives of female sex offenders in an effort to legitimize that sexual deviance by females who commit sexual crimes against children and teens is important in understanding women sexual offenders as they exist versus how society may want to portray female sexual offenders in terms of fitting their sexually deviant behavior into socially acceptable stereotypes that define female sexuality and sexual deviance. For example, when the focus is primarily on whether female sex offenders have a history of sexual victimization and when females who commit sexual crimes are allowed to focus on their victimization rather than on their offending, Turton states that "we are more likely to empathize with offenders who use this approach, finding the excuse for sexual offending more acceptable and thereby colluding with the rationale used" (p. 97) while ignoring or downplaying the sexual offenses and the sexually deviant behavior. Another aspect of the "female sexual offender as victim" is that by focusing on the past victimization of a female offender, when and if it does exist, the female offender essentially takes on the role of the victim whereby the child victim can be readily dismissed or the harm suffered minimized because the past victimization of the adult female takes precedence (Turton, 2007).

As discussed previously, female sex offenders as members of society are often aware of the societal stereotypes that allow them to excuse, justify, and dismiss their sexual crimes, even when their sexual offending is clearly illegal, unethical, and harmful.[5] Social and cultural stereotypes of female sexuality[6] tend to support the denial of female sexual deviance by suggesting that sexual crimes against children by females are not sexually motivated or that the sexual behavior is not abusive.[7] These stereotypes are in direct contradiction to what survivors of female sexual abuse report.[8] As pointed out by Turton (2007), many survivors remember that they recognized the sexual intent of the offenses at the time they were being committed against them by the women who were committing the sexual crime. As one woman recalled, "My mother and her brothers and father all became sexual around the words 'bottoms' or 'spanking.' My mother indulged in a lot of spanking that didn't really hurt. She rubbed and fondled our buttocks a lot and with a lot of sexual pleasure. There was a special smile she had for this and I saw it again when my sister had children. She did exactly the same to them but everyone thought it was innocent" (Turton, 2007, p. 108). Victim accounts of female sexual deviance indicate that it is essential to evaluate deviant sexual arousal in the assessment, treatment, and management of women sexual offenders and to include objective measures of deviant sexual arousal and reports from their victims rather than relying only on the reports of female offenders who may be inclined to deny sexual arousal in order to align themselves with social norms and stereotypes and to convince themselves that the harm they cause to their victim is minimal. When female sexual deviance is not recognized and understood as part of the sexual offending patterns of women, it can also leave their victims with a greater sense of confusion and loss of where to turn for support and help. As noted by one female victim,

> [After being sexually assaulted by a female,] I felt I had no place to go. I felt like I couldn't go to a sexual assault centre and say "I've been raped by a woman." I didn't think I would receive respect or attention or if I would be told that that just wasn't so. It's harder to have your story believed if the perpetrator is a woman. It made me feel very alone. (Denov, 2003a, p. 311)

Sexual offending against children is linked to viewing children and teens as sex objects, and this is especially true when the sexualization of children and teens is reinforced by having power and control over the child that in turn becomes a part of the offender's sexual gratification.[9] Turton (2007) presents the case of a grandmother who sexually offended against her 11-year-old granddaughter and was suspected of sexually abusing her two daughters and other grandchildren. The grandmother, rather than admitting to her sexual deviance, tried to place blame on the granddaughter as indicated by such comments as the victim "begged for sex, she wanted it, asked for it, she could have left at anytime" (p. 105). Rationales that female sexual offenders use to deny or dismiss their sexual deviance are similar to the rationales of male sexual offenders in their attempts to deny their sexual deviance and avoid responsibility for the sexual offenses they commit.[10] Duncan (2004) identifies four types of denial that sex offenders are known to use: (a) *denial of facts*, where the offender attempts to deny that the sexual offending was actually sexual abuse or denies that a crime was committed; (b) *denial of awareness*, where the offender reports that he or she was not aware or conscious of committing sexual abuse; (c) *denial of impact*, where the offender lacks empathy with a victim and denies the harm he or she caused to the victim; and (d) *denial of accountability*, where the offender attempts to place responsibility for the abuse onto the victim. The fourth pattern of denial—denial of accountability—is often quoted in news articles where women who commit sexual offenses against teens are referred to as having "consensual sexual relations" rather than as committing a sexual crime against an underage teen.[11] These patterns of denial become a way of excusing sexual deviance directed toward children and teens and consequently can make it easier for male and female sex offenders to continue their sexual offending.[12]

The sexual deviance of women who commit sexual offenses against children is of course implied in the sexual crimes they commit; however, it is interesting that a direct discussion of a woman's sexual motivation for committing her sexual crime is decidedly absent from a majority of the research.[13] This is especially notable in light of the gratification that orgasm has for human beings, including people who have committed sexual offenses.[14] An example of motivations other than deviant sexual arousal is provided by Vandiver (2006a) who explains that "while sexual gratification has been explored as a possible cause of women sexual offending, it does not appear to be a sole motivating factor" (p. 70). Instead of a sexual motivation, it is proposed that for females a need exists to connect with another person and that child sexual abuse is one avenue for meeting this emotional need"[15] Explanations that focus on emotional needs being inappropriately met through a child tend to negate sexual arousal or orgasmic responses for female sex offenders and romanticize the sexual crime. If sexual motivations and responses do exist, they may be viewed as rare or secondary to the "need to connect," and therefore have little motivational significance to female sexual offending and by extension in the risk assessment, management, and treatment of female sexual offenders. Another aspect critical to the discussion of female sexual deviance is the idea that (a) female sexual offenders cannot have multiple motivations for committing their sexual offenses, including deviant sexual arousal, and (b) these multiple motivations can occur in the context of a distorted view of children and teens as viable sexual partners or (c) deviant sexual arousal could not also be coupled with using children for economic gain in terms of coercing children into prostitution or using children in pornography.[16] Perhaps "emotional motivation" is further support of the observation by Fedoroff et al. (1999) that researchers find what they are looking for, and if they are not looking for female sexual deviance in the among the motivations for female sexual offending, then female sexual crimes will simply be explained as "the need to connect with another human being." Finally, what is most problematic about the absence of a discussion or evaluation about female sexual deviance is that researchers and others who engage in this absence can become complicit in dismissing the risk potential that deviant sexual interests have as motivational factors for female sexual offending, especially sexual offenses against children and teens.

What does appear to be an aspect of female sexual deviance is the sexualization of children and teens, which allows the female abuser to fantasize and imagine a sexual dynamic between her and the victim, and this in turn may be reinforced through masturbation and sexual fantasies.[17] As discussed by Turton (2007), the pleasure of orgasm is one reinforcing factor that allows deviant sexual behavior to be repeated, and there seems little doubt that at least some women sexual abusers have a similar drive for sexual gratification as male perpetrators and that they may have a diverse sex object choice or even a preference for children. Turton suggests that "we have to assume that a combination of opportunity, excitement, pleasure, power and orgasm breaks down the expected barriers of internal controls and ignites the desire to sexually abuse" (p. 116), while society and cultural stereotypes can maintain a propensity toward ignoring female sexual deviance and its role in the sexual crimes that females are capable of committing.[18]

Hislop (2001) indicates that while little is known about the sexual functioning of the female child molester, she seems to lack sexual boundaries, indicates sexual identity confusion, and exhibits paraphilias. Hislop cites a study by Davin (1999) that indicated that among the 30 independent female offenders and the 46 co-offending female offenders in the study, more than 25 percent of the independent female offenders and at least 5 percent of the co-offenders experienced orgasm while offending. Hislop indicates that in her previous study of female sex offenders, the women indicated a variety of sexual experiences that included a large number of male partners and sexual contact with women and that the women's stated preference for heterosexual or homosexual relationships often did not match their reported histories of actual sexual behavior. Hislop referred to this group of women as "omnisexual," defined as "little ability to establish and/or enforce sexual preferences or boundaries" (p. 137).

In their review of the literature on female sexual offenders, both Gannon and Rose (2008) and Johansson-Love and Fremouw (2006) substantiate that female sex offenders do not seem to show a preference in terms of the victim's gender; therefore, it is likely that girls as well as boys can be at equal risk of sexual victimization by a female. A lack of established sexual preference may in part be explained by the higher erotic plasticity (i.e., sexual fluidity) noted in females and cited by Baumeister and Stillman (2006). The case for a type of higher erotic plasticity in female sexual offenders can be drawn to begin to develop a preliminary theoretical framework that would help to understand the lack of a victim-gender preference that is being reported in current studies on female sexual offenders. The work and studies cited by Baumeister and Stillman, indicate that studies find that lesbians are more likely than gay males to have had heterosexual sex and that lesbians are more likely to have heterosexual relationships even after having been exclusively gay for years indicate a higher erotic plasticity for some females. To demonstrate this variability in same-sex and other-sex attraction as it might apply to females, Baumeister and Stillman cite evidence that suggests that "there is more consensual same-gender activity in women's than in men's prisons, and women seem to make the transition much more smoothly and easily from an exclusively heterosexual orientation prior to their imprisonment, to homosexual while in prison, and then back to heterosexual upon release from prison than do men" (p. 347). In studies on sexual arousal in the laboratory, the authors note that "lesbian and heterosexual women were aroused as a result of seeing both male-male and female-female sexual acts" and that in another study "women indicated that they were aroused by a greater variety of stimuli than were men" (p. 353). Therefore, if females have higher erotic plasticity, it may be that females who commit sexual offenses against children and teens are a sub-type of females with high erotic plasticity, and that there may be a group of women who sexually offend against children and teens who are less likely to show a gender preference in their victimization of children. Therefore there may be a group of females that are at risk of offending against a male or female child when their erotic plasticity includes sexual arousal toward children and teens. Put another way, higher erotic plasticity for a sub-group of females and sexual interests in children and/or teens may translate into less rigidity when it comes to gender preference for females who commit child sexual abuse. Therefore, females who meet these criteria and have other risk factors as well are more likely to offend against either males or females because their erotic plasticity differs from that of males, who exhibit low erotic plasticity in their sexual offending patterns against children (i.e., males who show a victim-gender preference).

OVERVIEW OF EMERGING TYPOLOGIES

Typologies of sexual offenders are important in terms of developing prevention strategies that educate the public about sexual offenders and in the development of rehabilitation/treatment programs to prevent sexual reoffending.[19] Research to develop typologies of females who commit sexual offenses is not at the same stage of mature empirical development that is currently available for males who commit sexual offenses.[20] While there are several studies that have proposed typologies, they have either used relatively small sample sizes or have not been validated in terms of their reliability for replication across studies.[21] Additionally, researchers have not consistently used comparison samples or control groups, which are essential in distinguishing characteristics of female sexual offenders from other groups of females (see Faller, 1987; Matthews, 1989; Nathan & Ward, 2002; Sandler & Freeman, 2009; Vandiver & Kercher, 2004). Similar to the early studies on male sexual offenders, typologies for female sex offenders are simplistic, narrow, and limited to convenience samples, such as those provided by state sex offender registries or women imprisoned for sexual offenses or women in the community participating in sex offender treatment programs.[22] Additionally, studies have not provided information on female sexual offenders in the child protection population and who may not be on the sex offender registry, nor have studies provided information regarding the offender's relationship to the victim, which is important in distinguishing incest offenders from non–incest offenders.[23] Studies on female typologies have also not provided information on the sexual offense patterns of females that would include motivations for sexual offending as well as a woman's criminal history other than sexual offenses (Gannon & Rose, 2008; Johansson-Love & Fremouw, 2006).

Vandiver and Kercher (2004) are viewed as having conducted the first empirical study of female sex offenders whereby statistical analysis was conducted on data that were available on 471 convicted female sex offenders from the sex offender registry in Texas, meaning that females not included in the registry were not available for analysis and female sex offenders on other state registries were not included. Vandiver and Kercher identified the following six typologies of female sex offenders from the Texas registry. The first is the heterosexual nurturer whose average age was 30 years old and primarily victimized 12-year-old males. The second is the noncriminal homosexual offender whose average age was 32 years old and victimized 13-year-old females. The third is the female sexual predator whose average age was 29 years old and victimized 11-year-old males. The fourth is the young adult child exploiter whose average age was 28 years old and who victimized primarily children around the age of seven but did not show a particular gender preference in her targeted victim. Vandiver and Kercher hypothesized that this group of offenders were likely to be mothers who molested their own children. The fifth is the homosexual criminal subtype whose average age was stated as being in the thirties and whose victim was likely to be in his or her thirties. This offender showed a preference for adult female victims, and offenses included forcing adult victims into prostitution. The sixth is the aggressive homosexual offender described as an older female who tended to sexually assault another adult female of a comparable age (31 years of age) in the context of a domestic relationship. In reviewing the typologies suggested by Vandiver and Kercher there appears to be *three possible typologies* in this group of female sex offenders in Texas: (a) females who sexually offend against children 13 years of age and younger and who may or may not show a gender preference in victim, (b) females who sexually offend against adult females that may include forcing women into prostitution, and (c) females who sexually offend against a same-sex partner in a domestic relationship. The typologies by Vandiver and Kercher did not consistently distinguish the relationship that the female offender had with her child victim that would help identify incestuous offenders from nonincestuous offenders, and none of the typologies consistently indicated motivations for the sexual offending or whether violence was involved in the sexual offense. Additionally, the sexual offenses against children were not distinguished by type of sexual offense in terms of direct physical sexual abuse of a child or whether the female sexual offender committed other types of sexual offenses, such as sexual exploitation (e.g., prostitution and pornography). This distinction is important in terms of determining the type of risk that women pose to children and teens and whether economic gain (e.g., forcing a child into prostitution or using a child for pornography) is a risk factor for future sexual offending. Economic gain may not always be a motivation for sexual offending and child exploitation. For example, a mother that I worked with in 1987 lost custody of her children because she repeatedly sent nude photos of her children to a convicted male sex offender who was in prison. There was no indication by law enforcement or Child Protective Services that this mother committed these sexual offenses for economic gain; rather, she did so to engage in deviant sexual behavior with the convicted male sex offender. She would also allow the convicted sex offender to speak with her children when he called the home even though she knew this was in violation of the protective order for her children. He was found masturbating in his cell at the prison where he was incarcerated holding the photographs of the children. This convicted male sex offender admitted to deviant sexual fantasies during his telephone calls with the children. This mother could be considered an accomplice who engaged in behavior that promoted sexually deviant behaviors that encompassed child sexual exploitation.[24]

The use of "homosexual" in the description of typologies by Vandiver and Kercher (2004) is considered problematic in terms of placing a focus on nondeviant sexual orientation (i.e., homosexuality) rather than on the deviant sexual behavior and sexual offenses committed. Language in sex offender typology (male or female) that includes nondeviant sexual orientation (i.e., homosexual) could be construed as discriminatory toward lesbians (or male homosexuals if used in the language of male sex offender typology), and it has the potential to mislead the public into thinking that nondeviant sexual orientation is dominant in sexual offending patterns for males and females rather than indicating that a pedophilic individual has a sexual preference toward male children or female children or toward both gender of children. Research of male sex offenders has not indicated that sexual offending is linked to nondeviant sexual orientation or arousal, and emerging research on females does not indicate this either.[25] The focus of this discussion is, as is the earlier discussion on language, an attempt to ensure that language in female sex offender typologies is not sexist or potentially discriminatory toward a nondeviant sexual orientation or does not mislead the public regarding homosexuality.

A study by Sandler and Freeman (2007) attempted to test the analyses and findings of Vandiver and Kercher's (2004) typologies and found that the 390 female sex offenders registered in New York State were similar to Vandiver and Kercher's sample on demographic variables, such as offender age and race and victim age. However, Sandler and Freeman also found that the cluster of characteristics that determined their six types of female sex offenders differed substantially from those found by Vandiver and Kercher. Sandler and Freeman identified two distinct categories of female hebephile:[26] (a) the *criminally limited hebephile*, who targeted primarily males but also had offended against females, and (b) the *criminally prone hebephile*, and while both groups shared similar characteristics, the criminally limited hebephile targeted an older child victim whose average age was 13.7 years, while the criminally prone hebephile targeted a younger child victim whose average age was 7.3 years. The term "hebephile" places emphasis on the sexual deviance of the female sex offender toward children and young teens, and this is distinctly different from the homosexual terminology used by Vandiver and Kercher (2004). Sandler and Freeman suggest that future studies include offender age and victim age as distinguishing characteristics of female sex offenders. They also suggest that databases limited to convicted female sex offenders "may not be generalizable to sex offenders whose crimes and/or criminal histories allowed them to plead to lesser, non-sexual offenses, or female sex offenders who never become known to authorities. Furthermore, the results may not generalize to states with substantially different criminal codes or registry requirements" (p. 87).

An article out of Australia by Deering and Mellor (2007) offers a review of the various categories of typologies that have been proposed and presents a multidimensional approach in the development of female sex offender typologies. A multidimensional approach may be more useful for clinicians that provide risk assessment evaluations and treatment services to female sex offenders as well as to probation and parole officers who oversee the community management of convicted female sex offenders. Lawson (1993), in her critique of the research on female sex offenders, suggests that for research to be useful, it is essential that it reflect clinical application that can be used in the field and that it is essential that researchers and clinicians work together to develop valid typologies. Lawson suggests that clinicians and researchers must be informed by one another and appreciate the contribution that each perspective offers to understanding female sexual offending and that both have a role in providing a meaningful contribution to the identification and treatment of females committing sexual abuse. A study by Gannon, Rose, and Ward (2008) is the first to propose a comprehensive model of the offense process of female sexual offending across three dimensions: (a) comprehensive social history and personal background of female sexual offenders, (b) the preoffense period (i.e., events occurring one year prior to the offense period, and (c) the offense and postoffense period (i.e., factors occurring at the time of the offense or immediately following the offense).

In cross-referencing the categories of female sex offenders who offend against children and teens and have been described in the research, there appears to be four broad categories of typologies for female sexual offenders, with possible subcategories contained in these four broader categories.[27] A summary of the four broad categories with examples of subcategories tend to lend themselves to the following:

1. *Adult child exploiter* is an adult female who is a non–family member who exploits her dominant relationship, trust, and authority status with a child or adolescent and targets primarily youth in her care or where there is an established relationship. Depending on pedophilic or hebephilic orientation or other type of sexual deviance, she may exploit and offend against either a male or a female child age 16 years and younger. Dominant in this category is the cognitive distortion that may be distinct to this category of female offender in terms rationalizing her sexual offending as based on a mutual attraction rather than based on the manipulation and exploitation of a minor for her own sexual and emotional gratification. This offender is considered at high risk because of a potential for deviant sexual arousal, exploitive beliefs, and grooming of the victim. She may have a more extensive history of sexual offenses than indicated at the time of her arrest.
2. *Developmentally delayed female offender*[28] is an adult female diagnosed by a standardized test as having a cognitive/intellectual impairment or diminished intellectual capacity. This category would include both family and non–family members. This female offender is considered at high risk of reoffending because of impaired cognitive ability poor judgment. This category recognizes the impact of chronic developmental problems, organic syndromes, and developmental dependencies primary to the sexual offending along with the risk of sexual victimization and other types of traumas. This category may contain *coerced offender by either a male or female co-offender* and *accomplice/cooperative offender* when the offender is a mother, and the maternal offender is either an active accomplice, passive accomplice, or interchanges between these roles (see the following discussion).
3. *Maternal sexual offender* is an adult female who commits sexual offenses against her own child or a child otherwise in her care as a maternal caretaker. She may be predisposed to sexual offending because of a childhood history of repeated and severe sexual abuse that occurred along with other types of child maltreatment

and childhood traumas. This category of maternal offender may also be at high risk for committing other types of child maltreatment other than sexual abuse that can also include physical violence. This category may also have a history of sexual offending and physical violence in adolescence or other criminal history as a juvenile. This category would include a *subcategory of coerced offender* when two conditions are met: (a) documentation by law enforcement or other verifiable source (other than woman offender) for domestic violence between the adults and (b) documentation of child sexual abuse by an adult partner independent of the mother; the adult partner may be male or female. This category also includes the *sub-category of the accomplice/cooperative offender*, who offends independently and with an adult partner, male or female, and/or who offends in a group of adult offenders, male or female. The maternal offender may be likely to offend against both male and female children without a particular gender preference and evaluation should assess for this potential offending pattern with victims and potential victims within the family.

4. *Violent female sex offender* would be an adult female who uses primarily physical aggression and violence in the commission of her sexual crimes, and her criminal history may include multiple sexual crimes and sexually deviant acts committed against children, teens, and adults. She may also have a documented history of other types of child maltreatment, domestic violence, and other crimes in her criminogenic history that may or may not be documented by law enforcement as convictions. This may be a more psychopathic offender because of multiple offending patterns and the use of a violence with the intent to cause harm, and this type of offender would be considered at high risk of reoffending and of violent offenses in particular.

The typologies described are not meant to be definitive; rather, they are offered as a framework to begin to understand the types of adult female child sexual offenders who are emerging in the literature as their sexual offenses become known to law enforcement, child protection services, criminal justice, and mental health practitioners.

TREATMENT COMPONENTS WITH FEMALE SEXUAL OFFENDERS

Susan Strickland (2008) provided a study of 60 female sex offenders incarcerated in the state of Georgia who were compared to 70 nonsexual female offenders in an effort to provide a framework for the treatment of female sexual offenders. The measures that Strickland used included (a) subscales of the Multiphasic Sex Inventory—II (female version) to determine a profile of personality disorder indicators, emotional neediness, social and sexual inadequacies, and cognitive distortions and immaturity; (b) the Substance Abuse Subtle Screening Inventory—3 to assess chemical dependency, defensiveness, and attributes of substance abuse; and (c) the Childhood Trauma Questionnaire—Brief Version to assess the type and severity of childhood trauma experienced. The instruments were administered in groups of 25 women, and the women were given three hours to complete all the inventories.

An equal number of women from both groups indicated that they had sex with both men and women even though the non–sex-offending group identified as primarily homosexual. None of the women from either group identified as having gender identity issues. Both groups of women offenders endorsed needing accurate sexual knowledge, indicating that they would benefit from education on human sexuality. Strickland (2008) indicated that "neither the sex offender group nor the non-sex offender group had adequate knowledge about sexual anatomy, physiology and sexual functioning" (p. 480). This finding was also indicated by Saradjian (1996); that is, although female sex offenders "have been involved in a great deal of sexual activity in their lives, they often have very limited knowledge about sex and sexuality. As a result of their life experience, the knowledge they do have is frequently distorted or completely inaccurate" (p. 233). While no significant differences were found between the two groups on the alcohol scale, the sex offender group did have a higher mean score, indicating that they did use alcohol more often but how alcohol related to their sexual offenses, if at all, was not described.

Regarding childhood trauma, while both groups of women reported childhood traumas, the sex-offending women "suffered significantly higher rates of total childhood trauma in terms of greater emotional abuse and physical neglect, and the sex-offending group scored higher on the subscale measuring childhood sexual abuse" (Strickland, 2008, p. 480). No distinctive personality disorders were indicated for either group of female offenders. This lack of distinction on personality characteristics may have reflected the inability of the personality measure used by Strickland to distinguish between the two groups or may indicate that female offenders as a group are more similar to each other in personality characteristics given that both groups have a history of childhood trauma that would affect personality development. As far as personality tendencies, the sex-offending group did show multiple personality characteristics that include schizoid, borderline, and dependent personality features, while the non–sex-offending group showed multiple personality characteristics that included antisocial and histrionic personality features, but again these differences were not found to distinguish between the two groups per se. Both groups of female offenders scored highest in the categories of "marked lack of accountability, and a blaming outlook," and scores indicated that both groups of female offenders indicated "emotional immaturity, feelings of being victimized and mistreated throughout life" (p. 482). Strickland suggests that both groups of women "engage in a victim-stance response style, including a pattern of blaming others for their circumstances," which indicates a tendency to not take responsibility for their offenses (p. 483).

The findings by Strickland (2008) are summarized as follows: (a) severity of childhood trauma and sexual abuse in particular are significant risk factors for the future development of sexually deviant behaviors for females in adulthood; (b) female sexual abusers experienced greater physical abuse as children than did the nonsexual offenders and were deprived of guidance and social skills needed to form supportive, healthy adult relationships; (c) female sexual offenders exhibited more inhibitions, insecurities, and inferiorities in the areas of social and sexual contacts; (d) severe, repeated sexual abuse in childhood may play a role in the development of sexually deviant interest in children; and (e) female sexual abusers who are mothers are more likely to exhibit role reversal in the parenting of their children, characterized by an overdependence on children to meet emotional needs. Strickland recommends that female sex offenders be provided sex offender–specific treatment that includes information on human sexuality, attention to sexual deviance, trauma resolution, social skills, and information and guidance on consenting and age-appropriate sexual relationships.

While it is likely that female sexual offenders who match the profile of the female sexual offenders in Strickland's (2008) study would benefit from sex offender–specific treatment that includes the previously mentioned components, it also true that female sex offenders will benefit the most when sex offender–specific treatment begins first with a comprehensive assessment of the sexual offending patterns that brought the female to treatment and to the attention of criminal justice.[29] The components of assessment would include identifying (a) events/triggers that lead to the offending, (b) beliefs that support the offending, (c) the way in which a female targeted and groomed the child or teen or how the absence of grooming enabled the sexual abuse, (d) the role that sexual fantasy played in the sexual offending, and (e) the emotional, sexual and cognitive response to the sexual offending. And, while group treatment for some components of female sexual offending would be appropriate, such as education on human sexuality, information and guidance on consenting and age-appropriate sexual relationships, cognitive distortions, and offending beliefs, other aspects of female sex offender treatment, such as deviant sexual arousal and addressing the specific sex offenses committed, may be better addressed individually to maintain confidentiality and personal boundaries and to contain deviant sexual arousal and fantasy that may be experienced by other female sex offenders in a group setting at least initially.[30] Also, as suggested by Saradjian (1996),[31] some treatment targets for female sexual offenders would be similar to those targeted with male sexual offenders, including denial and minimization, offense-supportive beliefs and attitudes, developing cognitive and emotional empathy skills, and prevention of reoffending. In addition, offense patterns in terms of whether women sex offenders committed their sexual crimes on their own or within a pattern of co-offending with others (male or female) would also need to be addressed but without the assumption that women who commit sexual crimes are coerced by males, and that female sexual offenders who sexually offend with others, although a reported minority at this point in time, may have different treatment needs than women who sexually offend alone.[32] Most important is that attention is paid to providing adequate risk assessment for female sexual offenders based on their individual assessment and that risk assessment occur in a conservative framework in order to avoid underestimating the risk that female sexual offenders pose to children and teens, especially given the societal context where sex-role stereotypes about sexual offending are known to exist.[33] Finally, as with all sex offender treatment, the goal is to prevent future sexual offending; therefore, evaluation of female sex offender treatment programs should include a component to assess the outcomes of a specific treatment for a particular individual or group of female sex offenders in order to identify what works and what does not work in the prevention of female sexual crimes and in particular crimes against the most vulnerable of potential victims, our children.

THE POSSIBILITY OF PREVENTING CHILD SEXUAL ABUSE

Child sexual abuse is a worldwide social, family, and public health problem.[34] Sexual abuse affects victims throughout their lifetimes with a wide range of adverse physical and behavioral health problems that can include disrupted academic performance, depression, substance abuse, eating disorders, post-traumatic stress disorder, sexually transmitted infection, and risky sexual behavior.[35] As a persistent trauma in the life of a young person, it can even shorten life expectancy by increasing the risk of chronic disease and stress-related illness.[36] Child sexual abuse has also been identified as a potential risk factor for future sexual offending. While this risk relationship is not fully understood, it does appear to exist for some individuals who experienced severe and repeated sexual abuse in their childhood along with other types of childhood maltreatment.[37] It is because of the multiple health costs and risk of future sexual offending that preventing child sexual abuse is essential. Not only do children and teens deserve to live in a world where adults do not take advantage of them, but they deserve to live in a world where they are cared for by the adults who surround them. Parents and other family members have the primary responsibility for acting to keep children safe and away from known sexual offenders. This means that women, as well as men, who are at risk for committing sexual offenses need to stop, think, and act to prevent their sexual offending. The cycle of family sexual abuse will not end as long as adults continue to perpetuate it or family members choose to ignore child sexual abuse because it is an unpleasant topic to discuss and bring into the open.[38]

Considerable advances have been made over the past several decades to educate the public and raise awareness about the potential risk to children by men intent on committing child and teen sexual abuse. While these efforts have certainly made a difference in the lives of children and teens, they have not kept pace with advancing the public's knowledge about the risk to children and teens from women intent on committing child and teen sexual abuse. Raising awareness about female sexual offending is one of the first steps in prevention. In order to accomplish this goal, the myths and stereotypes surrounding female sexual offending must be addressed, challenged, and remedied. To accomplish this goal, it is not necessary to reinvent the wheel. That is, current prevention education programs regarding sexual offending by males simply need to incorporate information about female sexual offending. However, these programs and the individuals responsible for them need to do so without gender bias or without promoting a specific political agenda other than the agenda to prevent child sexual abuse. This means that education and information about female sexual offending must be provided in an accurate and straightforward manner without minimizing or excusing the sexual crimes that women commit. Given that child sexual abuse most often occurs by a family member or someone the family knows, it is essential that communities work together to provide education about identifying and stopping child sexual abuse when it is occurring and that social norms that promote the sexualization of children and teens change toward social norms that promote a healthy respect and regard for our youth by both adult men and women as well as between adolescents and children. Wherever children and teens are at is where prevention education should be provided and adults need to be willing to provide this education.

Preventing child sexual abuse by females becomes possible when there is an increase in societal awareness that women do in fact commit sexual crimes and an acceptance that female sexual abuse is harmful to children and teens. This requires that female sexual abuse not be minimized, especially when it occurs against an adolescent, whether the adolescent is a male or a female. When society no longer denies female sexual abuse or the harm that females cause to their victims, it will become safe for children to tell about females who are abusing and exploiting them. Accountability for sexual crimes committed is just as important for females as it is for males; therefore, equitable treatment by the judicial system is essential to legitimizing that female sexual offending is not to be tolerated or condoned in societies and that just because females may commit fewer sexual crimes does not negate the importance of addressing the accountability for the sexual crimes that women commit.

Dispelling myths about female sexual offending and the gender bias and stereotypes that surround female sexual crimes is essential to improving the recognition of female sexual offenders. With recognition comes the opportunity to stop female sexual offenders and to prevent their sexual offending from continuing. However, recognition alone is not enough if there are few adults willing to act on behalf of children, report female sexual offenders, and make the safety and well-being of children and teens the priority. Screening for female sexual abuse by pediatricians, family physicians, and nurse practitioners will also support the detection of female sexual offending and provide the opportunity to extend needed support to both the victim and the female offender.

Asking someone about their behavior or talking to someone who presents identifiable risks for sexual offending is not the same as accusing someone of being a sexual offender. In fact, asking and talking may be the most viable methods of preventing the thoughts of sexual offending from becoming the acts of sexual offending—secrecy about sexual offending is complicit in the acts of sexual crimes. Asking and listening to someone who may be thinking about sexual offending can also provide the opportunity for that individual to seek the help they need not to commit a sexual crime against a child or teen. After all, it is the person intent on committing a sexual crime who has the ultimate responsibility for preventing child sexual abuse. As awareness is raised about female sexual offending, the opportunity arises for females who are currently committing sexual crimes or who are at risk of sexual offending to seek help and move away from these destructive patterns.

The American Association of University Women (AAUW) recommends that schools take an active role with parents in addressing and preventing sexual harassment. While the AAUW recognizes that one of the striking differences between its 1993 study[39] and the 2001 study[40] is that more schools have a policy prohibiting sexual harassment, what is discouraging is that even with these policies, sexual harassment continues. What this finding indicates is that a policy that is not implemented and practiced as a viable program will do little to prevent the sexualization and sexual harassment of students and consequently the sexual abuse of students in their educational environments. Indeed, policies that collect dust on a shelf are policies that may as well have not been written in the first place. At the same time, schools alone will not get the job done as far as promoting healthy and respectful interactions between students and adults in their school environments. Parents and students must also participate in ending sexual harassment and other types of sexual offenses in their schools. The following are five suggestions by Duncan (2009)[41] to help schools prevent sexual abuse, exploitation, and harassment of students:

1. Provide prevention education that includes bystander training for all school faculty and personnel where the focus is to train adults before training students and where this training occurs once a year, every year. On-going training and education helps everyone be safe at school and affirms the guidelines and rules for respectful, social interaction that encourages learning and academic outcomes.
2. Develop and distribute written policies and procedures to screen all employees, including volunteers, temporary, and part-time personnel, when hired and again at periodic times throughout a person's tenure with the school.
3. Develop and distribute written guidelines about respectable student-to-adult interaction, student-to-student interaction and adult-to-adult interaction and assure that safety policies that outline responses to reports of inappropriate, unethical, and criminal violations are contained in these guidelines. Include parents and students for input and review and provide annual reports as to the outcomes of these written guidelines so that prevention becomes a reality within the ever-changing environment of the school.
4. Monitor behavior of personnel through peer group councils that promote prevention and early intervention. The goal of the peer group councils should be to promptly report any inappropriate behavior, breaches in policy, or crossing of boundaries. All reports of sexual crimes should be made to legal authorities for investigation and not taken upon by the school to investigate. This requires knowledge of sexual crimes as defined by state laws and not as they are interpreted by schools and parents.
5. Make prevention a priority in school environments.

When adults are having a problem understanding or following appropriate boundaries and behavioral standards, it is their responsibility to ask for help and assistance before a crime is committed and a student or young person is harmed. These same guidelines can be followed by any organization working with or providing services to youth, including faith-based and religious organizations, athletic and sports leagues, and youth volunteer and mentoring organizations, such as Big Brothers Big Sisters, Boy Scouts, and Girl Scouts—in other words any organization involved with youth.

The Center for Sex Offender Management (CSOM) is a valuable resource for professionals working in the field of preventing sexual offending and working to provide oversight to convicted sex offenders living in communities. The overarching goal of CSOM is to enhance public safety and prevent further victimization by improving the management of sex offenders in the community. Through these activities, CSOM places a high priority on past and potential victim safety by promoting effective management strategies of convicted sex offenders when they reside in the community. CSOM also recognizes that sex offenders are not like other offenders and that specialized training is required for professionals charged with the oversight and monitoring of sex offenders in the community in order to effectively prevent re-offending. CSOM also focuses on keeping the public informed about sex offender management practices and policies and how to make best use of tools like sex offender registries without misusing them. CSOM encourages local law enforcement and prevention educators to teach others about how best to protect themselves and their children from sexual assault. CSOM recommends that communities and organizations work together, share their strengths, and direct their energies toward the common goal of ending sexual victimization.

Finally, education about human sexuality is essential in the prevention of child sexual abuse. Teaching the difference between consent and coercion and between exploration and exploitation and establishing sexual values that mirror respect for self and others are among the essentials of healthy human functioning. Comprehensive education about human sexuality should be required for everyone!

CHAPTER SUMMARY

While there is increasing attention being paid to female sexual offenders, there is still a distinct reluctance to pay attention to deviant sexual arousal patterns of females that commit sexual offenses. Female sexual deviance is an essential component to fully understanding the sexual offending patterns of women who commit sexual crimes, especially crimes against children and teens. Masturbation to sexual fantasies of children and teens along with the role pornography might have in female sexual offending has yet to be determined. For example, a study by Kernsmith and Kernsmith (2009) found that pornography use among females was a significant predictor for female sexual coercion and aggression. Obviously, further research into the role of pornography and female sexual deviance is needed, but the fact that the study was recently published is an indication of the increasing recognition and interest in determining the antecedents of female sexual aggression and sexual crimes committed by females.

While typologies of female sexual offenders are emerging in the research literature, it is clear that these typologies are limited to the samples of female sexual offenders from which the study draws. For example, typologies that are proposed from criminal justice samples of female sexual offenders may be distinctly different from those in the child protection system, and these distinctions need to be kept in mind when drawing tentative conclusions about emerging typologies.[42] Another consideration is that a majority of the research on female sexual offenders has tended to study white females, indicating that further research is needed about female sexual offending among other ethnic groups. The study by Duncan and Williams (1998) indicated that sexual offending against boys by African American females may be more prevalent than past studies have indicated since so few studies have been conducted about child sexual abuse in the African American community. The study by the U.S. Department of Justice indicated that African American and Hispanic women committed sexual crimes against youth in juvenile correctional facilities. More information is needed regarding child sexual by females among ethnic groups and by female sexual offenders that exist within these youth settings, such as correctional facilities, in particular.[43] Understanding the potential link between sexual victimization by a female and the risk for later sexual offending along with other adverse outcomes from female sexual offending is needed for early intervention and prevention.

The assessment and treatment of female sexual offenders is one of the cornerstones of protecting children and teens from sexual abuse by females. However, given that risk assessment, treatment development, and evaluation of treatment programs is still new, it is not possible at the present time to determine whether these efforts are currently successful or whether they will become successful into the future. Given the similarities between female and male sex offenders it is important that consideration be given to applying what is known to be effective with male sexual offenders for example, risk assessment tools, and whether a similar approach might also be effective with female sexual offenders. It may be that some of the current practices with male sex offenders are applicable to female sex offenders with some modification and that a completely different approach with females may not be necessary simply because of a difference in gender.[44] What is essential is that current prevention education programs and the assessment, treatment and management of female sexual offenders in the community are aimed at preventing sexual offending and victimization by females.[45]

Appendices

Appendix A

Adversarial Beliefs Inventory©
(ABI—Heterosexual Females)©

Response Scale for Items:

1—Strongly agree, 2—Mostly agree, 3—Slightly agree, 4—Disagree, 5—Slightly disagree, 6—Mostly disagree, 7—Neither agree nor disagree

Item	Circle One Response						
1. It is impossible to trust a man.	1	2	3	4	5	6	7
2. Men always want sex from a woman.	1	2	3	4	5	6	7
3. Dominating a man is sexually powerful.	1	2	3	4	5	6	7
4. Manipulating a man is necessary to get what you want from the relationship.	1	2	3	4	5	6	7
5. Women have been dominated by men for too long.	1	2	3	4	5	6	7
6. Never tell the truth about your sexual experiences to a man.	1	2	3	4	5	6	7
7. It is impossible to be honest with a man about your sexual past.	1	2	3	4	5	6	7
8. Never tell a man you have a sexually transmitted infection.	1	2	3	4	5	6	7
9. Lying to a man is necessary to stay ahead in the relationship.	1	2	3	4	5	6	7

10. A sexually liberated woman controls the relationship.	1	2	3	4	5	6	7
11. It is not wrong to seduce a man to get back at another woman.	1	2	3	4	5	6	7
12. Never let a man have the upper hand in the relationship.	1	2	3	4	5	6	7
13. I have seduced a man simply because I could.	1	2	3	4	5	6	7
14. I have had sex with a man to make another man jealous.	1	2	3	4	5	6	7
15. I would end the relationship if a man refused me sex.	1	2	3	4	5	6	7
16. I have gotten a man drunk to have sex with him.	1	2	3	4	5	6	7
17. A woman has the right to have sex at any time.	1	2	3	4	5	6	7
18. Men who get a woman aroused have no right to refuse her sex.	1	2	3	4	5	6	7
19. A man says "No" to sex even when he means "Yes".	1	2	3	4	5	6	7
20. Crying is a sure way to get what you want from a man.	1	2	3	4	5	6	7

The lower the score the greater the likelihood of adversarial sexual beliefs toward males.

Karen A Duncan. Correspondence should be sent to karenduncan@theright2besafe.org.

Appendix B

Beliefs about Male Rape© (BAMR)©

Response Scale for Items:

1—Strongly agree, 2—Mostly agree, 3—Slightly agree, 4—Disagree, 5—Slightly disagree, 6—Mostly disagree, 7—Neither agree nor disagree

Item	Circle One Response						
1. It is physically impossible for a woman to rape a man.	1	2	3	4	5	6	7
2. Men always want sex from a woman.	1	2	3	4	5	6	7
3. A sexually aggressive woman is more desirable.	1	2	3	4	5	6	7
4. A woman can get so horny that she has to have sex.	1	2	3	4	5	6	7
5. Women have to dominate men otherwise men will take advantage of women.	1	2	3	4	5	6	7
6. A liberated woman goes after sex.	1	2	3	4	5	6	7
7. If a man did not want to have sex, he could stop it.	1	2	3	4	5	6	7
8. Sexually dominating an unwilling man is sexually arousing.	1	2	3	4	5	6	7

9. A man is who does not want sex with a woman is not a man.	1	2	3	4	5	6	7
10. If a man has an erection it means he wants sex.	1	2	3	4	5	6	7

The lower the score the greater the endorsement of the male rape myth.

Karen A Duncan (November 2009). Correspondence should be sent to karenduncan@theright2besafe.org.

Appendix C

Justification of Sexual Aggression (JSA—Heterosexual Female)©

Response Scale for Items:

1—Strongly agree, 2—Mostly agree, 3—Slightly agree, 4—Disagree, 5—Slightly disagree, 6—Mostly disagree, 7—Neither agree nor disagree

Item	Circle One Response						
1. Sometimes a woman has to use physical force to get what she wants sexually from a man.	1	2	3	4	5	6	7
2. All men like women to sexually control them.	1	2	3	4	5	6	7
3. Dominating a man makes sex more stimulating.	1	2	3	4	5	6	7
4. Manipulating a man for sex is not a big deal.	1	2	3	4	5	6	7
5. Touching a man sexually while is he intoxicated is not a problem for men.	1	2	3	4	5	6	7
6. Teen boys benefit from sex with women older than them.	1	2	3	4	5	6	7
7. Teen girls should be able to experiment sexually with a man.	1	2	3	4	5	6	7
8. A 12-year-old boy should be shown how to enjoy sex by a woman.	1	2	3	4	5	6	7

9. Most men like rough sex.	1	2	3	4	5	6	7
10. Men want sex even when they say "No".	1	2	3	4	5	6	7
11. It's not illegal to get a man drunk and have sex with him.	1	2	3	4	5	6	7
12. Women are prudes who think casual sex is wrong.	1	2	3	4	5	6	7
13. Men are always ready for sex.	1	2	3	4	5	6	7
14. Most men do not want to talk about their feelings.	1	2	3	4	5	6	7
15. A man who is vulnerable is a wimp.	1	2	3	4	5	6	7

The lower the score the greater the endorsement for sexual aggression.

Developed by Karen A Duncan (November 2009). Correspondence should be sent to karenduncan@theright2besafe.org.

Appendix D

Assessment of Sexual Assertiveness© (ASA)©

Response Scale for Items:

1—Strongly agree, 2—Mostly agree, 3—Slightly agree, 4—Disagree,
5—Slightly disagree, 6—Mostly disagree, 7—Neither agree nor disagree

Item	Circle One Response						
1. It is important to be sober when communicating about sex in a relationship.	1	2	3	4	5	6	7
2. I tell someone directly whether I am interested in having sex so there are no misunderstandings.	1	2	3	4	5	6	7
3. Talking about my sexual decisions gives me sexual confidence.	1	2	3	4	5	6	7
4. I tell my partner what I want and need sexually.	1	2	3	4	5	6	7
5. Birth control is the responsibility of both men and women.	1	2	3	4	5	6	7
6. I ask about sexually transmitted infections with a person I am dating.	1	2	3	4	5	6	7
7. I do not let anyone pressure me into sex.	1	2	3	4	5	6	7
8. I have told a partner when I had a sexually transmitted infection.	1	2	3	4	5	6	7

9. Condoms are a condition for me to consent to sex with a partner.	1	2	3	4	5	6	7
10. I value my partner talking to me about their sexual desires.	1	2	3	4	5	6	7

What is your personal definition of sexual assertiveness?

____

____

The lower the score the greater the endorsement of sexual assertiveness.

Developed by Karen A Duncan (November 2009). Correspondence should be sent to karenduncan@theright2besafe.org.

Notes

CHAPTER 1

1. Allen, C. (1991). *Women and men who sexually abuse children: A comparative analysis.* Orwell, VT: The Safer Society Press.
2. Deering, R., & Mellor, D. (2007). Female-perpetrated child sex abuse: Definitional and categorisational analysis. *Psychiatry, Psychiatry and Law, 14*(2), 218–226; Rand, M. (2009, September). *Criminal victimization, 2008* (NCJ 227777). Washington, DC: U.S. Department of Justice, Office of Justice Programs.
3. Johansson-Love, J., & Fremouw, W. (2006). A critique of the female sexual perpetrator research. *Aggression and Violent Behavior, 11,* 12–26.
4. Hunt, L. M. (2006). *Females who sexually abuse in organisations working with children. Characteristics, international and Australian prevalence rates: Implications for child protection.* Melbourne: Child Wise.
5. Smith, A., Saewyc, E., Albert, M., MacKay, L., Northcott, M., & The McCreary Centre Society. (2007). *Against the odds: A profile of marginalized and street-involved youth in BC.* Vancouver: The McCreary Centre Society.
6. Home Office. 2002. *Protecting the public, strengthening protection against sex offenders and reforming the law on sexual offences* (CM 5668). London: The Stationery Office.
7. Andersson, N., & Ho-Foster, A. (2008). 13,915 reasons for equity in sexual offences legislation: A national school-based survey in South Africa. *International Journal for Equity in Health, 9*(20), 1–6.

8. Fazel, S., Sjostedt, G. Grann, M., & Langstrom, N. (2008). Sexual offending in women and psychiatric disorder: A national case-control study. *Archives of Sexual Behavior.*
9. Johansson-Love, J., & Fremouw, W. (2006). A critique of the female sexual perpetrator research. *Aggression and Violent Behavior, 11,* 12–26; Krahe, B., Waizenhofer, E., & Moller, I. (2003). Women's sexual aggression against men: Prevalence and predictors. *Sex Roles, 49,* 219–232; Kaufman, K., Wallace, A., Johnson, C., & Reeder, M. (1995). Comparing female and male perpetrators' modus operandi. *Journal of Interpersonal Violence, 10*(3), 322–333; Sandler, J., & Freeman, N. (2009). Female sex offender recidivism: A large-scale empirical analysis. *Sexual Abuse: A Journal of Research and Treatment, 21*(4), 455–473.
10. Denov, M. (2004a). The long-term effects of child sexual abuse by female perpetrators: A qualitative study of male and female victims. *Journal of Interpersonal Violence, 19*(10), 1137–1156; Krug, R. (1989). Adult male report of childhood sexual abuse by mothers: Case descriptions, motivations and long-term consequences. *Child Abuse and Neglect, 13,* 111–119; Lisak, D. (1994). The psychological impact of sexual abuse: Content analysis of interviews with male survivors. *Journal of Traumatic Stress, 7*(4), 525–548; Peluso, E., & Putnam, N. (1996). Case study: Sexual abuse of boys by females. *Journal of the American Academy of Child and Adolescent Psychiatry, 35*(1), 51–54; Reckling, A. (2004). Mother-daughter incest: When survivors become mothers. *Journal of Trauma Practice, 3*(2), 49–72; Rosencrans, B. (1997). *The last secret.* Brandon, VT: The Safer Society Press (as cited by Salter, p. 77).
11. Dube, S., Anda, R., Whitfield, C. Brown, D., Felitti, V. Dong, M., et al. (2005). Long-term consequences of childhood sexual abuse by gender of victim. *American Journal of Preventive Medicine, 28*(5), 430–438. This report is from the Adverse Child Experience Study (ACES) study, a longitudinal study out of San Diego, California. The ACES has identified childhood sexual abuse as one of four adverse child experiences linked to adverse health consequences across the life span. The ACES study is sponsored by the Centers for Disease Control and Prevention (Washington, DC) and the Health Maintenance Organization Kaiser Permanente, Department of Preventive Medicine (San Diego). There are 7,970 men and 9,367 women in the study. To view the reports, go to http://www.cdc.gov/nccdphp/ACE.
12. Centers for Disease Control. (2004). *Sexual violence prevention: Beginning the dialogue.* Atlanta: Author.
13. National Sexual Violence Resource Center publications (available at http://www.nsvrc.org/publications/nsvrc-publications).
14. National Coalition to Prevent Child Sexual Exploitation. (2008). *The National Plan to Prevent the Sexual Exploitation of Children.*
15. Kevin Fagan, *San Francisco Chronicle,* e-mail correspondence on November 16, 2009, following telephone interview on November 13, 2009.
16. Prior to 2007, forced sex with male children in South Africa counted not as rape but as "indecent assault," a much less serious offense with less serious legal consequences (see Andersson and Ho-Foster, 2008).

17. Smith, A., Saewyc, E., Albert, M., MacKay, L., Northcott, M., & The McCreary Centre Society. (2007). *Against the odds: A profile of marginalized and street-involved youth in BC.* Vancouver: The McCreary Centre Society.
18. The McCarty Centre Society was founded in 1977 and is a nongovernment, non-profit organization committed to improving the health of British Columbian youth through research, education, and community-based projects.
19. Child Wise is a not-for-profit organization, working to prevent, protect, and reduce the sexual abuse and exploitation of children in Australia and overseas (http://childwise.net/index.php).
20. Sandler, J., & Freeman, N. (2007). Typology of female sex offenders: A test of Vandiver and Kercher. *Sex Abuse, 19,* 73–89.
21. The Crown Prosecution Services, "Vanessa George and Angela Allen Sentenced," December 15, 2009 (available at http://cps.gov.uk/news/press_releases/161_09).
22. Saul J., & Audage, N. (2007). *Preventing child sexual abuse within youth-serving organizations: Getting started on policies and procedures.* Atlanta, GA: Centers for Disease Control and Prevention, National Center for Injury Prevention and Control.
23. Beck, A., Adams, D., & Guerino, P. (2008, July). *Sexual violence reported by juvenile correctional authorities, 2005–06* (NCJ215337). Washington, DC: U.S. Department of Justice, Office of Justice Programs, Bureau of Justice Statistics.
24. Referral for prosecution may not necessarily lead to prosecution (see Stroud, Martens, & Berker, 2000), and prosecution may not necessarily lead to incarceration. A majority of sex offenders, male and female, are residing within communities and not necessarily incarcerated. See Center for Sex Offender Management, *Fact sheet: What you need to know about sex offenders* (available at http://www.csom.org/pubs/needtoknow_fs.pdf).
25. Crime statistics are based on a particular crime being reported to law enforcement and not necessarily on the actual number of crimes committed because not all crime is reported. For a crime to be included in national crime data, it must first be reported (http://www.FBI.com). According to the Center for Sex Offender Management (CSOM), not all convicted sex offenders attend treatment programs to assist in preventing their reoffending. CSOM estimates that 20,000 sex offenders are released into local communities each year (http://www.csom.org/pubs/Comp_Approach_Brief.pdf).
26. Federal Bureau of Investigation, *Crimes against children* (available at http://www.fbi.gov/hq/cid/cac/registry.htm).
27. Kilpatrick, D. G. (2004). *Making sense of rape in America: Where do the numbers come from and what do they mean?* (Violence Against Women Supplement Meeting). Atlanta, GA: Centers for Disease Control and Prevention.
28. Nielson, T. (1983). Sexual abuse of boys: Current perspectives. *Personnel and Guidance Journal, 62,* 139–142; Nelson, E. D. (1994). Females who sexually abuse children: A discussion of gender stereotypes and symbolic assailants. *Qualitative Sociology, 17*(1), 63–88; Peter, T. (2006). Mad, bad, or victim? Making sense of mother-daughter sexual abuse. *Feminist Criminology, 1*(4), 283–302.

29. Greenfield, L., & Snell, T. (1999). *Women offenders* (NCJ 175688). Washington, DC: U.S. Department of Justice, Office of Justice Programs, Bureau of Justice Statistics (revised October 3, 2000); Snyder, H., & Sickmund, M. (2006). *Juvenile offenders and victims: 2006 national report.* Washington, DC: U.S. Department of Justice, Office of Justice Programs, Office of Juvenile Justice and Delinquency Prevention.
30. Allen, C. (1991). *Women and men who sexually abuse children: A comparative analysis.* Orwell, VT: The Safer Society Press.
31. Snyder, H., & Sickmund, M. (2006). *Juvenile offenders and victims: 2006 national report.* Washington, DC: U.S. Department of Justice, Office of Justice Programs, Office of Juvenile Justice and Delinquency Prevention.
32. Center for Sex Offender Management. (2007a, March). *Female sex offenders.* Washington, DC: U.S. Department of Justice, Office of Justice Programs.
33. Ibid., pp. 6–7.
34. Ibid., pp. 8–10.
35. Ibid.
36. Ibid.
37. The Crown Prosecution Services, "Vanessa George and Angela Allen Sentenced," December 15, 2009 (available at http://cps.gov.uk/news/press_releases/161_09).
38. "Colin Blanchard from Smallbridge, Rochdale, Vanessa George from Efford, Plymouth, and Angela Allen from Bulwell, Nottinghamshire, pleaded guilty to a string of child sex offenses," *Messenger Newspaper*, October 2, 2009 (available at http://www.messengernewspapers.co.uk/news/4661391.Trio_admit_string_of_child_sex_offences).
39. Allen, C. (1990). Women as perpetrators of child sexual abuse: Recognition barriers. In A. Horton, B. Johnson, L. Roundy, & D. Williams (Eds.), *The incest perpetrator: A family member no one want to treat.* Newbury Park, CA: Sage.
40. Johnson, S. A. (2007). *Physical abusers and sexual offenders: Forensic and clinical strategies.* New York: Taylor and Francis Group.
41. Kaplan, M., & Green, A. (1995). Incarcerated female sex offenders: A comparison of sexual histories with eleven female sex offenders. *Sexual Abuse: A Journal of Research and Treatment, 7,* 287–300.
42. Fazel, S., Sjostedt, G. Grann, M., & Langstrom, N. (2008). Sexual offending in women and psychiatric disorder: A national case-control study. *Archives of Sexual Behavior.*
43. Ibid., p. 3.
44. Kaufman, K., Wallace, A., Johnson, C., & Reeder, M. (1995). Comparing female and male perpetrators' modus operandi. *Journal of Interpersonal Violence, 10*(3), 322–333.
45. Basile, K., Chen, J., Black, M., & Saltzman, L. (2007). Prevalence and characteristics of sexual violence victimization among U.S. adults, 2001–2003. *Violence and Victims, 22*(4), 437–448.
46. Henry J. Kaiser Family Foundation. (n.d.). *National survey of adolescents and young adults: Sexual health knowledge, attitudes and experience publication* (#3218) (available at the Kaiser Family Foundation Web site at http://www.kff.org).

47. Hopper, J. (1998). Prevalence of the sexual abuse of boys. *Child Abuse Statistics, Research, and Resources* (available at http://www.jimhopper.com/abstracts).
48. Kilpatrick, D. G. (2004). *Making sense of rape in America: Where do the numbers come from and what do they mean?* (Violence Against Women Supplement Meeting). Atlanta, GA: Centers for Disease Control and Prevention.
49. Lawson, C. (1993). Mother-son sexual abuse: Rare or underreported? A critique of the research. *Child Abuse and Neglect, 17,* 261–269.
50. Muehlenhard, C., & Cook, S. (1988). Men's self-reports of unwanted sexual activity. *Journal of Sex Research, 24,* 58–72; Nathan, P., & Ward, T. (2002). Female sex offenders: Clinical and demographic features. *The Journal of Sexual Aggression, 8*(1), 5–21.
51. Incarcerated offenders were not necessarily incarcerated for sex crimes.
52. Macchietto, J. (1991). Aspects of male victimization and female aggression: Implications for counseling men. *Journal of Mental Health Counseling, 14*(3), 375–392.
53. Duncan, K. (2006, September 28). *Does gender matter: Female sex offenders and the impact to victims.* Paper presented at the Association for the Treatment of Sexual Abusers (ATSA) Conference, Chicago, IL. This paper discusses the gender bias inherent in the literature on child sexual abuse and victimization and addresses the attention that is needed in prevention education programs regarding female sexual offenders. The paper also discusses the pathway between male sexual offending for those males who experienced sexual abuse by a female.
54. Centers for Disease Control. (2004). *Sexual violence prevention: Beginning the dialogue.* Atlanta, GA: Author.
55. Anderson, P. B. (1998). Women's motives for sexual initiation and aggression. In P. Anderson & C. Struckman-Johnson (Eds.), *Sexually aggressive women: Current perspectives and controversies.* New York: Guilford Press; Anderson, P. B. (1996). Correlates of college women's self-reports of heterosexual aggression. *Sexual Abuse: A Journal of Research and Treatment, 8*(2), 121–131; Archer, J. (2000). Sex differences in aggression between heterosexual partners: A meta-analytic review. *Psychological Bulletin, 126*(5), 651–680.
56. Kaufman, K., Wallace, A., Johnson, C., & Reeder, M. (1995). Comparing female and male perpetrators' modus operandi. *Journal of Interpersonal Violence, 10*(3), 322–333.
57. Ibid., p. 324.
58. Bunting, L. (2005). *Females who sexually offend against children: Responses of child protection and criminal justice systems.* London: National Society for the Prevention of Cruelty to Children.
59. Girshick, L. (2001). *No more denying: Facing woman to woman sexual violence* (available at http://www.loribgirshick.com/booklet.html).
60. *Sexual Offences Act 2003* of Great Britain is available through The Crown Prosecution Service at http://www.cps.gov.uk/legal/s_to_u/sexual_offences_act.
61. Levine, K. (2006). No penis, no problem. *Fordham Urban Law Journal,* January, 2006 Issue.
62. Gannon, Rose, and Ward (2008) identified a group of adult female sex offenders ($N = 5$) in the prison population they studied that offended in groups of three or

more people. When offending against a female, the women identified revenge and humiliation of the victim as the motivation for planning physical aggression and that, during the commission of the physical violence, sexual violence was committed as well.

63. "Girl gang-raped for two hours at homecoming dance while a dozen people watched and did nothing," New York Daily News.com, October 27, 2009.
64. Salter, A. (2003). *Predators, pedophiles, rapists and other sex offenders: Who they are, how they operate, and how we can protect ourselves and our children.* New York: Basic Books.
65. Denov, M. (2003a). The myth of innocence: Sexual scripts and the recognition of child sexual abuse by female perpetrators. *Journal of Sex Research, 40*(3), 303–314; Pearson, P. (1998). *When she was bad: How and why women get away with murder.* New York: Penguin Books. Pearson's book is grounded in crime statistics, criminal justice data, forensic research, and anthropological studies on female aggression.
66. Corcoran, J. (2004). Treatment outcome research with the non-offending parents of sexually abused children: A critical review. *Journal of Child Sexual Abuse, 13*(2), 59–84; James, B., & Nasjleti, M. (1983). *Treating sexually abused children and their families.* Palo Alto, CA: Consulting Psychologists Press; Lev-Wiesel, R. (2006). Intergenerational transmission of sexual abuse? Motherhood in the shadow of incest. *Journal of Child Sexual Abuse, 15*(2), 75–101.
67. It is important to differentiate the various feminist scholarship and the premises that underlie their frameworks. For example, radical feminist scholarship is different from third-wave feminism and Marxist feminism (see hooks, 2000; Price & Sokoloff, 2004). Radical feminism is the framework that purports that rape and sexual assault occurs because of patriarchal societies that oppress women through sexual dominance, so it is unable to account for sexual violence as it is committed by women and girls without reference to this sociopolitical context of male dominance.
68. Brownmiller, S. (1975). *Against our will: Men, women and rape.* New York: Simon & Schuster; Herman, J. (1981). *Father-daughter incest.* Cambridge, MA: Harvard University Press.
69. Bjorkqvist, K. (1994). Sex differences in physical, verbal and indirect aggression: A review of recent research. *Sex Roles, 30*(3/4), 177–188; Burbank, V. (1994). Cross-cultural perspectives on aggression in women and girls: An introduction. *Sex Roles, 30*(3/4), 169–176; Coleman, V. (1994). Lesbian battering: The relationship between personality and perpetration of violence. *Violence and Victims, 9*(2), 139–152; Condy, S., Templer, D., Brown, R., & Veaco, L. (1987). Parameters of sexual contact of boys with women. *Archives of Sexual Behavior, 16*(5), 379–394; Dellasega, C., & Nixon, C. (2002). *12 strategies that will end female bullying.* New York: Simon & Schuster; Denov, M. (2003a). The myth of innocence: Sexual scripts and the recognition of child sexual abuse by female perpetrators. *Journal of Sex Research, 40*(3), 303–314; Duncan, K. (2005a). The impact of child sexual abuse on parenting: A female perspective (Article 58). *VISTAS: Compelling Perspectives on Counseling 2005, 58,* 267–270; Dutton, D., & Nicholls, T.

(2005). The gender paradigm in domestic violence research and theory: Part 1—The conflict of theory and data. *Aggression and Violent Behavior, 10,* 680–714; Fromuth, M.E., & Burkhart, B.R. (1987). Childhood sexual victimization among college men: Definitional and methodological issues. *Violence and Victims, 2*(4), 241–253.

70. Interview with Laura Symon on January 10, 2009, and October 23, 2009. The first three quotes are from e-mails with Laura Symon, a therapist in Evansville, Indiana, who works with sexual offenders and has worked with female sexual offenders. The quotes are from female sexual offenders.
71. Quotes are from convicted female sex offenders published in the study by Gannon, Rose, and Ward (2008).
72. U.S. Department of Health and Human Services, Administration on Children, Youth and Families. (2009). *Child maltreatment 2007.* Washington, DC: U.S. Government Printing Office. For many victims, the efforts of the child protective system in the United States have not been successful in preventing subsequent victimization. Through the Child and Family Services Reviews, the Children's Bureau has established the current national standard for the absence of maltreatment recurrence as 94.6 percent.
73. Duncan, K. (2004). *Healing from the trauma of childhood sexual abuse: The journey for women.* Westport, CT: Praeger.
74. Dube, S., Anda, R., Whitfield, C. Brown, D., Felitti, V. Dong, M., et al. (2005). Long-term consequences of childhood sexual abuse by gender of victim. *American Journal of Preventive Medicine, 28*(5), 430–438.
75. Turton (2007), in her discussion about gender stereotypes, identifies that when professionals reframe female sexual offending into socially constructed norms of female–male behavior, they are possibly colluding in decreasing the responsibility the female has in the commission of her sexual crimes (see Turton's chapter on professionals). Therefore, it would seem a prudent recommendation that researchers exercise some caution in labeling female sex offenders as male coerced until further studies on this aspect of female sexual offending is available.
76. Sandler and Freeman identified a sample of 1,466 females convicted of a sexual offense in New York State. This study is significant in that it may be the first large-scale empirical study on reoffending rates among a population of convicted female sex offenders.
77. Abel, G., & Harlow, N. (2002). The Abel and Harlow Child Molestation Study, excerpted from *The stop child molestation book* (2002), published by Xlibris.
78. Gannon, T., Rose, M., & Ward, T. (2008). A descriptive model of the offense process for female sexual offenders. *Sexual Abuse: A Journal of Research and Treatment, 20*(3), 352–374.
79. McNaulty, R.D., & Burnette, M. (2006a). *Sex and sexuality: Vol. 1. Sexual deviation and sexual offenses.* Westport, CT: Praeger.
80. The National Incident-Based Reporting System (NIBRS) was developed by the Federal Bureau of Investigation (FBI). The NIBRS data include participating counties (not all counties) from 21 states and Washington, DC. Even though the

data are not as inclusive as the Uniform Crime Reports, they provide incident-based-level information for each crime reported to the FBI, making it possible to separate out solo offenders from co-offenders (to review an explanation of the NIBRS, go to the FBI's Web site at http://www.FBI.com).

81. O'Dell, L. (2003). The "harm" story in childhood sexual abuse: Contested understanding, disputed knowledges. In P. Reavey & S. Warner (Eds.), *New feminist stories of child sexual abuse: Sexual scripts and dangerous dialogues.* London: Routledge.
82. Salter, A. (2003). *Predators, pedophiles, rapists and other sex offenders: Who they are, how they operate, and how we can protect ourselves and our children.* New York: Basic Books.
83. Rosencrans, B. (1997). *The last secret.* Brandon, VT: The Safer Society Press (as cited by Salter, p. 77).
84. Bunting, L. (2007). Dealing with a problem that doesn't exist? Responses to female perpetrated child sexual abuse. *Child Abuse Review, 16,* 252–267.
85. Boroughs, D. (2004). Female sexual abusers of children. *Children and Youth Services Review, 26,* 481–487.
86. Kaufman, K., Wallace, A., Johnson, C., & Reeder, M. (1995). Comparing female and male perpetrators' modus operandi. *Journal of Interpersonal Violence, 10*(3), 322–333.
87. Correctional Service of Canada. (1995). *Case studies of female sex offenders in the Correctional Service of Canada.* Ottawa: Author. Case studies of 19 females convicted of sexual offenses in the Canadian prison system (retrieved August 8, 2008, from http://www.csc-scc.gc.ca/text/pblct/so/female/female-01-eng.shtml).
88. Ferguson, C., & Meehan, D. (2005). An analysis of females convicted of sex crimes in the state of Florida. *Journal of Child Sexual Abuse, 14*(1), 75–89.
89. "Weeping Suspect Accused of Girl's Rape, Murder," *San Francisco Chronicle,* April 15, 2009, sec. A, p. 1.
90. Groth, N. (1979a). *Men who rape: The psychology of the offender.* New York: Plenum Press; Hare, R. D. (1996). Psychopathy: A clinical construct whose time has come. *Criminal Justice and Behavior, 23,* 25–54; Pincus, J. (2001). *Basic instincts: What makes killers kill.* New York: Norton.
91. U.S. Department of Health and Human Services, Administration on Children, Youth and Families. (2009). *Child maltreatment 2007.* Washington, DC: U.S. Government Printing Office.
92. Crewdson, J. (1988). *By silence betrayed: Sexual abuse of children in America.* New York: Harper & Row; Dong, M., Anda, R., Dube, S., Giles, W., & Felitti, V. (2003). The relationship of exposure to childhood sexual abuse to other forms of abuse, neglect, and household dysfunction during childhood. *Child Abuse and Neglect, 27,* 625–639.
93. Fullilove, M., Fullilove, R., Smith, M., Winkler, K., Michael, C., Panzer, P., et al. (1993). Violence, trauma, and posttraumatic stress disorder among women drug users. *Journal of Traumatic Stress, 6*(4), 533–543.
94. Duncan, K. (2004). *Healing from the trauma of childhood sexual abuse: The journey for women.* Westport, CT: Praeger.

95. Greenfield, L., & Snell, T. (1999). *Women offenders* (NCJ 175688). Washington, DC: U.S. Department of Justice, Office of Justice Programs, Bureau of Justice Statistics (revised October 3, 2000) (available at http://www.ojp.usdoj.gov/bjs/pub/pdf/wo.pdf); Widom, C., & Hiller-Sturmhofel, S. (2001). Alcohol abuse as a risk factor for and consequence of child abuse. *Alcohol Research and Health, 25*(1), 52–57.
96. Faller, K. C. (1987). Women who sexually abuse children. *Violence and Victims, 2*(4) 263–276; Johansson-Love, J., & Fremouw, W. (2006). A critique of the female sexual perpetrator research. *Aggression and Violent Behavior, 11,* 12–26.
97. Boroughs, D. (2004). Female sexual abusers of children. *Children and Youth Services Review, 26,* 481–487; Gannon, T., & Rose, M. (2008). Female child sexual offenders: Towards integrating theory and practice. *Aggression and Violent Behavior, 13,* 442–461; Johansson-Love, J., & Fremouw, W. (2006). A critique of the female sexual perpetrator research. *Aggression and Violent Behavior, 11,* 12–26.
98. Langevin, R., Wright, P., & Handy, L. (1989). Characteristics of sex offenders who were sexually victimized as children. *Annals of Sex Research, 2,* 227–253; Lisak, D. (1994). The psychological impact of sexual abuse: Content analysis of interviews with male survivors. *Journal of Traumatic Stress, 7*(4), 525–548; Groth, N., & Burgess, A. (1980). Male rape: Offenders and victims. *American Journal of Psychiatry, 13*(7), 806–810; for a more recent study in Britain, see Glasser et al. (2001); Whitaker, D., Le, B., Hanson, R. K., Baker, C., McMahon, P., Ryan, G. (2008). Risk factors for the perpetration of child sexual abuse: A review and meta-analysis. *Child Abuse and Neglect, 32,* 529–548.
99. Boroughs, D. (2004). Female sexual abusers of children. *Children and Youth Services Review, 26,* 481–487; Gannon, T., & Rose, M. (2008). Female child sexual offenders: Towards integrating theory and practice. *Aggression and Violent Behavior, 13,* 442–461; Johansson-Love, J., & Fremouw, W. (2006). A critique of the female sexual perpetrator research. *Aggression and Violent Behavior, 11,* 12–26.
100. It may be that the male offenders of violent crimes (nonsexual crimes) had not been asked if they had experienced sexual abuse in childhood, which would explain the lower percentage in this study as compared to other studies.
101. See Miller, Turner, and Henderson (2009) for a review on latent profile analysis.
102. Bandura, A. (1986). *Social foundations of thought and action: A social cognitive theory.* Englewood Cliffs, NJ: Prentice Hall.
103. Bloom, B., Owen, B., & Covington, S. (2005, May). *Gender-responsive strategies for women offenders: A summary of research, practice and guiding principles for women offenders.* Washington, DC: U.S. Department of Justice, National Institute of Corrections; Duncan, K. (2006, September 28). *Does gender matter: Female sex offenders and the impact to victims.* Paper presented at the Association for the Treatment of Sexual Abusers (ATSA) Conference, Chicago, IL; Greenfield, L., & Snell, T. (1999). *Women offenders* (NCJ 175688). Washington, DC: U.S. Department of Justice, Office of Justice Programs, Bureau of Justice Statistics (revised October 3, 2000) (available at http://www.ojp.usdoj.gov/bjs/pub/pdf/wo.pdf).

104. Malamuth, N. (1998). The confluence model as an organizing framework for research on sexually aggressive men: Risk, moderators, imagined aggression and pornography consumption. In R. Green & E. Donnerstein (Eds.), *Aggression: Theoretical and empirical reviews*. New York: Academic Press.
105. World Health Organization. (2007). *Key facts on the cycles of violence: The relationship between childhood maltreatment and the risk of later becoming a victim or perpetrator of violence.* Geneva: Author (available at http://www.euro.who.int/document/E90619.pdf).
106. Widom, C., & Hiller-Sturmhofel, S. (2001). Alcohol abuse as a risk factor for and consequence of child abuse. *Alcohol Research and Health, 25*(1), 52–57.
107. Fazel, S., Sjostedt, G., Grann, M., & Langstrom, N. (2008). Sexual offending in women and psychiatric disorder: A national case-control study. *Archives of Sexual Behavior.*
108. Bloom, B., Owen, B., & Covington, S. (2005, May). *Gender-responsive strategies for women offenders: A summary of research, practice and guiding principles for women offenders.* Washington, DC: U.S. Department of Justice, National Institute of Corrections.
109. Duncan, K. (2005b). The relationship between posttraumatic stress disorder and substance abuse in women with a history of childhood sexual abuse trauma (Article 60). *VISTAS: Compelling Perspectives on Counseling 2005, 58,* 267–270; Najavits, L., et al. (1998). Cocaine dependence with and without PTSD among subjects in the National Institute on Drug Abuse Collaborative Cocaine Treatment Study. *American Journal of Psychiatry, 155*(2), 214–219; Widom, C., & Hiller-Sturmhofel, S. (2001). Alcohol abuse as a risk factor for and consequence of child abuse. *Alcohol Research and Health, 25*(1), 52–57.
110. Hare, R. D. (1996). Psychopathy: A clinical construct whose time has come. *Criminal Justice and Behavior, 23,* 25–54.
111. Bunting, L. (2005). *Females who sexually offend against children: Responses of child protection and criminal justice systems.* London: National Society for the Prevention of Cruelty to Children; Bunting, L. (2007). Dealing with a problem that doesn't exist? Responses to female perpetrated child sexual abuse. *Child Abuse Review, 16,* 252–267; Christopher, K., Lutz-Zois, E., & Reinhardt, A. (2007). Female sexual offenders: Personality pathology as a mediator of the relationship between childhood sexual abuse history and sexual abuse perpetration against others. *Child Abuse and Neglect, 31,* 871–883.
112. Oliver, B. (2007). Preventing female-perpetrated sexual abuse. *Journal of Trauma, Violence and Abuse, 8*(1), 19–32.
113. Johansson-Love, J., & Fremouw, W. (2006). A critique of the female sexual perpetrator research. *Aggression and Violent Behavior, 11,* 12–26.
114. National Public Radio, "Sexual abuse often taboo for black boys," July 13, 2009.
115. Duncan, L., & Williams, L. (1998). Gender role socialization and male-on-male vs. female-on-male child sexual abuse. *Sex Roles, 39*(9/10), 765–785. This is a significant study on the sexual abuse of African American boys by female sex

offenders especially in light of the scarcity of studies on the sexual abuse of African American children.

116. Eighty-nine percent of the male participants were African American.
117. A recent study by Springman, Wherry, and Notaro (2006) indicates that *cross-race dyads result in improved disclosure* (more disclosing) than same-race dyads in cases of child sexual abuse (see Bibliography for article reference).
118. Clarification of these findings was substantiated through e-mail correspondence with the primary author of the study, Lauren Duncan, on December 1, 2009.
119. Condy, S., Templer, D., Brown, R., & Veaco, L. (1987). Parameters of sexual contact of boys with women. *Archives of Sexual Behavior, 16*(5), 379–394; Hannon, R., Hall, D., Nash, H., Formati, J., & Hopson, T. (2000). Judgments regarding sexual aggression as a function of aggressor and victim. *Sex Roles, 43*(5/6), 311–322.
120. Finkelhor, D. (1984). *Child sexual abuse: New theory and research.* New York: Free Press; Ford, H. (2006). *Women who sexually abuse children.* West Sussex: Wiley.
121. The authors, Duncan and Williams (1998), performed additional multiple regression analyses to control for home environment as a possible factor of abuse outcomes and found identical patterns with the exception of a case that showed that, when including the home abuse variable, the relationship between CF abuse and adult perpetration emerged.
122. Glasser, M., Kolvin I., Campbell, D., Glasser, A., Leitch, I., & Farrelly, S. (2001). Cycle of child sexual abuse: Links between being a victim and becoming a perpetrator. *British Journal of Psychiatry, 179,* 482–494; Langevin, R., Wright, P., & Handy, L. (1989). Characteristics of sex offenders who were sexually victimized as children. *Annals of Sex Research, 2,* 227–253; Whitaker, D., Le, B., Hanson, R. K., Baker, C., McMahon, P., Ryan, G., (2008). Risk factors for the perpetration of child sexual abuse: A review and meta-analysis. *Child Abuse and Neglect, 32,* 529–548.
123. A recent study by Jespersen, Lalumiere, and Seto (2009) found a higher prevalence of a sexual abuse history among adult sex offenders than among non–sex offenders, a higher prevalence of sexual abuse history among sex offenders against children, and a higher prevalence of physical abuse for both groups of sex offenders. The study has similarities to the previous research of Finkelhor and Russell (1984) and a study by Dong, Anda, Dube, Giles, and Felitti (2003) that found that physical abuse was prominent in the matrix of traumas that children experience in childhood. It would be important for future studies investigating the sexual offense histories of adult male sex offenders to include a gender analysis of original offender and the potential types of abuse that adult male sex offenders experienced in their childhoods, as this information could be relevant to treatment and risk reduction for future offending, whether sexual offenses or other types of interpersonal violence (see Bibliography).
124. Bandura, A. (1986). *Social foundations of thought and action: A social cognitive theory.* Englewood Cliffs, NJ: Prentice Hall.

125. Rand, M. (2009, September). *Criminal victimization, 2008* (NCJ 227777). Washington, DC: U.S. Department of Justice, Office of Justice Programs.
126. Kellogg, N. (2005). The American Academy of Pediatrics: Clinical report. The evaluation of sexual abuse in children. *Pediatrics, 116*(2), 506–512; Leder, M., Emans, S., Hafler, J., & Rappaport, L. (1999). Addressing sexual abuse in the primary care setting. *Pediatrics, 104*(2), 270–275.
127. hooks, b. (2000). *Feminist theory: From margin to center* (2nd ed.). Cambridge, MA: South End Press.
128. Skrypnek, B., & Snyder, M. (1982). On the self-perpetuating nature of stereotypes about women and men. *Journal of Experimental Social Psychology, 18,* 277–291.
129. Examples of sex role stereotypes regarding male/female sexual behavior are "females as victims and males as offenders," "male as aggressor and female as resistor" or "male as dominant and female as passive," and "men seek sex and women avoid sex."
130. Nelson, E. D. (1994). Females who sexually abuse children: A discussion of gender stereotypes and symbolic assailants. *Qualitative Sociology, 17*(1), 63–88.
131. Interview with adult woman sexually abused as a child by a female educator and coach (October 2009).
132. Allen, C. (1990). Women as perpetrators of child sexual abuse: Recognition barriers. In A. Horton, B. Johnson, L. Roundy, & D. Williams (Eds.), *The incest perpetrator: A family member no one want to treat.* Newbury Park, CA: Sage; Hetherton, J., & Beardsall, L. (1998). Decisions and attitudes concerning child sexual abuse: Does the gender of the perpetrator make a difference to child protection professionals? *Child Abuse and Neglect, 22*(12), 1265–1283.
133. Duncan, L., & Williams, L. (1998). Gender role socialization and male-on-male vs. female-on-male child sexual abuse. *Sex Roles, 39*(9/10), 765–785.
134. Denov, M. (2001b). A culture of denial: Exploring professional perspectives on female sex offending. *Canadian Journal of Criminology, 43,* 303–329.
135. Miller, H., Turner, K., & Henderson, C.E. (2009). Psychopathology of sex offenders: A comparison of males and females using latent profile analysis. *Criminal Justice and Behavior, 36*(8), 778–792.
136. Hetherton, J., & Beardsall, L. (1998). Decisions and attitudes concerning child sexual abuse: Does the gender of the perpetrator make a difference to child protection professionals? *Child Abuse and Neglect, 22*(12), 1265–1283.
137. Skrypnek, B., & Snyder, M. (1982). On the self-perpetuating nature of stereotypes about women and men. *Journal of Experimental Social Psychology, 18,* 277–291.
138. Deaux, K., & Lafrance, M. (1998). Gender. In D. T. Gilbert, S.T. Fiske, & G. Lindzey (Eds.), *Handbook of social psychology* (Vol. 2). Boston: McGraw-Hill.
139. Ferguson, C., & Meehan, D. (2005). An analysis of females convicted of sex crimes in the state of Florida. *Journal of Child Sexual Abuse, 14*(1), 75–89.
140. Montaldo, C. (n.d.). *Mary Kay Letourneau* (available at http://crime.about.com/od/history/p/Letourneau.htm).

141. Interview with adult female sexually abused by a woman (September 20, 2008).
142. Macchietto (1991) provides an excellent summary on the technique of reframing in working with males who have been sexually abused or experienced physical violence by females.
143. Young, V. (1993b). Women abusers: A feminist view. In M. Elliott (Ed.), *Female sexual abuse of children*. New York: Guilford Press.
144. Abel, G., Gore, D., Holland E., Camp N., Becker, J., & Rathnew J. (1989). The measurement of the cognitive distortions of child molesters. *Annals of Sex Research, 2,* 135–152.
145. Young, V. (1993b). Women abusers: A feminist view. In M. Elliott (Ed.), *Female sexual abuse of children*. New York: Guilford Press.
146. Turton, J. (2007). *Child abuse, gender and society.* New York: Routledge.

CHAPTER 2

1. Holzworth-Munroe, A. (2005). Female perpetration of physical aggression against an intimate partner: A controversial new topic of study. *Violence and Victims, 20,* 2, 251–259; Fry, D. P., & Gabriel, A. H. (1994). Preface: The cultural construction of gender and aggression. *Sex Roles, 30*(3/4), 165–167. Both articles are from an anthropological perspective of human aggression with the basic premise that either gender is capable of aggressive behavior.
2. Miller, A. (1985). *Thou shalt not be aware: Society's betrayal of the child.* London: Pluto. Alice Miller has written extensively on the abuse of children by mothers and fathers.
3. Henning, Renauer, and Holdford (2007) have suggested four subtypes of women offenders convicted of intimate partner violence: no prior violence, primary victim, primary aggressor, and primary aggressor not identified.
4. Geraci, L. (1986). *Making shelters safe for lesbians.* In K. Lobel (Ed.), *Naming the violence: Speaking out about lesbian battering.* Seattle: The Seal Press; Girshick, L. (2001). *No more denying: Facing woman to woman sexual violence.* (available at http://www.loribgirshick.com/booklet.html); VanderLaan, D., & Vasey, P. (2009). Patterns of sexual coercion in heterosexual and non-heterosexual men and women. *Archives of Sexual Behavior, 38*(6), 987–999.
5. Dong, M., Anda, R., Dube, S., Giles, W., & Felitti, V. (2003). The relationship of exposure to childhood sexual abuse to other forms of abuse, neglect, and household dysfunction during childhood. *Child Abuse and Neglect, 27,* 625–639. This is one of the outcome studies from the Adverse Child Experience Study, a longitudinal study on the long-term health effects of four types of adverse childhood experiences (see Chapter 1 reference to Dube et al., 2005). Two of the adverse experiences identified by the researchers are child sexual abuse and domestic violence. (see also Gil-Gonzales, Vives-Casas, Ruiz, Carrasco-Portino, & Alvarez-Dardet, 2007).

6. Harold, G., Fincham, F., Osborne, L., & Conger, R. (1997). Mom and dad are at it again: Adolescent perceptions of marital conflict and adolescent psychological Distress. *Developmental Psychology, 33,* 333–350; Fincham, F., Grych, J., & Osborne, L. (1994). Does marital conflict cause children maladjustment? Directions and challenges for longitudinal research. *Journal of Family Psychology, 8,* 128–140.
7. Moore and Pepler's study compared mothers residing at a domestic violence shelter with mothers who were not residing at a domestic violence. They found that mothers from both groups used threats and insults at about the same frequency and that the children from both groups suffered comparable harm. This study indicates that it is not just physical violence that endangers child's well-being and emotional safety and that mothers who are not reported to be experiencing domestic violence engage in verbal and psychological abuse of children.
8. Dutton, D., & Nicholls, T. (2005). The gender paradigm in domestic violence research and theory: Part 1—The conflict of theory and data. *Aggression and Violent Behavior, 10,* 680–714.
9. Macchietto, J. (1991). Aspects of male victimization and female aggression: Implications for counseling men. *Journal of Mental Health Counseling, 14*(3), 375–392.
10. Ramisetty-Mikler, S., Caetano, R., & McGrath, C. (2007). Sexual aggression among white, black, and Hispanic couples in the U.S.: Alcohol use, physical assault, and psychological aggression as its correlates. *American Journal of Drug and Alcohol Abuse, 33,* 31–43.
11. Holzworth-Munroe, A. (2005). Female perpetration of physical aggression against an intimate partner: A controversial new topic of study. *Violence and Victims, 20,*(2), 251–259; Straus, M. A. (1999a). The controversy over domestic violence by women: A methodological, theoretical, and sociology of science analysis. In X. B. Arriaga & S. Oskamp (Eds.), *Violence in intimate relationships.* Thousand Oaks, CA: Sage; Straus, M. (1999b). Physical assault by wives: A major social problem. In R. Gelles & D. Loseke (Eds.), *Current controversies on family violence.* Newbury Park, CA: Sage.
12. World Health Organization. (2007). *Key facts on the cycles of violence: The relationship between childhood maltreatment and the risk of later becoming a victim or perpetrator of violence* (available at http://www.euro.who.int/document/E90619.pdf).
13. U.S. Department of Health and Human Services, Administration on Children, Youth and Families. (2009). *Child maltreatment 2007.* Washington, DC: U.S. Government Printing Office.
14. Ibid., p. 23.
15. Ibid., p. 29. A similar level of maltreatment by mothers is also indicated in the 2006 report issued by the U.S. Department of Health and Human Services.
16. Ibid., p. 55.
17. Ibid., p. 56

18. World Health Organization. (2006). *Preventing child maltreatment: A guide to taking action and generating evidence.* Geneva: Author. World Health Organization. (2003). *Violence prevention the evidence: Changing cultural and social norms that support violence.* Geneva: Author.
19. Oliver, B. (2007). Preventing female-perpetrated sexual abuse. *Journal of Trauma, Violence and Abuse, 8*(1), 19–32.
20. van Dam, C. (2001). *Identifying child molesters: Preventing child sexual abuse by recognizing the patterns of the offenders.* New York: Haworth Press.
21. Crewdson, John. 1988. *By silence betrayed: Sexual abuse of children in America.* New York: Harper & Row; Denov, M. (2003a). The myth of innocence: Sexual scripts and the recognition of child sexual abuse by female perpetrators. *Journal of Sex Research, 40*(3), 303–314.
22. Ogilvie, B. (2004). *Mother-daughter incest: A guide for helping professions.* New York: Haworth Press.
23. Denov, M. (2004b). *Perspectives on female sex offending: A culture of denial.* Burlington, VT: Ashgate. Denov, M. (2004a). The long-term effects of child sexual abuse by female perpetrators: A qualitative study of male and female victims. *Journal of Interpersonal Violence, 19*(10), 1137–1156.
24. Denov, M. (2004b). *Perspectives on female sex offending: A culture of denial.* Burlington, VT: Ashgate.
25. Denov, M. (2004a). The long-term effects of child sexual abuse by female perpetrators: A qualitative study of male and female victims. *Journal of Interpersonal Violence, 19*(10), 1137–1156.
26. Duncan, K. (2004). *Healing from the trauma of childhood sexual abuse: The journey for women.* Westport, CT: Praeger.
27. Peter, T. (2006). Mad, bad, or victim? Making sense of mother-daughter sexual abuse. *Feminist Criminology, 1*(4), 283–302; Denov, M. (2004a). The long-term effects of child sexual abuse by female perpetrators: A qualitative study of male and female victims. *Journal of Interpersonal Violence, 19*(10), 1137–1156. Denov, M. (2001). A culture of denial: Exploring professional perspectives on female sex offending. *Canadian Journal of Criminology, 43,* 303–329.
28. The article provides a comprehensive yet succinct history of the influences that have prevailed to influence at what point in time the trauma of child sexual abuse has been identified and accepted or identified and denied.
29. Dong, M., Anda, R., Dube, S., Giles, W., & Felitti, V. (2003). The relationship of exposure to childhood sexual abuse to other forms of abuse, neglect, and household dysfunction during childhood. *Child Abuse and Neglect, 27,* 625–639.
30. Interview with Circuit Court Judge K. Mark Loyd on December 11, 2009, at Judge Loyd's Chambers located at the Johnson County Court House (Franklin, IN).
31. Kasl, C. D. (1990). Female perpetrators of sexual abuse: A feminist view. In M. Hunter (Ed.), *The sexually abused male: Volume 1. Prevalence, impact and treatment.* Lexington, MA: Lexington Books.

32. Peter, T. (2006). Mad, bad, or victim? Making sense of mother-daughter sexual abuse. *Feminist Criminology, 1*(4), 283–302. This article is a qualitative study on how daughters, sexually abused by their mothers, perceive their mother—mentally ill, evil, or a victim of sexual abuse; it offers an insightful look into the level of secrecy and shame that daughters have experienced because of society's denial and a lack of research on maternal sexual abuse.
33. Snyder, H., & Sickmund, M. (2006). *Juvenile offenders and victims: 2006 national report.* Washington, DC: U.S. Department of Justice, Office of Justice Programs, Office of Juvenile Justice and Delinquency Prevention; Snyder, H. N. (2000). *Sexual assault of young children as reported to law enforcement: Victim, offender and incident characteristics* (NCJ 182990). Washington, DC: U.S. Department of Justice, Office of Justice Programs, Bureau of Justice Statistics.
34. DeMause, L. (1974). The evolution of childhood. In L. DeMause (Ed.), *The history of childhood.* New York: Psychohistory Press.
35. Herman, J. (1981). *Father-daughter incest.* Cambridge, MA: Harvard University Press.
36. DeMause, L. (1991). The universality of incest. *Journal of Psychohistory, 19*(2) (available at http://www.psychohistory.com/htm/05_history.html). Citation from the letters of Sigmund Freud in *The origins of psychoanalysis: Letters to Wilhelm Fliess, drafts and notes: 1887–1902.* New York: Basic Books, 1954, p. 220.
37. This view is also cited by feminist writer bell hooks (2000) and feminists who view themselves as third-wave feminists (see Peter, 2006).
38. See Chapter 1 in reference to the explanation of the crime database used by Vandiver (2006b) in her study of female solo offenders and Lawson (1993), Kilpatrick (2004), and Hopper (2009) for analysis on the problems with crime rates and prevalence studies regarding child sexual abuse and other types of sexual victimization. Child sexual abuse and other sexual offenses are viewed as the least likely type of crime to be reported. Given the cultural bias against believing that females commit sexual crimes and the lack of direct questions about female perpetrators in general population surveys, sexual crimes by females are considered even less likely to be reported than sexual crimes committed by males.
39. Kilpatrick, D. G. (2004). *Making sense of rape in America: Where do the numbers come from and what do they mean?* Atlanta, GA: Centers for Disease Control and Prevention.
40. Allen, C. (1991). *Women and men who sexually abuse children: A comparative analysis.* Orwell, VT: The Safer Society Press.
41. Fry, D. P., & Gabriel, A. H. (1994). Preface: The cultural construction of gender and aggression. *Sex Roles, 30*(3/4), 165–167; Gagnon, J. H. (1990). The explicit and implicit use of the scripting perspective in sex research. In J. Bancroft, C. M. Davis, & D. Weinstein (Eds.), *Annual review of sex research* (Vol. 1, pp. 1–43). Mount Vernon, IA: Society for the Scientific Study of Sex; Nielson, T. (1983). Sexual abuse of boys: Current perspectives. *Personnel and Guidance Journal, 62,* 139–142.

42. Denov, M. (2004a). The long-term effects of child sexual abuse by female perpetrators: A qualitative study of male and female victims. *Journal of Interpersonal Violence, 19*(10), 1137–1156.
43. Saradjian, J., with Helga Hanks (1996). *Women who sexually abuse children: from research to clinical practice.* New York: Wiley.
44. McCarty, L.M. (1986). Mother-child incest: Characteristics of the offender. *Child Welfare, 65*(5), 447–458. This study is worth reviewing not only because of McCarty's seminal work regarding maternal sexual abuse but also because her findings remain relevant today in the emerging typologies of female sex offenders.
45. Ibid.
46. Because researchers do not consistently identify the relationship between the offender and the victim in their studies on sexual offending, it is difficult to ascertain information specific to maternal sexual abuse versus sexual abuse committed by women other than mothers. This criticism of research on female sexual offending has also been cited by Banning (1989) and Lawson (1993). However, when placing reported case studies alongside prevalence data that are available on female sex offenders in the context of the criminal justice report by Snyder (2000) on child sexual victimization, it is reasonable to assume at this point in time that the majority of reported female sex offenders are in fact mothers and other women who are in a primary role of caregiver with children. It is hoped that research methods on sexual offending will improve over time with one improvement in particular being an agreement to include the relationship between the victim and offender in studies on female sexual offending.
47. Kellogg, N. (2005). The American Academy of Pediatrics: Clinical report. The evaluation of sexual abuse in children. *Pediatrics, 116*(2), 506–512; Leder, M., Emans, S., Hafler, J., & Rappaport, L. (1999). Addressing sexual abuse in the primary care setting. *Pediatrics, 104*(2), 270–275.
48. Clinical notes of Karen A. Duncan, May 1998.
49. See Faller (1987); Gannon, Rose, and Ward (2008); Hislop (2001); Kaplan and Green (1995); McCarty (1986); Mitchell and Morse (1998); Ogilvie (2004); Reckling (2005); and Rosencrans (1997), Saradjian & Hanks, 1996), Tardiff, et al. (2005).
50. Sarrel, P., & Masters, W. (1982). Sexual molestation of men by women. *Archives of Sexual Behavior, 11*(2), 117–131.
51. As previously mentioned by Bunting (2005) and Miller, Turner, and Henderson (2009), accurate risk assessment for female sex offenders is needed, as it does not exist at the present time. This author has experienced a lack of resources to recommend to individuals who attend my trainings on female sex offenders. Probation and parole officers usually share that they use risk assessments developed for male sex offenders and adapt them to use with female sex offenders. Given the similarities that do exist between male and female sex offenders, it is not inconceivable that current risk assessments for males could be adapted and applied to females, while research into their use with females is recommended along with developing female specific risk assessment tools.

52. Duncan, K. (2004). *Healing from the trauma of childhood sexual abuse: The journey for women.* Westport, CT: Praeger; Lisak, D. (1994). The psychological impact of sexual abuse: Content analysis of interviews with male survivors. *Journal of Traumatic Stress, 7*(4), 525–548.
53. Duncan, K. (2004). *Healing from the trauma of childhood sexual abuse: The journey for women.* Westport, CT: Praeger.
54. National Child Traumatic Stress Network, Justice System Consortium. (2009). *Helping traumatized children: Tips for judges.* Los Angeles: National Center for Child Traumatic Stress (available at http://www.nctsnet.org/nctsn_assets/pdfs/Judges FactSheet.pdf).
55. Igelman, R.S., Ryan, B.E., Gilbert, A. M., Bashant, C., & North, K. (2008). Best practices for serving traumatized children and families. *Juvenile and Family Court Journal, 59*(4), 35–47.
56. Morrison, S., & Greene, E. (1992). Juror and expert knowledge of child sexual abuse. *Child Abuse and Neglect, 16*(4), 595–613.
57. Banning, A. (1989). Mother–son incest: Confronting a prejudice. *Child Abuse and Neglect, 13,* 563–570.
58. Lisak, D. (1994). The psychological impact of sexual abuse: Content analysis of interviews with male survivors. *Journal of Traumatic Stress, 7*(4), 525–548.
59. Education about defining personal boundaries and examples of boundary violations are essential in reducing the risk of revictimization in families where sexual abuse has occurred. It is also critical to monitor a family's use of boundaries and how they respond when mild boundary violations occur, as less serious boundary violations may be an indication of more serious boundary violations in the family when others are not present or may lead to more serious boundary violations. This aspect of safety planning is essential to include in a reunification plan with families where reunification is implemented and evaluated through the stages of treatment with victims, offenders, and other family members. Since families where sexual abuse occurs often lack information about what characterizes a healthy family (i.e., nonabusive), it is also important to include information and examples of what it means to be a healthy family. For an example of information on healthy family characteristics visit The Right To Be safe at http://www.theright2besafe.org and go to the links "Resources" and "Handouts."
60. U.S. Department of Health and Human Services, Administration on Children, Youth and Families. (2009). *Child maltreatment 2007.* Washington, DC: U.S. Government Printing Office. In 2007, nearly 70 percent (69.9%) of child fatalities were caused by one or more parents. More than one-quarter (27.1%) of fatalities were perpetrated by the mother acting alone. Child fatalities where the relationship of the offender was not identified accounted for 16.4 percent.
61. Miller, A. (1985). *Thou shalt not be aware: Society's betrayal of the child.* London: Pluto.
62. Reckling, A. (2004). Mother-daughter incest: When survivors become mothers. *Journal of Trauma Practice, 3*(2), 49–72.

63. Denov, M. (2004a). The long-term effects of child sexual abuse by female perpetrators: A qualitative study of male and female victims. *Journal of Interpersonal Violence, 19*(10), 1137–1156.
64. See Denov (2004a) and Ogilvie (2004).
65. Duncan, K. (2005a). The impact of child sexual abuse on parenting: A female perspective (Article 58). *VISTAS: Compelling Perspectives on Counseling 2005, 58,* 275–277. Alexandria, VA: American Counseling Association.
66. Denov, M. (2004a). The long-term effects of child sexual abuse by female perpetrators: A qualitative study of male and female victims. *Journal of Interpersonal Violence, 19*(10), 1137–1156.
67. Mitchell, J., & Morse, J. (1998). *From victims to survivors: Reclaimed voices of women sexually abused in childhood by females.* Washington, DC: Taylor and Francis Group; Krug, R. (1989). Adult males report of childhood sexual abuse by mothers: Case descriptions, motivations and long-term consequences. *Child Abuse and Neglect, 13,* 111–119.
68. Hislop, J. (2001). *Female sex offenders: What therapists, law enforcement and child protection services need to know.* Ravensdale, WA: Issues Press.
69. Greeting Card Association, *Mother's Day* (available at http://www.greetingcard.org/about.php?ID=121).
70. Margaret Miles, in her article "God's love, mother's milk: An image of salvation" (*Christian Century,* 2008) references prominent theologians who describe God's love for humanity as that of "a mother who offers care and provision to her dependent child, both in her womb and in its early experience in the world" and that "God's care as closely resembling that of a mother: The mother's service is nearest, readiest, and surest: nearest because it is most natural; readiest because it is most loving; surest because it is truest (Showings, Long text 59)." (Miles's article is available at http://findarticles.com/p/articles/mi_m1058/is_125/ai_n24256359/?tag=content;col1).
71. Kevin Fagan, interviewed by telephone and e-mail on November 13, 2009. Fagan is an award-winning journalist with the *San Francisco Chronicle.* Correspondence and contact with Fagan followed his article on the arrest of Melissa Huckaby for the kidnapping, rape, and murder of eight-year-old Sandra Cantu.
72. Cited by Peter (2005, p. 284) from a study by Longdon (1993).

CHAPTER 3

1. Brownmiller, S. (1975). *Against our will: Men, women and rape.* New York: Simon and Schuster, p. 8.
2. Fry, D. P., & Gabriel, A. H. (1994). Preface: The cultural construction of gender and aggression. *Sex Roles, 30*(3/4), 165–167.
3. Hamel, J. (2009). Toward a gender-inclusive conception of intimate partner violence research and theory: Part 2—New directions. *International Journal of Men's Health, 8*(1), 41–59.

4. Dobash, R. P., & Dobash, E. R. (1978). *Wives: The "appropriate" victims of marital violence. Reflection on violence against women: Classic papers* (available at http://www.mincava.umn.edu/classics).
5. Dobash, R. P., Dobash, E. R., Wilson, M., & Daly, M. (1992). The myth of sexual symmetry in marital violence. *Social Problems, 391*(1), 71–91; Dobash, R. P., & Dobash, E. R. (1978). *Wives: The "appropriate" victims of marital violence. Reflection on violence against women: Classic papers* (available at http://www.mincava.umn.edu/classics); Ehrmin, J. (1996). No more mother blaming: A feminists nursing perspective on the mother's role in father-daughter incest. *Archives of Psychiatric Nursing, 10*(4), 252–260; and, for the alternate view see Pearson, P. (1998). *When she was bad: How and why women get away with murder*. New York: Penguin Books; Peter, T. (2006). Mad, bad, or victim? Making sense of mother-daughter sexual abuse. *Feminist Criminology, 1*(4), 283–302.
6. Smith, A., Saewyc, E., Albert, M., MacKay, L., Northcott, M., & The McCreary Centre Society. (2007). *Against the odds: A profile of marginalized and street-involved youth in BC.* Vancouver: The McCreary Centre Society; Rand, M. (2009, September). *Criminal victimization, 2008* (NCJ 227777). Washington, DC: U.S. Department of Justice, Office of Justice Programs; Snyder, H. N. (2000). *Sexual assault of young children as reported to law enforcement: Victim, offender and incident characteristics* (NCJ 182990). Washington, DC: U.S. Department of Justice, Office of Justice Programs, Bureau of Justice Statistics.
7. Dowd, L., Leisring, P., & Rosenbaum, A. (2005). Partner aggressive women: Characteristics and treatment attrition. *Violence and Victims, 20*(2), 219–233.
8. Struckman-Johnson, C., & Struckman-Johnson, D. (1998). The dynamics and impact of sexual coercion of men by women. In P. B. Anderson & C. Struckman-Johnson (Eds.), *Sexually aggressive women: Current perspectives and controversies.* New York: Guilford Press.
9. Ibid.
10. Ibid.
11. Straus, M., & Ramirez, I. (2002, July 30). *Gender symmetry in prevalence, severity, and chronicity of physical aggression against dating partners by university students in Mexico and USA.* Paper presented at the XV World Meeting of the International Society for Research on Aggression. Montreal.
12. Oswald, D., & Russell, B. (2006). Perceptions of sexual coercion in heterosexual dating relationships: The role of aggressor gender and tactics. *Journal of Sex Research, 43,* 87–95.
13. As cited by Oswald and Russell (2006) and Struckman-Johnson and Struckman-Johnson (2003).
14. Anderson, P., & Struckman-Johnson, C. (Eds.). (1998). *Sexually aggressive women.* London: Guilford Press; Capaldi, D., Kim, H., & Shortt, J. (2004). Women's involvement in aggression in young adult romantic relationships. In M. Pullatz (Ed.), *Aggression, antisocial behavior, and violence among girls.* New York: Guilford Press; Denov, M. (2001). A culture of denial: Exploring professional perspectives on female sex offending. *Canadian Journal of Criminology, 43,* 303–329;

Muehlenhard, C. L. (1998). The importance and danger of studying sexually aggressive women. In E. Anderson & C. Struckman-Johnson (Eds.), *Sexually aggressive women: Current perspectives and controversies*. New York: Guilford Press; Macchietto, J. (1991). Aspects of male victimization and female aggression: Implications for counseling men. *Journal of Mental Health Counseling, 14*(3), 375–392.

15. Muehlenhard, C. L. (1998). The importance and danger of studying sexually aggressive women. In E. Anderson & C. Struckman-Johnson (Eds.), *Sexually aggressive women: Current perspectives and controversies.* New York: Guilford Press.
16. Burbank, V. (1994). Cross-cultural perspectives on aggression in women and girls: An introduction. *Sex Roles, 30*(3/4), 169–176; Fry, D. P., & Gabriel, A. H. (1994). Preface: The cultural construction of gender and aggression. *Sex Roles, 30*(3/4), 165–167.
17. White, J., & Kowalski, R. (1994). Deconstructing the myth of the nonaggressive female: A feminist analysis. *Psychology of Women Quarterly, 18,* 477–498.
18. Mosher, D., & Tomkins, S. (1988). Scripting the macho man: Hypermasculine socialization and enculturation. *Journal of Sex Research, 25,* 60–84.
19. Gagnon, J. H. (1990). The explicit and implicit use of the scripting perspective in sex research. In J. Bancroft, C. M. Davis, & D. Weinstein (Eds.), *Annual review of sex research* (Vol. 1). Mount Vernon, IA: Society for the Scientific Study of Sex.
20. Jackson, S. (1978). The social context of rape: Sexual scripts and motivation. *Women's Studies International Quarterly, 1,* 27–38.
21. Capaldi, D., Kim, H., & Shortt, J. (2004). Women's involvement in aggression in young adult romantic relationships. In M. Pullatz (Ed.), *Aggression, antisocial behavior, and violence among girls*. New York: Guilford Press.
22. Allgier, E., & Lamping, J. (1998). Theories, politics and sexual coercion. In P. B. Anderson & C. Struckman-Johnson (Eds.), *Sexually aggressive women: Current perspectives and controversies.* New York: Guilford Press; Shea, M. E. (1998). When the tables are turned: Verbal sexual coercion among college women. In P. Anderson & C. Struckman-Johnson (Eds.), *Sexually aggressive women: Current perspectives and controversies.* New York: Guilford Press; Sisco, M., & Figueredo, A. (2008). Similarities between men and women in non-traditional aggressive sexuality: Prevalence, novel approaches to assessment and treatment applications. *Journal of Sexual Aggression, 14*(3), 253–266; Young, V. (1993b). Women abusers: A feminist view. In M. Elliott (Ed.), *Female sexual abuse of children.* New York: Guilford Press.
23. Greene, K., & Faulkner, S. (2005). Gender, belief in the sexual double standard, and sexual talk in heterosexual dating relationships. *Sex Roles, 53*(3/4), 239–251.
24. See Larimer, Lydum, Anderson, and Turner (1999); Sarrel and Masters (1982); and Waldner-Haugrud and Magruder (1995).
25. Byers, E. S. (1996). How well does the traditional sexual script explain sexual coercion? Review of a program of research. *Journal of Psychology and Human Sexuality, 8*(1/2), 7–25.

26. Archer, J. (2000). Sex differences in aggression between heterosexual partners: A meta-analytic review. *Psychological Bulletin, 126*(5), 651–680.
27. Fry, D. P., & Gabriel, A. H. (1994). Preface: The cultural construction of gender and aggression. *Sex Roles, 30*(3/4), 165–167.
28. Klein, O., & Snyder, M. (2003). Stereotypes and behavioral confirmation: From interpersonal to intergroup perspectives. *Advances in Experimental Social Psychology, 35,* 153–234.
29. Muehlenhard, C. L. (1998). The importance and danger of studying sexually aggressive women. In E. Anderson & C. Struckman-Johnson (Eds.), *Sexually aggressive women: Current perspectives and controversies.* New York: Guilford Press.
30. hooks, b. (2000). *Feminist theory: From margin to center* (2nd ed.). Cambridge, MA: South End Press.
31. Lisak, D. (1994). The psychological impact of sexual abuse: Content analysis of interviews with male survivors. *Journal of Traumatic Stress, 7*(4), 525–548; Macchietto, J. (1991). Aspects of male victimization and female aggression: Implications for counseling men. *Journal of Mental Health Counseling, 14*(3), 375–392.
32. Struckman-Johnson, C., & Struckman-Johnson, D. (2003). Tactics of sexual coercion: When men and women won't take no for an answer. *Journal of Sex Research, 40*(1), 76–86.
33. Ibid., p. 84.
34. Oswald, D & Russell, B. (2002). Sexual coercion and victimization of college men : The role of love styles. *Journal of Interpersonal Violence, 17*(3), 273–285; Shea, M. E. (1998). When the tables are turned: Verbal sexual coercion among college women. In P. Anderson & C. Struckman-Johnson (Eds.), *Sexually aggressive women: Current perspectives and controversies.* New York: Guilford Press.
35. Struckman-Johnson, C., & Struckman-Johnson, D. (1994). Men pressured and forced into sexual experience. *Archives of Sexual Behavior, 23,* 93–114.
36. Byers, E. S., & O'Sullivan, L. (1998). Similar but different: Men's and women's experiences of sexual coercion. In P. B. Anderson & C. Struckman-Johnson (Eds.), *Sexually aggressive women: Current perspectives and controversies.* New York: Guilford Press.
37. The countries that participated in the study included Asian countries, Australia/New Zealand, Canada, Europe, Latin America, the Middle East, and the United States. For a list of the countries and sites in the countries, see Hines (2007, p. 410).
38. Doroszewicz, K., & Forbes, G. (2008). Experiences with dating aggression and sexual coercion among Polish college students. *Journal of Interpersonal Violence, 23*(1), 58–73.
39. Lottes, I., & Weinberg, M. (1996). Sexual coercion among university students: A comparison of the United States and Sweden. *Journal of Sex Research, 34,* 67–76.
40. O'Sullivan, L., Byers, E., & Finkelman, L. (1998). A comparison of male and female college students' experiences of sexual coercion. *Psychology of Women Quarterly, 22,* 177–195.

41. Jackson, S., Cram, F., & Seymour, F. (2000). Violence and sexual coercion in high school students' dating relationships. *Journal of Family Violence, 15,* 23–36.
42. Kilpatrick, D. G. (2004). *Making sense of rape in America: Where do the numbers come from and what do they mean?* Atlanta, GA: Centers for Disease Control and Prevention;
43. Centers for Disease Control. (2004). *Sexual violence prevention: Beginning the dialogue.* Atlanta: Author.
44. Clark, M. D., & Carroll, M. (2008). Acquaintance rape scripts of women and men: Similarities and Differences. *Sex Roles, 58,* 616–625.
45. Bertone, C., & Camoletto, R. (2009). Beyond the sex machine? Sexual practices and masculinity in adult men's heterosexual accounts. *Journal of Gender Studies, 18,* 369–386; Crawford, M., & Popp, D. (2003). Sexual double standards: A review and methodological critique of two decades of research. *Journal of Sex Research, 40,* 13–26; Greene, K., & Faulkner, S. (2005). Gender, belief in the sexual double standard, and sexual talk in heterosexual dating relationships. *Sex Roles, 53*(3/4), 239–251.
46. Lisak, D. (1994). The psychological impact of sexual abuse: Content analysis of interviews with male survivors. *Journal of Traumatic Stress, 7*(4), 525–548.
47. Ibid.
48. Struckman-Johnson, C., & Struckman-Johnson, D. (1998). The dynamics and impact of sexual coercion of men by women. In P. B. Anderson & C. Struckman-Johnson (Eds.), *Sexually aggressive women: Current perspectives and controversies.* New York: Guilford Press.
49. Muehlenhard, C. L. (1998). The importance and danger of studying sexually aggressive women. In E. Anderson & C. Struckman-Johnson (Eds.), *Sexually aggressive women: Current perspectives and controversies.* New York: Guilford Press.
50. Two major educational organizations, the Harvard School of Public Health and the National Center on Addiction and Substance Abuse at Columbia University, have worked cooperatively with other organizations concerned about the growing problem of college-age alcohol and drug use. Both of these educational organizations have issued reports throughout the years on college-age drinking/drug use and the adverse outcomes to college students. These reports are the primary sources of information to provide a context for the following discussion on alcohol consumption and the risk for sexual coercion among college students. After 14 years in existence, the Harvard School of Public Health College Alcohol Study (CAS) issued its final report that was authored by Wechsler and Nelson (2008). The primary purpose of this 14-year study was to learn about the type of drinking college students engage in and the resulting consequences to students and those around them as a consequence of alcohol consumption. The CAS established a definition for heavy drinking and created a gender-specific definition of binge drinking: for a male, the definition is five drinks and for a female is four drinks, including binge drinking on three or more occasions in the past two weeks, the number of drinking occasions in the past 30 days, the number

of drunken occasions in the past 30 days, and the usual number of drinks on a drinking occasion. These measures have been adopted by other studies, such as Monitoring the Future, Centers for Disease Control and Prevention Youth Risk Behavior Surveillance, National College Health Risk Behavior Survey, and the World Health Organization.

51. Struckman-Johnson, C., & Struckman-Johnson, D. (2003). Tactics of sexual coercion: When men and women won't take no for an answer. *Journal of Sex Research, 40*(1), 82.
52. National Center on Addiction and Substance Abuse at Columbia University. (2007). *Wasting the best and the brightest: Substance abuse at America's colleges and universities (2007)*. New York: Author; Wechsler, H., & Nelson, T. (2008). What we have learned from the Harvard School of Public Health College Alcohol Study: Focusing attention on alcohol consumption and the environmental conditions that promote it. *Journal of Studies on Alcohol and Drugs, 69,* 1–10; Wechsler, H3. (2000). *Binge drinking on America's college campuses: Findings from the Harvard School of Public Health College Alcohol Study.*. Harvard School of Public Health: Author
53. Ibid.
54. Ibid.
55. Wechsler, H., & Nelson, T. (2008). What we have learned from the Harvard School of Public Health College Alcohol Study: Focusing attention on alcohol consumption and the environmental conditions that promote it. *Journal of Studies on Alcohol and Drugs, 69,* 1–10.
56. Ibid.
57. Centers for Disease Control and Prevention. (2000). *Tracking the hidden epidemics: Trends in STDs in the United States, 2000.* Atlanta, GA: Author; Centers for Disease Control and Prevention. (2008, June 8). Youth Risk Behavior Surveillance—United States, 2007. *Morbidity and Mortality Weekly Report,* Surveillance Summaries (Vol. 57, No. SS-4).
58. National Center on Addiction and Substance Abuse at Columbia University. (2007). *Wasting the best and the brightest: Substance abuse at America's colleges and universities (2007)*. New York: Author.
59. Abbey, A. (2002). Alcohol-related sexual assault: A common problem among college students. *Journal on the Study of Alcohol and Drugs, 14,* 118–128.
60. National Sexual Violence Resource Center sexual assault reports on college campuses reported to law enforcement (available at http://www.nsvrc.org/publications/nsvrc-publications).
61. Sisco, M., & Figueredo, A. (2008). Similarities between men and women in nontraditional aggressive sexuality: Prevalence, novel approaches to assessment and treatment applications. *Journal of Sexual Aggression, 14*(3), 253–266.
62. Byers, E. S. (1996). How well does the traditional sexual script explain sexual coercion? Review of a program of research. *Journal of Psychology and Human Sexuality, 8*(1/2), 7–25.

63. Capaldi, D., Kim, H., & Shortt, J. (2004). Women's involvement in aggression in young adult romantic relationships. In M. Pullatz (Ed.), *Aggression, antisocial behavior, and violence among girls*. New York: Guilford Press.
64. Wechsler, H., & Nelson, T. (2008). What we have learned from the Harvard School of Public Health College Alcohol Study: Focusing attention on alcohol consumption and the environmental conditions that promote it. *Journal of Studies on Alcohol and Drugs, 69,* 1–10.
65. Kubik, E., & Hecker, J. (2005). Cognitive distortions about sex and sexual offending: A comparison of sex offending girls, delinquent girls, and girls from the community. *Journal of Child Sexual Abuse, 14*(4), 43–69.
66. Bandura, A. (1986). *Social foundations of thought and action: A social cognitive theory*. Englewood Cliffs, NJ: Prentice Hall.; Weitzman, E., Toben, N., & Wechsler, H. (2003). Taking up binge drinking in college: The influences of person, social group and environment. *Journal of Adolescent Health,* 32, 26–35
67. Wechsler, H., & Nelson, T. (2008). What we have learned from the Harvard School of Public Health College Alcohol Study: Focusing attention on alcohol consumption and the environmental conditions that promote it. *Journal of Studies on Alcohol and Drugs, 69,* 1–10; Weitzman, E., Toben, N., & Wechsler, H. (2003). Taking up binge drinking in college: The influences of person, social group and environment. *Journal of Adolescent Health, 32,* 26–35.
68. Collins, R. L., Parks, G. A., & Marlatt, G. A. (1985). Social determinants of alcohol consumption: The effects of social interaction and model status on the self-administration of alcohol. *Journal of Consulting and Clinical Psychology, 53,* 189–200; Larimer, M., Lydum, A., Anderson, B., & Turner, A. (1999). Male and female recipients of unwanted sexual contact in a college student sample: Prevalence rates, alcohol use and depression symptoms. *Sex Roles, 40*(3/4), 295–308.
69. Struckman-Johnson, C., & Struckman-Johnson, D. (2003). Tactics of sexual coercion: When men and women won't take no for an answer. *Journal of Sex Research, 40*(1), 76–86.
70. Kalof, L., & Cargill, T. (1991). Fraternity and sorority membership and gender dominance attitudes. *Sex Roles, 25,* 419–425.
71. DeSantis, A. D. (2007). *Inside Greek U.: Fraternities, sororities, and the pursuit of pleasure, power and prestige.* Lexington: University Press of Kentucky.
72. Wuthrich, C. (2009). Reflections on personal responsibility: Sorority members at risk for interpersonal violence. *National Association of Student Personnel Administration (NASPA) Journal, 46*(2), 228–257.
73. Wechsler, H., & Nelson, T. (2008). What we have learned from the Harvard School of Public Health College Alcohol Study: Focusing attention on alcohol consumption and the environmental conditions that promote it. *Journal of Studies on Alcohol and Drugs, 69,* 1–10.
74. Smith, R., Pine, C., & Hawley, M. (1988). Social cognition about adult male victims of female sexual assault. *Journal of Sex Research, 24,* 101–241.

75. Struckman-Johnson, C. (1988). Forced sex on dates: It happens to men, too. *Journal of Sex Research, 24,* 234–241.
76. Wuthrich, C. (2009). Reflections on personal responsibility: Sorority members at risk for interpersonal violence. *National Association of Student Personnel Administration (NASPA) Journal, 46*(2), 228–257.
77. Larimer, M. E., Irvine, D. L., Kilmer, J. R., & Marlatt, G. A. (1997). College drinking and the Greek system: Examining the role of perceived norms for high-risk behavior. *Journal of College Student Development, 38*(6), 587–598.
78. Baron, R. S., Burgess, M. L., & Kao, C. F. (1991). Detecting and labeling prejudice: Do female perpetrators go undetected? *Personality and Social Psychology Bulletin, 17,* 115–123.
79. Abbey, A. (1991). Acquaintance rape and alcohol consumption on college campuses: How are they linked? *Journal of American College Health, 39,* 165–169.
80. Testa, M., & Dermen, K. (1999). The differential correlates of sexual coercion and rape. *Journal of Interpersonal Violence, 14*(5), 548–561; Wuthrich, C. (2009). Reflections on personal responsibility: Sorority members at risk for interpersonal violence. *National Association of Student Personnel Administration (NASPA) Journal, 46*(2), 228–257.
81. Byers, E. S., & O'Sullivan, L. (1998). Similar but different: Men's and women's experiences of sexual coercion. In P. B. Anderson & C. Struckman-Johnson (Eds.), *Sexually aggressive women: Current perspectives and controversies.* New York: Guilford Press; Struckman-Johnson, C., & Struckman-Johnson, D. (2003). Tactics of sexual coercion: When men and women won't take no for an answer. *Journal of Sex Research, 40*(1), 76–86.
82. Russell, B., & Oswald, D. (2002). Sexual coercion and victimization of college men: The role of love styles. *Journal of Interpersonal Violence, 17*(3), 273–285.
83. Larimer, M. E., Irvine, D. L., Kilmer, J. R., & Marlatt, G. A. (1997). College drinking and the Greek system: Examining the role of perceived norms for high-risk behavior. *Journal of College Student Development, 38*(6), 587–598.
84. Cook, S. L. (1995). Acceptance and expectation of sexual aggression in college students. *Psychology of Women Quarterly, 19,* 181–194.
85. Schewe, P., Adam, N., & Ryan, K. (2009). A qualitative analysis of the temptation to use force in sexual relationships. *Violence and Victims, 24*(2), 219–231.
86. Anderson, P. B. (1998). Women's motives for sexual initiation and aggression. In P. Anderson & C. Struckman-Johnson (Eds.), *Sexually aggressive women: Current perspectives and controversies.* New York: Guilford Press.
87. Burt, M. (1980). Cultural myths and supports for rape. *Journal of Personality and Social Psychology, 38,* 217–230.
88. Kubik, E., & Hecker, J. (2005). Cognitive distortions about sex and sexual offending: A comparison of sex offending girls, delinquent girls, and girls from the community. *Journal of Child Sexual Abuse, 14*(4), 43–69
89. Byers, E. S. (1996). How well does the traditional sexual script explain sexual coercion? Review of a program of research. *Journal of Psychology and Human Sexuality, 8*(1/2), 7–25; Sisco, M., & Figueredo, A. (2008). Similarities between men

and women in non-traditional aggressive sexuality: Prevalence, novel approaches to assessment and treatment applications. *Journal of Sexual Aggression, 14*(3), 253–266.

90. Sarwer, D., Kalichman, S., Johnson, J., Early, J., & Akram Ali, S. (1993). Sexual aggression and love styles: An exploratory study. *Archives of Sexual Behavior, 22*(3), 265–275.
91. National Center on Addiction and Substance Abuse at Columbia University. (2007). *Wasting the best and the brightest: Substance abuse at America's colleges and universities (2007)*. New York: Author; Abbey, A. (2002). Alcohol-related sexual assault: A common problem among college students. *Journal on the Study of Alcohol and Drugs, 14,* 118–128.
92. Collins, R. L., Parks, G. A., & Marlatt, G. A. (1985). Social determinants of alcohol consumption: The effects of social interaction and model status on the self-administration of alcohol. *Journal of Consulting and Clinical Psychology, 53,* 189–200.
93. Larimer, M., Lydum, A., Anderson, B., and Turner, A. (1999). Male and female recipients of unwanted sexual contact in a college student sample: Prevalence rates, alcohol use and depression symptoms. *Sex Roles, 40*(3/4), 295–308; Larimer, M. E., Irvine, D. L., Kilmer, J. R., & Marlatt, G. A. (1997). College drinking and the Greek system: Examining the role of perceived norms for high-risk behavior. *Journal of College Student Development, 38*(6), 587–598.
94. Struckman-Johnson, C., & Struckman-Johnson, D. (2003). Tactics of sexual coercion: When men and women won't take no for an answer. *Journal of Sex Research, 40*(1), 76–86.

CHAPTER 4

1. The quote is from a college student describing his experience of being on the receiving end of sexual coercion by one of his teachers in high school. Cited in Struckman-Johnson, C., & Struckman-Johnson, D. (1998). The dynamics and impact of sexual coercion of men by women. In P. B. Anderson & C. Struckman-Johnson (Eds.), *Sexually aggressive women: Current perspectives and controversies.* New York: Guilford Press.
2. American Association of University Women Educational Foundation. (2001). *Hostile hallways: Bullying, teasing and sexual harassment in school* (available at http://www.aauw.org).
3. van Dam, C. (2001). *Identifying child molesters: Preventing child sexual abuse by recognizing the patterns of the offenders.* New York: Haworth Press.
4. Russell, D. (1984). *Sexual exploitation: Rape, child sexual abuse and workplace harassment.* Beverly Hills, CA: Sage.
5. The report by the U.S. Department of Education defined educator sexual misconduct used the definition of educator sexual misconduct from the Ontario College of Teachers "Professional Advisory on Professional Misconduct Related to Sexual Abuse and Sexual Misconduct" (as cited by the U.S. Department of Education

[2004], p. 2) as a guide; educator sexual misconduct in this review is defined as any "behavior of a sexual nature which may constitute professional misconduct" (p. 1). Included in this broad listing are a continuum of the types of educator sexual conduct, including overt and covert actions: any conduct that would amount to sexual harassment under Title IX of the U.S. Education Amendments of 1972; any conduct that would amount to sexual abuse of a minor person under state criminal codes; any sexual relationship by an educator with a student, regardless of the student's age, with a former student under 18, and with a former student (regardless of age) who suffers from a disability that would prevent consent in a relationship; all students enrolled in the school and in any organization in which the educator holds a position of trust and responsibility are included; any activity directed toward establishing a sexual relationship, such as sending intimate letters; engaging in sexualized dialogue in person, via the Internet, in writing, or by phone; making suggestive comments; and dating a student. This definition includes criminal, civil, and professional codes of conduct and responds to the missing elements in much of the literature on child sexual abuse. This definition covers what is also commonly referred to as sexual abuse and/or sexual harassment of children. This definition is central to the development of future studies on educator sexual misconduct.

6. U.S. Department of Education, Office of the Under Secretary. (2004). *Educator sexual misconduct: A synthesis of existing literature.* Washington, DC: Author.
7. American Association of University Women Educational Foundation. (2001). *Hostile hallways: Bullying, teasing and sexual harassment in school* (available at http://www.aauw.org).
8. Rubin, S., & Biggs, J. (1999). *Teachers that sexually abuse students: An administrative and legal guide.* Lancaster, PA: Technomic Publishing Company.
9. Rand, M. (2009, September). *Criminal victimization, 2008* (NCJ 227777). Washington, DC: U.S. Department of Justice, Office of Justice Programs.
10. Allen, C. (1990). Women as perpetrators of child sexual abuse: Recognition barriers. In A. Horton, B. Johnson, L. Roundy, & D. Williams (Eds.), *The incest perpetrator: A family member no one want to treat.* Newbury Park, CA: Sage; Allen, H. (1987). *Justice unbalanced: Gender, psychiatry and judicial decisions.* Milton Keynes: Open University Press.
11. Snyder, H. N. (2000). *Sexual assault of young children as reported to law enforcement: Victim, offender and incident characteristics* (NCJ 182990). Washington, DC: U.S. Department of Justice, Office of Justice Programs, Bureau of Justice Statistics; Tardiff, M., Auclair, N., Jacob, M., & Carpenter, J. (2005). Sexual abuse perpetrated by adult and juvenile females: An ultimate attempt to resolve a conflict associated with maternal identity. *Child Abuse and Neglect, 29,* 153–167.
12. Alaggia, R., & Millington, G. (2008). Male child sexual abuse: A phenomenology of betrayal. *Journal of Clinical Social Work, 36,* 265–275; Alaggia, R. (2005). Disclosing the trauma of child sexual abuse: A gender analysis. *Journal of Loss and Trauma, 10,* 453–470.

13. Duncan, K. (2004). *Healing from the trauma of childhood sexual abuse: The journey for women.* Westport, CT: Praeger.
14. Matthews, J. (1993). Working with female sexual abusers In M. Elliott (Ed.), *Female sexual abuse of children.* New York: Guilford Press; Matthews, R. (1989). *Female sexual offenders: An exploratory study.* Brandon, VT: The Safer Society Press. Matthews was the first to coin the terms "teacher/lover" for a category of female sexual offenders.
15. Duncan, K. (2006, September 28). *Does gender matter: Female sex offenders and the impact to victims.* Paper presented at the Association for the Treatment of Sexual Abusers Conference, Chicago, IL.
16. CNN, Larry King, interview with Mary Kay Letourneau and Vili Fualaau (available at http://transcripts.cnn.com/TRANSCRIPTS/0606/05/lkl.01.html).
17. Duncan, K. (2004). *Healing from the trauma of childhood sexual abuse: The journey for women* (chapter 2 and appendix A). Westport, CT: Praeger.
18. Ibid., chapter 4 on chronic shock symptoms and dissociation.
19. Duncan, K. (2004). *Healing from the trauma of childhood sexual abuse: The journey for women.* Westport, CT: Praeger.
20. *Female coach sentenced in sex case*, KGO-TV, San Francisco, February 15, 2006 (available at http://abclocal.go.com/kgo/story?section=news/local&id=3911563).
21. Ibid.
22. Chow, E., & Choy, A. (2002). Clinical characteristics and treatment response to SSRI in a female pedophile. *Archives of Sexual Behavior, 31*(2), 211–215; Hall, R., & Hall, R. (2007). A profile of pedophilia: Definition, characteristics of offenders, recidivism, treatment outcomes and forensic issues. *Mayo Clinic Proceedings, 82*(4), 457–471 (available at http://www.mayoclinicproceedings.com/content/82/4/457.full.pdf+html); Sandler, J., & Freeman, N. (2007). Typology of female sex offenders: A test of Vandiver and Kercher. *Sex Abuse, 19,* 73–89.
23. Rubin, S., & Biggs, J. (1999). *Teachers that sexually abuse students: An administrative and legal guide.* Lancaster, PA: Technomic Publishing Company.
24. Abel, G., & Harlow, N. (2002). The Abel and Harlow Child Molestation Study excerpted from *The Stop Child Molestation Book* (2002), published by Xlibris; Abel, G., Gore, D., Holland E., Camp N., Becker, J., & Rathnew J. (1989). The measurement of the cognitive distortions of child molesters. *Annals of Sex Research, 2,* 135–152.
25. Rosencrans, B. (1997). *The last secret.* Brandon, VT: The Safer Society Press; Sgroi, S., & Sargent, N. (1993). Impact and treatment issues for victims of childhood sexual abuse by female perpetrators, In M. Elliott (Ed.), *Female sexual abuse of children.* New York: Guilford Press.
26. Baron, R.S., Burgess, M.L., & Kao, C.F. (1991). Detecting and labeling prejudice: Do female perpetrators go undetected? *Personality and Social Psychology Bulletin, 17,* 115–123.

27. Duncan, K. (2006, September 28). *Does gender matter: Female sex offenders and the impact to victims.* Paper presented at the Association for the Treatment of Sexual Abusers (ATSA) Conference, Chicago, IL.
28. Andersson, N., & Ho-Foster, A. (2008). 13,915 reasons for equity in sexual offences legislation: A national school-based survey in South Africa. *International Journal for Equity in Health, 9*(20), 1–6.
29. Deering, R., & Mellor, D. (2007). Female-perpetrated child sex abuse: Definitional and categorisational analysis. *Psychiatry, Psychiatry and Law, 14*(2), 218–226.
30. National Campaign to Prevent Teen and Unplanned Pregnancy. (n.d.). *Sex and tech: results from a survey of teen and young adults* (available at http://www.TheNationalCampaign.org).
31. Duncan, K. (2009, November). Speaking out. Stepping up: Preventing abuse in our schools. *Indianapolis Woman Magazine.*
32. American Psychological Association, Task Force on the Sexualization of Girls. (2007). *Report of the APA Task Force on the Sexualization of Girls.* Washington, DC: Author (available at http://www.apa.org/pi/wpo/sexualization.html).
33. Rapsey, R., & Murachver, T. (2006). Adolescent sexuality. In R. D. McNaulty & M. Burnette (Eds.), *Sex and sexuality: Vol. 1. Sexual deviation and sexual offenses.* Westport, CT: Praeger.
34. Duncan, K. (2009, November). Speaking out. Stepping up: Preventing abuse in our schools. *Indianapolis Woman Magazine.*
35. American Association of University Women Educational Foundation. (1993). *Hostile hallways: The AAUW survey on sexual harassment in America's schools.* Washington, DC: Author (available at http://www.aauw.org).
36. American Association of University Women Educational Foundation. (2001). *Hostile hallways: Bullying, teasing and sexual harassment in school* (available at http://www.aauw.org).
37. American Association of University Women Educational Foundation. (2004). *Harassment free hallways: How to stop sexual harassment in school: A Guide for students, parents, and schools* (available at http://www.aauw.org).
38. American Association of University Women Educational Foundation. (2001). *Hostile hallways: Bullying, teasing and sexual harassment in school* (available at http://www.aauw.org).
39. Levine, K. (2006). No penis, no problem. *Fordham Urban Law Journal.*
40. American Association of University Women Educational Foundation. (2001). *Hostile Hallways: Bullying, teasing and sexual harassment in school* (available at http://www.aauw.org).
41. Ibid.
42. Jackson, S., Cram, F., & Seymour, F. (2000). Violence and sexual coercion in high school students' dating relationships. *Journal of Family Violence, 15,* 23–36.
43. American Association of University Women Educational Foundation. (2001). *Hostile hallways: Bullying, teasing and sexual harassment in school* (available at http://www.aauw.org).

44. Wechsler, H., & Nelson, T. (2008). What we have learned from the Harvard School of Public Health College Alcohol Study: Focusing attention on alcohol consumption and the environmental conditions that promote it. *Journal of Studies on Alcohol and Drugs, 69,* 1–10.
45. American Association of University Women Educational Foundation. (2004). *Harassment free hallways: How to stop sexual harassment in school: A guide for students, parents, and schools* (available at http://www.aauw.org).
46. Hopper, J. (1998). *Prevalence of the sexual abuse of boys* (available at http://www.jimhopper.com/abstracts).
47. Duncan, L., & Williams, L. (1998). Gender role socialization and male-on-male vs. female-on-male child sexual abuse. *Sex Roles, 39*(9/10), 765–785.
48. Media Education Foundation (available at http://www.mediaed.org/wp/links).
49. American Psychological Association, Task Force on the Sexualization of Girls. (2007). *Report of the APA Task Force on the Sexualization of Girls.* Washington, DC: Author (available at http://www.apa.org/pi/wpo/sexualization.html).

CHAPTER 5

1. Saradjian, J., with Helga Hanks. (1996). *Women who sexually abuse children: From research to clinical practice.* New York: Wiley.
2. Wright, L., & Hatcher, A. (2006). Treatment of sex offenders. In R. McNaulty & N. M. Burnette (Eds.), *Sex and sexuality: Sexual deviation and sexual offenses* (Vol. 3). Westport, CT: Praeger.
3. Gannon, T., & Rose, M. (2008). Female child sexual offenders: Towards integrating theory and practice. *Aggression and Violent Behavior, 13,* 442–461; Johansson-Love, J., & Fremouw, W. (2006). A critique of the female sexual perpetrator research. *Aggression and Violent Behavior, 11,* 12–26.
4. Allen, C. (1990). Women as perpetrators of child sexual abuse: Recognition barriers. In A. Horton, B. Johnson, L. Roundy, & D. Williams (Eds.), *The incest perpetrator: A family member no one want to treat.* Newbury Park, CA: Sage; Allen, H. (1987). *Justice unbalanced: Gender, psychiatry and judicial decisions.* Milton Keynes: Open University Press; Bunting, L. (2007). Dealing with a problem that doesn't exist? Responses to female perpetrated child sexual abuse. *Child Abuse Review, 16,* 252–267.
5. Levine, K. (2006). No penis, no problem. *Fordham Urban Law Journal.*
6. Denov, M. (2004b). *Perspectives on female sex offending: A culture of denial.* Burlington, VT: Ashgate.
7. Turton, J. (2007). *Child abuse, gender and society.* New York: Routledge.
8. Elliott, M. (1993b). What survivors tell us, In M. Elliott (Ed.), *Female sexual abuse of children.* New York: Guilford Press; Rosencrans, B. (1997). *The last secret.* Brandon, VT: The Safer Society Press.
9. Saradjian, J., with Helga Hanks. (1996). *Women who sexually abuse children: From research to clinical practice.* New York: Wiley.

10. Duncan, K. (2004). *Healing from the trauma of childhood sexual abuse: The journey for women.* Westport, CT: Praeger.
11. *Female coach sentenced in sex case*, KGO-TV, San Francisco, February 15, 2006 (available at http://abclocal.go.com/kgo/story?section=news/local&id=3911563).
12. Duncan, K. (2004). *Healing from the trauma of childhood sexual abuse: The journey for women.* Westport, CT: Praeger.
13. Fedoroff, J., Fishel, A., & Fedoroff, B. (1999). A case series of women evaluated for paraphilic sexual disorders. *Canadian Journal of Human Sexuality, 8*(2), 127–140.
14. Wright, L., & Hatcher, A. (2006). Treatment of sex offenders. In R. McNaulty & N. M. Burnette (Eds.), *Sex and sexuality: Sexual deviation and sexual offenses* (Vol. 3). Westport, CT: Praeger.
15. It is interesting that emotional gratification has been explored as a motivating factor for female sexual offending with less recognition sexual that sexual motivations can be equally relevant for female sexual offending.
16. Vandiver, D. (2006a). Female sex offenders. In R. D. McNaulty & M. Burnette (Eds.), *Sex and sexuality: Sexual deviation and sexual offenses* (Vol. 3, pp. 47–80). Westport, CT: Praeger.
17. Fedoroff, J., Fishel, A., & Fedoroff, B. (1999). A case series of women evaluated for paraphilic sexual disorders. *Canadian Journal of Human Sexuality, 8*(2), 127–140; Saradjian, J., with Helga Hanks. (1996). *Women who sexually abuse children: From research to clinical practice.* New York: Wiley; Sgroi, S., & Sargent, N. (1993). Impact and treatment issues for victims of childhood sexual abuse by female perpetrators. In M. Elliott (Ed.), *Female sexual abuse of children.* New York: Guilford Press; Turton, J. (2007). *Child abuse, gender and society.* New York: Routledge.
18. Turton, J. (2007). *Child abuse, gender and society.* New York: Routledge.
19. Miller, H., Turner, K., & Henderson, C. E. (2009). Psychopathology of sex offenders: A comparison of males and females using latent profile analysis. *Criminal Justice and Behavior, 36*(8), 778–792.
20. Gannon, T., & Rose, M. (2008). Female child sexual offenders: Towards integrating theory and practice. *Aggression and Violent Behavior, 13,* 442–461; Johansson-Love, J., & Fremouw, W. (2006). A critique of the female sexual perpetrator research. *Aggression and Violent Behavior, 11,* 12–26.
21. Johansson-Love, J., & Fremouw, W. (2006). A critique of the female sexual perpetrator research. *Aggression and Violent Behavior,* 11, 12– 26.
22. Sandler, J., & Freeman, N. (2007). Typology of female sex offenders: A test of Vandiver and Kercher. *Sex Abuse, 19,* 73–89; Vandiver, D., & Kercher, G. (2004). Offender and victim characteristics of registered female sexual offenders in Texas: A proposed typology of female sexual offenders. *Sexual Abuse: A Journal of Research and Treatment, 16*(2), 121–137.
23. Sandler, J., & Freeman, N. (2007). Typology of female sex offenders: A test of Vandiver and Kercher. *Sex Abuse, 19,* 73–89.

24. Case files from Karen A. Duncan, 1987.
25. Reference to Association for the Treatment of Sexual Abusers publication "Pedophiles and Child Molesters: The Differences" (available at http://www.atsa.com). For a review of adult male sex offender typologies, see Johnson (2007) and Schwartz and Cellini (1995).
26. Hebephile refers to an individual with a deviant sexual interest toward pubescent young people, and the victim's age-group may be distinguished as 11 to 14 for girls and 15 or 16 for boys (see Anderson, 2007; McCarty, 1988).
27. For a review of the research by Faller, Gannon, and Rose; Johansson and Fremouw; McCarty, Matthews, Sandler, and Freeman; and Vandiver and Kercher, see the Bibliography.
28. Faller, K.C. (1987). Women who sexually abuse children. *Violence and Victims, 2*(4), 263–276, identified a group of females who were of borderline intelligence, as did McCarty, L.M. (1986). Mother-child incest: Characteristics of the offender. *Child Welfare, 65*(5), 447–458.
29. Saradjian, J., with Helga Hanks. (1996). *Women who sexually abuse children: From research to clinical practice.* New York: Wiley.
30. Maletzky, B. M. (1991). *Treating the sex offender.* London: Sage.
31. Saradjian, J., with Helga Hanks. (1996). *Women who sexually abuse children: From research to clinical practice.* New York: Wiley.
32. Faller, K.C. (1987). Women who sexually abuse children. *Violence and Victims, 2*(4), 263–276.
33. Bunting, L. (2005). *Females who sexually offend against children: Responses of child protection and criminal justice systems.* London: National Society for the Prevention of Cruelty to Children.
34. World Health Organization. (2006). *Preventing child maltreatment: A guide to taking action and generating evidence.* Geneva: Author.
35. Dube, S., Anda, R., Whitfield, C., Brown, D., Felitti, V., Dong, M., et al. (2005). Long-term consequences of childhood sexual abuse by gender of victim. *American Journal of Preventive Medicine, 28*(5), 430–438.
36. Dong, M., Anda, R., Dube, S., Giles, W., & Felitti, V. (2003). The relationship of exposure to childhood sexual abuse to other forms of abuse, neglect, and household dysfunction during childhood. *Child Abuse and Neglect, 27,* 625–639.
37. Whitaker, D., Le, B., Hanson, R. K., Baker, C., McMahon, P., Ryan, G. (2008). Risk factors for the perpetration of child sexual abuse: A review and meta-analysis. *Child Abuse and Neglect,* 32, 529–548.
38. Duncan, K. (2004). *Healing from the trauma of childhood sexual abuse: The journey for women.* Westport, CT: Praeger.
39. American Association of University Women Educational Foundation. (1993). *Hostile hallways: The AAUW survey on sexual harassment in America's schools* (available at http://www.aauw.org).
40. American Association of University Women Educational Foundation. (2001). *Hostile hallways: Bullying, teasing and sexual harassment in school* (available at http://www.aauw.org).

41. Duncan, K. (2009, November). Speaking out. Stepping up: Preventing abuse in our schools. *Indianapolis Woman Magazine.*
42. Bader, S., Scalora, M. Casady, T., & Black, S. (2008). Female sexual abuse and criminal justice intervention: A comparison of child protective service and criminal justice samples. *Child Abuse and Neglect, 32,* 111–119.
43. Beck, A., Adams, D., & Guerino, P. (2008, July). *Sexual violence reported by juvenile correctional authorities, 2005–06* (NCJ215337). Washington, DC: U.S. Department of Justice, Office of Justice Programs, Bureau of Justice Statistics.
44. Miller, H., Turner, K., & Henderson, C. E. (2009). Psychopathology of sex offenders: A comparison of males and females using latent profile analysis. *Criminal Justice and Behavior, 36*(8), 778–792.
45. Quinsey, V., & Lalumiere, M. (2001). *Assessment of sexual offenders against children* (2nd ed.). APSAC Study Guides 1. Thousand Oaks, CA: American Professional Society on the Abuse of Children and Sage; Wright, L., & Hatcher, A. (2006). Treatment of sex offenders. In R. McNaulty & N. M. Burnette (Eds.), *Sex and sexuality: Sexual deviation and sexual offenses* (Vol. 3). Westport, CT: Praeger.

Bibliography

Abbey, A. (1991). Acquaintance rape and alcohol consumption on college campuses: How are they linked? *Journal of American College Health, 39,* 165–169.

Abbey, A. (2002). Alcohol-related sexual assault: A common problem among college students. *Journal on the Study of Alcohol and Drugs, 14,* 118–128.

Abbey, A., Ross, L. T., & McDuffie, D. (1994). Alcohol's role in sexual assault. In R. R. Watson (Ed.), *Drug and alcohol abuse reviews: Vol. 5. Addictive behaviors in women.* Totowa, NJ: Humana Press.

Abel, G., Gore, D., Holland E., Camp N., Becker, J., & Rathnew J. (1989). The measurement of the cognitive distortions of child molesters. *Annals of Sex Research, 2,* 135–152.

Abel, G., & Harlow, N. (2002). The Abel and Harlow Child Molestation Study excerpted from *The stop child molestation book.* Published by Xlibris.

Alaggia, R. (2005). Disclosing the trauma of child sexual abuse: A gender analysis. *Journal of Loss and Trauma, 10,* 453–470.

Alaggia, R., & Millington, G. (2008). Male child sexual abuse: A phenomenology of betrayal. *Journal of Clinical Social Work, 36,* 265–275.

Allen, C. (1990). Women as perpetrators of child sexual abuse: Recognition barriers. In A. Horton, B. Johnson, L. Roundy, & D. Williams (Eds.). *The incest perpetrator: A family member no one want to treat.* Newbury Park, CA: Sage.

Allen, C. (1991). *Women and men who sexually abuse children: A comparative analysis.* Orwell, VT: The Safer Society Press.

Allen, H. (1987). *Justice unbalanced: Gender, psychiatry and judicial decisions.* Milton Keynes: Open University Press.

Allgier, E., Lamping, J. (1998). Theories, politics and sexual coercion. In P. B. Anderson & C. Struckman-Johnson (Eds.), *Sexually aggressive women: Current perspectives and controversies*. New York: Guilford Press.

American Association of University Women Educational Foundation. (1993). *Hostile hallways: The AAUW survey on sexual harassment in America's schools.* Washington, DC: Author (available at http://www.aauw.org).

American Association of University Women Educational Foundation. (2001). *Hostile hallways: Bullying, teasing and sexual harassment in school* (available at http://www.aauw.org).

American Association of University Women Educational Foundation. (2004). *Harassment free hallways: How to stop sexual harassment in school: A guide for students, parents, and schools* (available at http://www.aauw.org).

American Psychiatric Association. (1994) *Diagnostic and statistical manual of mental disorders* (4th ed.). Washington, DC: Author.

American Psychological Association, Task Force on the Sexualization of Girls. (2007). *Report of the APA Task Force on the Sexualization of Girls.* Washington, DC: Author (available at http://www.apa.org/pi/wpo/sexualization.html).

Anderson, P. B. (1996). Correlates of college women's self-reports of heterosexual aggression. *Sexual Abuse: A Journal of Research and Treatment, 8*(2), 121–131.

Anderson, P. B. (1998). Women's motives for sexual initiation and aggression. In P. Anderson & C. Struckman-Johnson (Eds.), *Sexually aggressive women: Current perspectives and controversies.* New York: Guilford Press.

Anderson, P., & Aymani, R. (1993). Male and female differences in reports of women's heterosexual initiation and aggression. *Archives of Sexual Behavior, 28,* 243–253.

Anderson, P., & Struckman-Johnson, C. (Eds.). (1998). *Sexually aggressive women.* London: Guilford Press.

Andersson, N., & Ho-Foster, A. (2008). 13,915 reasons for equity in sexual offences legislation: A national school-based survey in South Africa. *International Journal for Equity in Health, 9*(20), 1–6.

Araji, S., & Finkelhor, D. (1986). Abusers: A review of the research. In D. Finkelhor, *A sourcebook on child sexual abuse.* Beverly Hills, CA: Sage.

Arata, C. M. (1998). To tell or not to tell: Current functioning of child sexual abuse survivors who disclosed their victimization. *Child Maltreatment, 3,* 63–71.

Archer, J. (1999). Assessment of the reliability of the Conflict Tactics Scale. *Journal of Interpersonal Violence, 14*(12), 1263–1289.

Archer, J. (2000). Sex differences in aggression between heterosexual partners: A meta-analytic review. *Psychological Bulletin, 126*(5), 651–680.

Association for the Treatment of Sexual Abusers. (n.d.). *Pedophiles and child molesters: The differences* (available at http://www.atsa.com).

Babcock, J., Miller, S., & Siard, C. (2003). Toward a typology of abusive women: Differences between partner-only and generally violent women in the use of violence. *Psychology of Women Quarterly, 13,* 46–59.

Bader, S., Scalora, M. Casady, T., & Black, S. (2008). Female sexual abuse and criminal justice intervention: A comparison of child protective service and criminal justice samples. *Child Abuse and Neglect, 32,* 111–119.

Bandura, A. (1986). *Social foundations of thought and action: A social cognitive theory.* Englewood Cliffs, NJ: Prentice Hall.

Banning, A. (1989). Mother–son incest: Confronting a prejudice. *Child Abuse and Neglect, 13,* 563–570.

Baron, R. S., Burgess, M. L., & Kao, C. F. (1991). Detecting and labeling prejudice: Do female perpetrators go undetected? *Personality and Social Psychology Bulletin, 17,* 115–123.

Basile, K., Chen, J., Black, M., & Saltzman, L. (2007). Prevalence and characteristics of sexual violence victimization among U.S. adults, 2001–2003. *Violence and Victims, 22*(4), 437–448.

Baumeister, R., & Stillman, T. (2006). Erotic plasticity: Nature, culture, gender and sexuality. In R. D. McNaulty & M. Burnette (Eds.), *Sex and sexuality: Sexual deviation and sexual offenses* (Vol. 1). Westport, CT: Praeger.

Beck, A., Adams, D., & Guerino, P. (2008, July). *Sexual violence reported by juvenile correctional authorities, 2005–06* (NCJ215337). Washington, DC: U.S. Department of Justice, Office of Justice Programs, Bureau of Justice Statistics.

Becker, J., Hall, S., & Stinson, J. (2001). Female sexual offenders: Clinical, legal and policy issues. *Journal of Forensic Psychology Practice, 1,* 29–50.

Bem, S. L. (1983). Gender schema theory and its implications for child development: Raising gender-aschematic children in a gender-schematic society. *Signs, 8,* 596–616.

Bender, L., & Blau, A. (1937). The reaction of children to sexual relations with adults. *American Journal of Orthopsychiatry, 7,* 500–518.

Bergen, R. K., Edleson, J. L., & Renzetti, C. M. (Eds.). (2005). *Violence against women: Classic papers.* Boston, MA: Pearson, Allyn and Bacon.

Berkowitz, A. (2004, October). *Working with men to prevent violence against women: Program modalities and formats* (Pt. 2). Applied Research Forum and the National Online Research Center on Violence Against Women available at http://new.vawnet.org/category/Documents.php?docid=414&category_id=496.

Bertone, C., & Camoletto, R. (2009). Beyond the sex machine? Sexual practices and masculinity in adult men's heterosexual accounts. *Journal of Gender Studies, 18,* 369–386.

Bifulco, A., Brown, G. W., & Adler, Z. (1990). Early sexual abuse and clinical depression in adult life. *British Journal of Psychiatry, 159,* 115–122.

Bjorkqvist, K. (1994). Sex differences in physical, verbal and indirect aggression: A review of recent research. *Sex Roles, 30*(3/4), 177–188.

Bloom, B., Owen, B., & Covington, S. (2005, May). *Gender-responsive strategies for women offenders: A summary of research, practice and guiding principles for women offenders.* Washington, DC: U.S. Department of Justice, National Institute of Corrections.

Blumenthal, S., Gudjonsson, G., & Burs, J. (1999). Cognitive distortions and blame attribution in sex offenders against adults and children. *Child Abuse and Neglect, 23,* 129–143.

Bookwala, J. (2002). Adult attachment styles and aggressive behaviors in dating relationships. *Journal of Social and Personal Relationships, 15,* 175–190.

Boroughs, D. (2004). Female sexual abusers of children. *Children and Youth Services Review, 26,* 481–487.

Bowlby, J. (1982). *Attachment and loss: Vol. 1. Attachment* (2nd ed.). London: Hogarth Press.

Bowlby, J. (1988). *A secure base.* New York: Basic Books.

Bradley, A., & Wood, J. (1996). How do children tell? The disclosure process in child sexual abuse. *Child Abuse and Neglect, 20,* 881–891.

Briere, J., & Zaidi, L. (1989). Sexual abuse histories and sequelae in female psychiatric emergency room patients. *American Journal of Psychiatry, 146*(12), 1602–1606.

Brownmiller, S. (1975). *Against our will: Men, women and rape.* New York: Simon and Schuster.

Buckingham, D., & Bragg, S. (2003). *Young people, media and personal relationships.* Broadcasting Standards Commission (available at http://www.bsc.org.uk).

Bumby, K., & Bumby, N. (1997). Adolescent female sexual offenders. In B. K. Schwartz & H. R. Cellini (Eds.), *The sex offender: Vol. 2. New insights, treatment innovations and legal developments.* Kingston, NJ: Civic Research Institute.

Bunting, L. (2005). *Females who sexually offend against children: Responses of child protection and criminal justice systems.* London: National Society for the Prevention of Cruelty to Children.

Bunting, L. (2007). Dealing with a problem that doesn't exist? Responses to female perpetrated child sexual abuse. *Child Abuse Review, 16,* 252–267.

Burbank, V. (1994). Cross-cultural perspectives on aggression in women and girls: An introduction. *Sex Roles, 30*(3/4), 169–176.

Burroughs, D. (2004). Female sexual abusers of children. *Children and Youth Services Review, 26,* 481–487.

Burt, M. (1980). Cultural myths and supports for rape. *Journal of Personality and Social Psychology, 38,* 217–230.

Byers, E. S. (1996). How well does the traditional sexual script explain sexual coercion? Review of a program of research. *Journal of Psychology and Human Sexuality, 8*(1/2), 7–25.

Byers, E. S., & O'Sullivan, L. (1998). Similar but different: Men's and women's experiences of sexual coercion. In P. B. Anderson & C. Struckman-Johnson (Eds.), *Sexually aggressive women: Current perspectives and controversies.* New York: Guilford Press.

Cano, A., Avery-Leaf, S., Cascardi, M., & O'Leary, K. (1998). Dating violence in two high school samples: Discriminating variables. *Journal of Primary Prevention, 18*(4), 431–446.

Capaldi, D., Kim, H., & Shortt, J. (2004). Women's involvement in aggression in young adult romantic relationships. In M. Pullatz (Ed.), *Aggression, antisocial behavior, and violence among girls.* New York: Guilford Press.

Carl, J., & VanDeusen, K. (2004). Risk factors for male sexual aggression on college campuses. *Journal of Family Violence, 19*(5), 279–289.

Carlson, B., Maciol, K., & Schneider, J. (2006). Sibling incest: Reports from forty-one survivors. *Journal of Child Sexual Abuse, 15*(4), 19–34.

Carney, M., Buttell, F., & Dutton, D. (2007). Women who perpetrate intimate partner violence: A review of the literature with recommendations for treatment. *Aggression and Violent Behavior, 12,* 108–115.

Carrado, M., George, M., Loxam, F., Jones, L., & Templar, D. (1996). Aggression in British heterosexual relationships: A descriptive analysis. *Aggressive Behavior, 22,* 401–415.

Center for Sex Offender Management. (2007a, March). *Female sex offenders.* Washington, DC: U.S. Department of Justice.

Center for Sex Offender Management. (2007b, July). *The importance of assessment in sex offender management: An overview of key principles and practices.* Washington, DC: U.S. Department of Justice.

Center for Sex Offender Management. (2008, November). *The comprehensive approach to sex offender management.* Washington, DC: U.S. Department of Justice.

Centers for Disease Control. (2004). *Sexual violence prevention: Beginning the dialogue.* Atlanta, GA: Author.

Centers for Disease Control and Prevention. (2000). *Tracking the Hidden Epidemics: Trends in STDs in the United States, 2000.* Atlanta, GA: Author.

Centers for Disease Control and Prevention. (2008, June 8). Youth risk behavior surveillance—United States, 2007. *Morbidity and Mortality Weekly Report,* Surveillance Summaries (Vol. 57, No. SS-4).

Chideckel, M. (1935). *Female sex perversions: The sexually aberrated woman a she is.* New York: Eugenics.

Child Welfare Information Gateway. (n.d.). *Sexual abuse.* Retrieved from http://www.childwelfare.gov/can/types/sexualabuse/.

Chow, E., & Choy, A. (2002). Clinical characteristics and treatment response to SSRI in a female pedophile. *Archives of Sexual Behavior, 31*(2), 211–215.

Christopher, K., Lutz-Zois, E., & Reinhardt, A. (2007). Female sexual offenders: Personality pathology as a mediator of the relationship between childhood sexual abuse history and sexual abuse perpetration against others. *Child Abuse and Neglect, 31,* 871–883.

Clark, M. D., & Carroll, M. (2008). Acquaintance rape scripts of women and men: Similarities and Differences. *Sex Roles, 58,* 616–625.

Cleckley, H. (1988). *The mask of sanity* (5th ed.). Thousand Oaks, CA: Sage.

Clements-Schreiber, M.E., Rempel, J.K., & Desmarais, S. (1998). Women's sexual pressure tactics and adherence to related attitudes: A step toward prediction. *Journal of Sex Research, 35,* 197–205.

CNN. (2006, June 5). *Larry King*. Interview with Mary Kay Letourneau and Vili Fualaau (available at http://transcripts.cnn.com/TRANSCRIPTS/0606/05/lkl.01.html).

Coker, A., Davis, K., Arias, I., Desai, S., Sanderson, M., Brandt, H., et al. (2002). Physical and mental health effects of intimate partner violence for men and women. *American Journal of Preventive Medicine, 23*(4), 260–268.

Coleman, V. (1994). Lesbian battering: The relationship between personality and perpetration of violence. *Violence and Victims, 9*(2), 139–152.

Collins, R. L., Parks, G. A., & Marlatt, G. A. (1985). Social determinants of alcohol consumption: The effects of social interaction and model status on the self-administration of alcohol. *Journal of Consulting and Clinical Psychology, 53,* 189–200.

Condy, S., Templer, D., Brown, R., & Veaco, L. (1987). Parameters of sexual contact of boys with women. *Archives of Sexual Behavior, 16*(5), 379–394.

Cook, S. L. (1995). Acceptance and expectation of sexual aggression in college students. *Psychology of Women Quarterly, 19,* 181–194.

Corcoran, J. (2004). Treatment outcome research with the non-offending parents of sexually abused children: A critical review. *Journal of Child Sexual Abuse, 13*(2), 59–84.

Correctional Service of Canada. (1995). *Case studies of female sex offenders in the Correctional Service of Canada.* Ottawa: Author. Retrieved August 8, 2008, from http://www.csc-scc.gc.ca/text/pblct/so/female/female-01-eng.shtml

Cortoni, F., & Hanson, R. (2005). *A review of recidivism rates of adult female sexual offenders.* Ottawa: Correctional Service of Canada.

Courtois, C. A. 1988. *Healing the incest wound: Adult survivors in therapy.* New York: Norton.

Crawford, M., & Popp, D. (2003). Sexual double standards: A review and methodological critique of two decades of research. *Journal of Sex Research, 40,* 13–26.

Crewdson, J. (1988). *By silence betrayed: Sexual abuse of children in America.* New York: Harper & Row.

Davin, P. (1999). Secrets revealed: A study of female sex offenders. In E. Bear (Ed.), *Female sexual abusers: Three views*. Brandon, VT: The Safer Society Press.

Davis, C., Yarber, W., Bauserman, R., Schreer, G., & Davis S. (Eds). (1998). *Handbook of sexuality-related measures*. Thousand Oak, CA: Sage Publications.

Deaux, K., & Lafrance, M. (1998). Gender. In D. T. Gilbert, S. T. Fiske, & G. Lindzey (Eds.), *Handbook of social psychology* (Vol. 2). Boston: McGraw-Hill.

Deering, R., & Mellor, D. (2007). Female-perpetrated child sex abuse: Definitional and categorisational analysis. *Psychiatry, Psychiatry and Law, 14*(2), 218–226.

Dellasega, C., & Nixon, C. (2002). *12 strategies that will end female bullying.* New York: Simon & Schuster.

DeMause, L. (1974). The evolution of childhood. In L. DeMause (Ed.), *The history of childhood.* New York: Psychohistory Press.

DeMause, L. (1991). The universality of incest. *Journal of Psychohistory, 19*(2) (available at http://www.psychohistory.com/htm/05_history.html).

Denov, M. (2001). A culture of denial: Exploring professional perspectives on female sex offending. *Canadian Journal of Criminology, 43,* 303–329.

Denov, M. (2003a). The myth of innocence: Sexual scripts and the recognition of child sexual abuse by female perpetrators. *Journal of Sex Research, 40*(3), 303–314.

Denov, M. (2003b). To a safer place? Victims of sexual abuse by females and their disclosures to professionals. *Child Abuse and Neglect, 27,* 47–61.

Denov, M. (2004a). The long-term effects of child sexual abuse by female perpetrators: A qualitative study of male and female victims. *Journal of Interpersonal Violence, 19*(10), 1137–1156.

Denov, M. (2004b). *Perspectives on female sex offending: A culture of denial.* Burlington, VT: Ashgate.

Denov, M., & Cortoni, F. (2006). Women who sexually abuse children. In C. Hilarski & J. S. Wodarski (Eds.), *Comprehensive mental health practice with sex offenders and their families.* Binghamton, NY: Haworth Press.

DeSantis, A. D. (2007). *Inside Greek U.: Fraternities, sororities, and the pursuit of pleasure, power and prestige.* Lexington: University Press of Kentucky.

Dobash, R. P., Dobash, E. R., Wilson, M., & Daly, M. (1992). The myth of sexual symmetry in marital violence. *Social Problems, 391*(1), 71–91.

Dobash, R. P., & Dobash, E. R. (1978). *Wives: The "appropriate" victims of marital violence. Reflection on violence against women: Classic papers* (available at http://www.mincava.umn.edu/classics).

Dong, M., Anda, R., Dube, S., Giles, W., & Felitti, V. (2003). The relationship of exposure to childhood sexual abuse to other forms of abuse, neglect, and household dysfunction during childhood. *Child Abuse and Neglect, 27,* 625–639.

Dooley, A. (2008). *Sexualization of youth helping to drive exploitation: Efforts must look at what's causing supply and demand* (available at http://www.unicef.ca/portal/Secure/Community/502/WCM/HELP/take_action/CSEC/Sexualization%20of%20youth%20helping%20to%20drive%20exploitation.pdf).

Doroszewicz, K., & Forbes, G. (2008). Experiences with dating aggression and sexual coercion among polish college students. *Journal of Interpersonal Violence,* 23(1), 58–73.

Dowd, L., Leisring, P., & Rosenbaum, A. (2005). Partner aggressive women: Characteristics and treatment attrition. *Violence and Victims, 20*(2), 219–233.

Dube, S., Anda, R., Whitfield, C., Brown, D., Felitti, V., Dong, M., et al. (2005). Long-term consequences of childhood sexual abuse by gender of victim. *American Journal of Preventive Medicine, 28*(5), 430–438.

Duncan, K. (2004). *Healing from the trauma of childhood sexual abuse: The journey for women.* Westport, CT: Praeger.

Duncan, K. (2005a). The impact of child sexual abuse on parenting: A female perspective (Article 58). *VISTAS: Compelling Perspectives on Counseling 2005, 58,* 275–277. Alexandria, VA: American Counseling Association.

Duncan, K. (2005b). The relationship between posttraumatic stress disorder and substance abuse in women with a history of childhood sexual abuse trauma (Article 60). *VISTAS: Compelling Perspectives on Counseling 2005, 58,* 267–270. Alexandria, VA: American Counseling Association.

Duncan, K. (2006, September 28). *Does gender matter: Female sex offenders and the impact to victims.* Paper presented at the Association for the Treatment of Sexual Abusers Conference, Chicago, IL.

Duncan, K. (2009, November). Special insert on preventing sexual violence: Article Speaking out. Stepping up: Preventing abuse in our schools. *Indianapolis Woman Magazine* (n.p.).

Duncan, L., & Williams, L. (1998). Gender role socialization and male-on-male vs. female-on-male child sexual abuse. *Sex Roles, 39*(9/10), 765–785.

Dutton, D., & Nicholls, T. (2005). The gender paradigm in domestic violence research and theory: Part 1—The conflict of theory and data. *Aggression and Violent Behavior, 10,* 680–714.

Editorial Board & Jen Calantone, Editor in Chief. (2010, March 31). A message from *The Eagle. The Eagle.* Retrieved from http://www.theeagleonline.com/opinion/story/a-message-from-the-eagle/.

Ehrmin, J. (1996). No more mother blaming: A feminists nursing perspective on the mother's role in father-daughter incest. *Archives of Psychiatric Nursing, 10*(4), 252–260.

Eldridge, H., & Saradjian, J. (2000). Replacing the function of abusive behaviors for the offender: Remaking relapse prevention in working with women who sexually abuse children. In D. R. Laws, S. M. Hudson, & T. Ward (Eds.), *Remaking relapse prevention with sex offenders: A sourcebook.* Thousand Oaks, CA: Sage.

Elliot, A., & Carnes, C. (2001). Reactions of nonoffending parents to the sexual abuse of their child: A review of the literature. *Child Maltreatment, 6*(4), 314–331.

Elliott, M. (Ed.). (1993a). *Female sexual abuse of children.* New York: Guilford Press.

Elliott, M. (1993b). What survivors tell us. In M. Elliott (Ed.), *Female sexual abuse of children.* New York: Guilford Press.

Evert, K. (1987). *When you're ready: Women healing from physical and sexual abuse by her mother.* MD: Launch Press.

Faith Trust Institute. (n.d.). *History of Violence Against Women Act of 1994* (available at http://www.ncdsv.org/images/HistoryofVAWA.pdf).

Faller, K. C. (1987). Women who sexually abuse children. *Violence and Victims, 2*(4), 263–276.

Faller, K. C. (1989). Characteristics of a clinical sample of sexually abused children: How boy and girl victims differ. *Child Abuse and Neglect, 13*(2), 281–291.

Faller, K. C. (1995). A clinical sample of women who have sexually abused children. *Journal of Child Sexual Abuse, 4*(3), 13–29.

Fazel, S., Sjostedt, G. Grann, M., & Langstrom, N. (2008). Sexual offending in women and psychiatric disorder: A national case-control study. *Archives of Sexual Behavior.* 39(1), 161–167.

Feder, L., & Henning, K. (2005). A comparison of male and female dually arrested domestic violence offenders. *Violence and Victims, 20*(2), 153–171.

Federal Bureau of Investigation. (n.d.). *Crimes against children* (available at http://www.fbi.gov/hq/cid/cac/registry.htm).

Fedoroff, J., Fishel, A., & Fedoroff, B. (1999). A case series of women evaluated for paraphilic sexual disorders. *Canadian Journal of Human Sexuality, 8*(2), 127–140.

Ferguson, C., & Meehan, D. (2005). An analysis of females convicted of sex crimes in the state of Florida. *Journal of Child Sexual Abuse, 14*(1), 75–89.

Fiebert, M., & Tucci, L. (1998). Sexual coercion: Men victimized by women. *Journal of Men's Studies, 6,* 127–133.

Fincham, F., Grych, J., & Osborne, L. (1994). Does marital conflict cause children maladjustment? Directions and challenges for longitudinal research. *Journal of Family Psychology, 8,* 128–140.

Fineran, S., & Bennett, L. (1999). Gender and power issues of peer sexual harassment among teenagers. *Journal of Interpersonal Violence, 14*(6), 626–641.

Finkelhor, D. (1984). *Child sexual abuse: New theory and research.* New York: Free Press.

Finkelhor, D. (1994). Current information on the scope and nature of child sexual abuse. *The Future of Children, 4*(2), 31–53.

Finkelhor, D., Araji, S., Baron, L., Peter, S. D., & Wyatt G. E. (1986). *A source book on child sexual abuse.* Thousand Oaks, CA: Sage.

Finkelhor, D., & Dziuba-Leatherman, J. (1994). Children as victims of violence: A national survey. *Pediatrics, 94*(4, Pt. 1), 413–420.

Finkelhor, D., Hotaling, G., Lewis, I. A., & Smith, C. (1990). Sexual abuse in a national survey of adult men and women: Prevalence, characteristics, and risk factors. *Child Abuse and Neglect, 14,* 19–28.

Finkelhor, D., & Russell, D. (1984). Women as perpetrators. In D. Finkelhor (Ed.), *Child sexual abuse: New theory and research.* New York: Free Press.

Finkelhor, D., Williams, L. M., & Burns, N. (1988). *Nursery crimes: Sexual abuse in day care.* Newbury Park, CA: Sage.

Ford, H. (2006). *Women who sexually abuse children.* West Sussex: Wiley.

Fowler, M. (2010, March 31). New sexual assault policies considered. *The Eagle.* Retrieved from http://www.theeagleonline.com/news/story/new-sexual-assault-policies-considered/.

Franklin, K. (2007). Sex offender industry sees invasion of "hebephile" hunters. *American Chronicle.* (available at http://www.americanchronicle.com/articles/view/45622).

Fritz, G. S., Stoll, K., & Wagner, N. A. (1981). A comparison of males and females who were sexually molested as children. *Journal of Sex Marital Therapy, 7,* 4–59.

Fromuth, M. E., & Burkhart, B. R. (1987). Childhood sexual victimization among college men: Definitional and methodological issues. *Violence and Victims, 2*(4), 241–253.

Fry, D. P., & Gabriel, A. H. (1994). Preface: The cultural construction of gender and aggression. *Sex Roles, 30*(3/4), 165–167.

Fullilove, M., Fullilove, R., Smith, M., Winkler, K., Michael, C., Panzer, P., et al. (1993). Violence, trauma, and posttraumatic stress disorder among women drug users. *Journal of Traumatic Stress, 6*(4), 533–543.

Gagnon, J. H. (1990). The explicit and implicit use of the scripting perspective in sex research. In J. Bancroft, C. M. Davis, & D. Weinstein (Eds.), *Annual review of sex research* (Vol. 1). Mount Vernon, IA: Society for the Scientific Study of Sex.

Gamez-Guadix, M., & Straus, M. (2009). *Childhood and adolescent victimization and sexual coercion and assault by male and female university students*. Family Research Laboratory, University of New Hampshire, Durham, NH 03824 available at http://pubpages.unh.edu/~mas2/CP91%20accepted%20Deviant%20 Behavior.pdf.

Gannon, T., & Rose, M. (2008). Female child sexual offenders: Towards integrating theory and practice. *Aggression and Violent Behavior, 13,* 442–461.

Gannon, T., Rose, M., & Ward, T. (2008). A descriptive model of the offense process for female sexual offenders. *Sexual Abuse: A Journal of Research and Treatment, 20*(3), 352–374.

Garbarino, J., & deLara, E. (2002). *And words can hurt forever.* New York: Simon & Schuster.

Gazzaniga, M. (2005). *The ethical brain.* New York: Dana Press.

George, M. (1994). Riding the donkey backwards: Men as the unacceptable victims of marital violence. *Journal of Men's Studies, 3*(2), 137–159.

Geraci, L. (1986). Making shelters safe for lesbians. In K. Lobel (Ed.), *Naming the violence: Speaking out about lesbian battering.* Seattle, WA: The Seal Press.

Gil-Gonzalez, D., Vives-Cases, C., Ruiz, M., Carrasco-Portino, M., & Alvarez-Dardet, C. (2007). Childhood experiences of violence in perpetrators as a risk factor of intimate partner violence: A systematic review. *Journal of Public Health, 30*(1), 14–22.

Gil-Rivas, V., Fiorentine, R., Anglin, M. D., & Taylor, E. (1997). Sexual and physical abuse: Do they compromise drug treatment outcomes? *Journal of Substance Abuse Treatment, 14*(4), 351–358.

Girl gang-raped for two hours at homecoming dance while a dozen people watched and did nothing. (2009, October 27). *New York Daily News.com.* (available at http://www.nydailynews.com/news/national/2009/10/27/2009-10-27_girl_gang_raped_for_two_hours_after_homecoming_dance__while_a_dozen_people_watch.html).

Girshick, L. (2001). *No more denying: Facing woman to woman sexual violence* (available at http://www.loribgirshick.com/booklet.html).

Girshick, L. (2002). *Woman-to-woman sexual violence: Does she call it rape?* Boston, MA: Northeastern University Press.

Glasser, M., Kolvin I., Campbell, D., Glasser, A., Leitch, I., & Farrelly, S. (2001). Cycle of child sexual abuse: Links between being a victim and becoming a perpetrator. *British Journal of Psychiatry, 179,* 482–494.

Glaze, L., & Bonczar, T. (2006). *Probation and parole in the United States, 2005.* Washington, DC: U.S. Department of Justice, Office of Justice Programs, Bureau of Justice Statistics.

Gontek, I. (2009, Spring). *Sexual violence against lesbian women in South Africa* (available at http://www.irnweb.org/siteFiles/Publications/308CB8F2AF7C696FB233B433CE3A4295.pdf).

Graffunder, C., Noonan, R., Cox, P., & Wheaton, J. (2004). Through a public health lens. Preventing violence against women: An update from the US Centers for Disease Control and Prevention. *Journal of Women's Health, 13*(1), 5–14.

Gray, H. M., & Foshee, V. (1997). Adolescent dating violence: Differences between one-sided and mutually violent profiles. *Journal of Interpersonal Violence, 12,* 126–141.

Greene, K., & Faulkner, S. (2005). Gender, belief in the sexual double standard, and sexual talk in heterosexual dating relationships. *Sex Roles, 53*(3/4), 239–251.

Greenfield, L., & Snell, T. (1999). *Women offenders* (NCJ 175688). Washington, DC: U.S. Department of Justice, Office of Justice Programs, Bureau of Justice Statistics (available at http://www.ojp.usdoj.gov/bjs/pub/pdf/wo.pdf).

Greeting Card Association, *Mother's Day* (available at http://www.greetingcard.org/about.php?ID=121).

Grice, D., Brady, K., Dustan, L., Malcolm, R., & Kilpatrick, D. (1995). Sexual and physical assault history and posttraumatic stress disorder in substance-dependent individuals. *American Journal on Addiction, 4*(4), 297–305.

Gries, L. T., Goh, D., & Cavanaugh, J. (1996). Factors associated with disclosure during child sexual abuse assessment. *Journal of Child Sexual Abuse, 5*(3), 1–19.

Groth, N. (1979a). *Men who rape: The psychology of the offender.* New York: Plenum Press.

Groth, N. (1979b). Sexual trauma in the life histories of rapists and child molesters. *Victimology: An International Journal, 4*(1), 10–16.

Groth, N., & Burgess, A. (1980). Male rape: Offenders and victims. *American Journal of Psychiatry, 13*(7), 806–810.

Hall, R., & Hall, R. (2007). A profile of pedophilia: Definition, characteristics of offenders, recidivism, treatment outcomes and forensic issues. *Mayo Clinic Proceedings, 82*(4), 457–471 (available at http://www.mayoclinicproceedings.com/content/82/4/457.full.pdf+html).

Hamel, J. (2009). Toward a gender-inclusive conception of intimate partner violence research and theory: Part 2—New directions. *International Journal of Men's Health, 8*(1), 41–59.

Hammock, G., & Richardson, D. (1993). Blaming drunk victims: Is it just world or sex role violation? *Journal of Applied Social Psychology, 23*(1), 1574–1586.

Hannon, R., Hall, D., Nash, H., Formati, J., & Hopson, T. (2000). Judgments regarding sexual aggression as a function of aggressor and victim. *Sex Roles, 43*(5/6), 311–322.

Hannon, R., Kuntz, T., Van Laar, S., & Williams, J. (1996). College students' judgments regarding sexual aggression during a date. *Sex Roles, 35,* 765–778.

Hanson, R. K., & Thornton, D. (2000). *Static-99: Improving actuarial risk assessments among sex offenders.* Retrieved October 7, 2006, from http://ww2.psepc-sppcc.gc.ca/publications/corrections/199902_e.pdf.

Hare, R. D. (1996). Psychopathy: A clinical construct whose time has come. *Criminal Justice and Behavior, 23,* 25–54.

Harold, G., Fincham, F., Osborne, L., & Conger, R. (1997). Mom and dad are at it again: Adolescent perceptions of marital conflict and adolescent psychological distress. *Developmental Psychology, 33,* 333–350.

Harris, A., & Musso, M. (2006). *Violence Against Women Act 2005* (available at http://www.center4research.org/vawa2005.html).

Hart, B. (2005). Lesbian battering: An examination (1986) and reflection to original paper. In R. K. Bergen, J. L. Edleson, & C. M. Renzetti (Eds.), *Violence against women: Classic papers.* Boston, MA: Pearson, Allyn and Bacon.

Hendrick, C., & Hendrick, S. (2003). Romantic love: Measuring Cupid's arrow. In S. Lopez & C. Snyder (Eds.), *Positive psychological assessment: A handbook of models and measures.* Washington, DC: American Psychological Association.

Henning, K., Renauer, B., & Holdford, R. (2007). Victim or offender? Heterogeneity among women arrested for intimate partner violence. *Journal of Family Violence, 21,* 351–368.

Henry J. Kaiser Family Foundation. (n.d.). *National Survey of Adolescents and Young Adults: Sexual Health Knowledge, Attitudes and Experience* (Publication 3218) (available at http://www.kff.org).

Herman, J. (1981). *Father-daughter incest.* Cambridge, MA: Harvard University Press.

Hess, A. (2010, March 29). American University student newspapers vandalized over "rape apology." *Washington City Paper.* Retrieved from http://www.washingtoncitypaper.com/blogs/sexist/2010/03/29/american-university-student-newspapers-vandalized-over-rape-apology/

Hetherton, J., & Beardsall, L. (1998). Decisions and attitudes concerning child sexual abuse: Does the gender of the perpetrator make a difference to child protection professionals? *Child Abuse and Neglect, 22*(12), 1265–1283.

Higgs, D., Canavan, M., & Meyer, W. (1992). Moving from defense to offense: The development of an adolescent female sex offender. *Journal of Sex Research, 29*(1), 131–139.

Hines, D. (2007). Predictors of sexual coercion against women and men: A multilevel multinational study of university students. *Archives of Sexual Behavior, 36*(3), 403–422.

Hines, D. & Saudino, K. (2003). Gender differences in psychological, physical and sexual aggression among college students using the revised conflict tactics scale. *Violence and Victims, 18*(2), 197–217.

Hislop, J. (2001). *Female sex offenders: What therapists, law enforcement and child protection services need to know.* Ravensdale, WA: Issues Press.

Holzworth-Munroe, A. (2005). Female perpetration of physical aggression against an intimate partner: A controversial new topic of study. *Violence and Victims, 20*(2), 251–259.

Home Office. (2002). *Protecting the public, strengthening protection against sex offenders and reforming the law on sexual offences* (CM 5668). London: The Stationery Office.

hooks, b. (2000). *Feminist theory: From margin to center* (2nd ed.). Cambridge, MA: South End Press. (Original work published 1984.)

Hopper, J. (1998). *Prevalence of the sexual abuse of boys* (available at http://www.jimhopper.com/abstracts).

Hopper, J. (2009). *Sexual abuse of males: Prevalence, possible lasting effects and resources* (available at http://www.jimhopper.com/male-ab).

Hunt, L. M. (2006). *Females who sexually abuse in organisations working with children. Characteristics, international and Australian prevalence rates: Implications for child protection.* Melbourne: Child Wise.

Hunter, J., & Matthews, R. (1997). Sexual deviance in females. In D. R. Laws and W. O'Donohue (Eds.), *Sexual deviance: Theory, assessment, and treatment.* New York: Guilford Press.

Igelman, R. S., Ryan, B. E., Gilbert, A. M., Bashant, C., & North, K. (2008). Best practices for serving traumatized children and families. *Juvenile and Family Court Journal, 59*(4), 35–47.

Jackson, S. (1978). The social context of rape: Sexual scripts and motivation. *Women's Studies International Quarterly, 1,* 27–38.

Jackson, S., Cram, F., & Seymour, F. (2000). Violence and sexual coercion in high school students' dating relationships. *Journal of Family Violence, 15,* 23–36.

James, B., & Nasjleti, M. (1983). *Treating sexually abused children and their families.* Palo Alto, CA: Consulting Psychologists Press.

Jespersen, A., Lalumiere, M., & Seto, M. (2009). Sexual abuse history among adult sex offenders and non-sex offenders: A meta-analysis. *Child Abuse and Neglect, 33*(3), 179–192.

Johansson-Love, J., & Fremouw, W. (2006). A critique of the female sexual perpetrator research. *Aggression and Violent Behavior, 11,* 12–26.

Johansson-Love, J., & Fremouw, W. (2009). Female sex offenders: A controlled comparison of offender and victim/crime characteristics. *Journal of Family Violence, 34,* 367–376.

Johnson, R., Ross, M., Wendell, T., Williams, M. Carvajal, R., & Peters, R. (2006). Prevalence of childhood sexual abuse among incarcerated males in county jail. *Child Abuse and Neglect, 30,* 75–86.

Johnson, S. A. (2007). *Physical abusers and sexual offenders: Forensic and clinical strategies.* New York: Taylor and Francis Group.

Jonason, P., & Marks, P. (2009). Common vs. uncommon sexual acts: Evidence for the sexual double standard. *Sex Roles, 60,* 357–365.

Jones, E. J. (1996). Introduction to the special section on attachment and psychopathology: Part I. *Journal of Consulting and Clinical Psychology, 64*(1), 5–7.

Kahn, A. S., Jackson, J., Kully, C., Badger, K., & Halvorsen, J. (2003). Calling it rape: Differences in experiences of women who do or do not label their sexual assault as rape. *Psychology of Women Quarterly, 27,* 233–242.

Kalof, L. (1993). Rape-supportive attitudes and sexual victimization experiences of sorority and nonsorority women. *Sex Roles, 29*(11/12), 767–780.

Kalof, L., & Cargill, T. (1991). Fraternity and sorority membership and gender dominance attitudes. *Sex Roles, 25,* 419–425.

Kaplan, M., & Green, A. (1995). Incarcerated female sex offenders: A comparison of sexual histories with eleven female sex offenders. *Sexual Abuse: A Journal of Research and Treatment, 7,* 287–300.

Kasl, C. D. (1990). Female perpetrators of sexual abuse: A feminist view. In M. Hunter (Ed.), *The sexually abused male: Vol. 1. Prevalence, impact and treatment.* Lexington, MA: Lexington Books.

Katz, J., Kuffel, S. W., & Coblentz, A. (2002). Are there gender differences in sustaining dating violence? An examination of frequency, severity, and relationship satisfaction. *Journal of Family Violence, 17,* 247–271.

Kaufman, K., Wallace, A., Johnson, C., & Reeder, M. (1995). Comparing female and male perpetrators' modus operandi. *Journal of Interpersonal Violence, 10*(3), 322–333.

Kellogg, N. (2005). The American Academy of Pediatrics: Clinical report. The evaluation of sexual abuse in children. *Pediatrics, 116*(2), 506–512.

Kernsmith, P., & Kernsmith, R. (2009). Female pornography use and sexual coercion perpetration. *Deviant Behavior, 30,* 589–610.

Kihyun, K., Noll, J., Putnam, F., & Trickett, P. (2007). Psychosocial characteristics of nonoffending mothers of sexually abused girls: Findings from a prospective multigenerational study. *Child Maltreatment, 12,* 338–351.

Kilpatrick, D. G. (2004). *Making sense of rape in America: Where do the numbers come from and what do they mean?* Atlanta, GA: Centers for Disease Control and Prevention.

Klein, O., & Snyder, M. (2003). Stereotypes and behavioral confirmation: From interpersonal to intergroup perspectives. *Advances in Experimental Social Psychology, 35,* 153–234.

Knepper, A. (2010, March 28). Dealing with AU's anti-sex brigade. *Eagle.* Retrieved from http://www.theeagleonline.com/opinion/story/dealing-with-aus-anti-sex-brigade/.

Koss, M. P., & Oros, C. J. (1982). Sexual experiences survey: A research instrument investigating sexual aggression and victimization. *Journal of Consulting and Clinical Psychology, 50,* 455–457.

Krahe, B. (2000). Sexual scripts and heterosexual aggression. In T. Eckes & M. Hanns (Eds.), *The developmental social psychology of gender.* Mahwah, NJ: Lawrence Erlbaum Associates.

Krahe, B., Waizenhofer, E., & Moller, I. (2003). Women's sexual aggression against men: Prevalence and predictors. *Sex Roles, 49,* 219–232.

Krause, T. (2005, November 23). "Lafave sign please." TBO.com News. Retrieved from http://news.tbo.com/news/MGBL1FT6DGE.html.

Krug, R. (1989). Adult males report of childhood sexual abuse by mothers: Case descriptions, motivations and long-term consequences. *Child Abuse and Neglect, 13,* 111–119.

Krug, E. G., et al. (Eds.). (2002). *World report on violence and health.* Geneva: World Health Organization.

Kubik, E., & Hecker, J. (2005). Cognitive distortions about sex and sexual offending: A comparison of sex offending girls, delinquent girls, and girls from the community. *Journal of Child Sexual Abuse, 14*(4), 43–69.

Longdon, C. (1993). A survivor and therapist's viewpoint, In M. Elliott (Ed.), *Female sexual abuse of children.* New York: Guilford Press.

Langevin, R., Wright, P., & Handy, L. (1989). Characteristics of sex offenders who were sexually victimized as children. *Annals of Sex Research, 2,* 227–253.

Larimer, M. E., Irvine, D. L., Kilmer, J. R., & Marlatt, G. A. (1997). College drinking and the Greek system: Examining the role of perceived norms for high-risk behavior. *Journal of College Student Development, 38*(6), 587–598.

Larimer, M., Lydum, A., Anderson, B., & Turner, A. (1999). Male and female recipients of unwanted sexual contact in a college student sample: Prevalence rates, alcohol use and depression symptoms. *Sex Roles, 40*(3/4), 295–308.

Lawson, C. (1993). Mother-son sexual abuse: Rare or underreported? A critique of the research. *Child Abuse and Neglect, 17,* 261–269.

Leder, M., Emans, S., Hafler, J., & Rappaport, L. (1999). Addressing sexual abuse in the primary care setting. *Pediatrics, 104*(2), 270–275.

Lee, J. A. (1973). *The colors of love.* Englewood Cliffs, NJ: Prentice Hall.

Levine, K. (2006). No penis, no problem. *Fordham Urban Law Journal,* 2006; Emory Public Law Research Paper No. 05-37. Available at SSRN: http://ssrn.com/abstract=869028.

Lev-Wiesel, R. (2006). Intergenerational transmission of sexual abuse? Motherhood in the shadow of incest. *Journal of Child Sexual Abuse, 15*(2), 75–101.

Lewin, L., & Bergin, C. (2001). Attachment behaviors, depression and anxiety in nonoffending mothers of child sexual abuse victims. *Child Maltreatment, 6,* 365–375.

Lewis, C., & Stanley, C. (2000). Women accused of sexual offences. *Behavioral Sciences and the Law, 18,* 73–81.

Lisak, D. (1994). The psychological impact of sexual abuse: Content analysis of interviews with male survivors. *Journal of Traumatic Stress, 7*(4), 525–548.

Lottes, I. (1991). The relationship between nontraditional gender roles and sexual coercion. *Journal of Psychology and Human Sexuality, 4,* 89–109.

Lottes, I., & Weinberg, M. (1996). Sexual coercion among university students: A comparison of the United States and Sweden. *Journal of Sex Research, 34,* 67–76.

Macchietto, J. (1991). Aspects of male victimization and female aggression: Implications for counseling men. *Journal of Mental Health Counseling, 14*(3), 375–392.

Macchietto, J. (1998). Treatment issues of adult male victims of female sexual aggression. In P. B. Anderson & C. Struckman-Johnson (Eds.), *Sexually aggressive women: Current perspectives and controversies.* New York: Guilford Press.

Main, M. (1996). Introduction to the special section on attachment and psychopathology: Part II. Overview of the field of attachment. *Journal of Consulting and Clinical Psychology, 64*(2), 5–7.

Malamuth, N. (1998). The confluence model as an organizing framework for research on sexually aggressive men: Risk, moderators, imagined aggression and pornography consumption. In R. Green & E. Donnerstein (Eds.) *Aggression: Theoretical and empirical reviews.* New York: Academic Press.

Maletzky, B. M. (1991). *Treating the sex offender.* London: Sage.

Margolin, L. (1987). The effects of mother-son incest. *Lifestyles, 8,* 104–114.

Marks, M., & Fraley, R. (2005). The sexual double standard: factor or fiction? *Sex Roles, 52,* 175–186.

Marks, M., & Fraley, R. (2006). Confirmation bias and the sexual double standard. *Sex Roles, 54*(1/2), 19–26.

Marvesti, J. (1986). Incestuous mothers. *American Journal of Forensic Psychiatry, 7,* 63–69.

Mathis, J. (1972). *Clear thinking about sexual deviations.* Chicago, IL: Nelson-Hall Company.

Matthews, J. (1993). Working with female sexual abusers. In M. Elliott (Ed.), *Female sexual abuse of children.* New York: Guilford Press.

Matthews, R. (1989). *Female sexual offenders: An exploratory study.* Brandon, VT: The Safer Society Press.

McCarty, L. M. (1986). Mother-child incest: Characteristics of the offender. *Child Welfare, 65*(5), 447–458.

McCloskey, K., & Raphael, D. (2005). Adult perpetrator gender asymmetries in child sexual assault victim selection: Results from the 2000 National Incident-Based Reporting System. *Journal of Child Sexual Abuse, 14*(4), 1–24.

McMullen, R. (1990). *Male rape: Breaking the silence of the last taboo.* Boston, MA: GMP Publishers.

McNaulty, R. D., & Burnette, M. (2006a). *Sex and sexuality: Vol. 1. Sexual deviation and sexual offenses.* Westport, CT: Praeger.

McNaulty, R. D., & Burnette, M. (2006b). *Sex and sexuality: Vol. 2. Sexual deviation and sexual offenses.* Westport, CT: Praeger.

McNaulty, R. D., & Burnette, M. (2006c). *Sex and sexuality: Vol. 3. Sexual deviation and sexual offenses.* Westport, CT: Praeger.

Medeiros, R., & Straus, M. (2006). Risk factors for physical violence between dating partners: Implications for gender-inclusive prevention and treatment of family violence. In J. Hamel & T. Nicholls (Eds.), *Family approaches in domestic violence: A practitioner's guide to gender-inclusive research and treatment.* New York: Springer Publishing.

Mendel, M. P. (1995). *The male survivor: The impact of sexual abuse.* Thousand Oaks, CA: Sage.

Messenger Newspaper. (2009, October 2). "Colin Blanchard from Smallbridge, Rochdale, Vanessa George from Efford, Plymouth, and Angela Allen from Bulwell, Nottinghamshire, pleaded guilty to a string of child sex offenses" (available at http://www.messengernewspapers.co.uk/news/4661391.Trio_admit_string_of_child_sex_offences).

Meyer, J. (2000). *History of sexual assault prevention efforts* (available at http://www.ccasa.org/documents/History_of_SAPE_Long_Version.pdf).

Mikler-Ramisetty, S., Caetano, R., & McGrath, C. (2007). Sexual aggression among white, black, and Hispanic couples in the U.S.: Alcohol use, physical assault and psychological aggression as its correlates. *American Journal of Drug and Alcohol Abuse, 33,* 31–43.

Miller, A. (1985). *Thou shalt not be aware: Society's betrayal of the child.* London: Pluto.

Miller, H., Turner, K., & Henderson, C. E. (2009). Psychopathology of sex offenders: A comparison of males and females using latent profile analysis. *Criminal Justice and Behavior, 36*(8), 778–792.

Mitchell, J., & Morse, J. (1998). *From victims to survivors: Reclaimed voices of women sexually abused in childhood by females.* Washington, DC: Taylor and Francis Group.

Moffatt, M. (1989). *Coming of age in New Jersey: College and American culture.* New Brunswick, NJ: Rutgers University Press.

Money, J. (2003). History, causality, and sexology. *Journal of Sex Research, 40*(3), 237–239.

Montaldo, C. (n.d.). *Mary Kay Letourneau* (available at http://crime.about.com/od/history/p/Letourneau.htm).

Moore, J., & Hagedorn, J. (2001, March). *Female gangs: A focus on research* (Juvenile Justice Bulletin). Washington, DC: U.S. Department of Justice, Office of Justice Programs, Office of Juvenile Justice and Delinquency Prevention.

Moore, T., & Pepler, D. (2006). Wounding words: Maternal verbal aggression and children's adjustment. *Journal of Family Violence, 21*(1), 89–93.

Morrison, S., & Greene, E. (1992). Juror and expert knowledge of child sexual abuse. *Child Abuse and Neglect, 16*(4), 595–613.

Mosher, D., & Tomkins, S. (1988). Scripting the macho man: Hypermasculine socialization and enculturation. *Journal of Sex Research, 25,* 60–84.

Moynihan, M., & Banyard, V. (2008). Community responsibility for preventing sexual violence: A pilot study with campus Greeks and intercollegiate athletes. *Journal of Prevention and Intervention in the Community, 30*(1/2), 23–38.

Muehlenhard, C. L. (1998). The importance and danger of studying sexually aggressive women. In E Anderson & C. Struckman-Johnson (Eds.), *Sexually aggressive women: Current perspectives and controversies.* New York: Guilford Press.

Muehlenhard, C., & Cook S. (1988). Men's self-reports of unwanted sexual activity. *Journal of Sex Research, 24,* 58–72.

Najavits, L., Gastfriend, M., Barger, J., Reif, S., Muenz, L., Blaine, M., et al. (1998). Cocaine dependence with and without PTSD among subjects in the National Institute on Drug Abuse Collaborative Cocaine Treatment Study. *American Journal of Psychiatry, 155*(2), 214–219.

Nansel, T. R., Overpeck, M., Pilla, R. S., Ruan, W. J., Simons-Morton, B., & Scheidt, P. (2001). Bullying behaviors among United States Youth: Prevalence and association with psychosocial adjustment. *Journal of the American Medical Association, 285*(16), 2094–2100.

Nathan, P., & Ward, T. (2002). Female sex offenders: Clinical and demographic features. *Journal of Sexual Aggression, 8*(1), 5–21.

National Campaign to Prevent Teen and Unplanned Pregnancy. (n.d.). *Sex and tech: Results from a survey of teen and young adults* (available at http://www.The NationalCampaign.org).

National Center on Addiction and Substance Abuse at Columbia University. (2007). *Wasting the best and the brightest: Substance abuse at America's colleges and universities.* New York: Author.

National Center on Addiction and Substance Abuse at Columbia University. (2003, February). *Teen tipplers: America's underage drinking epidemic* (Revised). New York: Author.

National Center for Injury Prevention and Control. (2003). *Costs of intimate partner violence against women in the United States.* Atlanta, GA: Author (available at http://www.cdc.gov/ncipc/pub-res/ipv_cost/ipv.htm).

National Child Traumatic Stress Network, Justice System Consortium. (2009). *Helping traumatized children: Tips for judges.* Los Angeles: Author (available at http://www.nctsnet.org/nctsn_assets/pdfs/JudgesFactSheet.pdf).

National Coalition to Prevent Child Sexual Exploitation. (2008, Washington, D.C.). *The national plan to prevent the sexual exploitation of children*, available through the National Center for Missing and Exploited Children at http://www.missingkids.com/missingkids/servlet/PublicHomeServlet?LanguageCountry=en_US. Author.

National Public Radio. (2009, July 13). Sexual abuse often taboo for black boys.

National Resource Center. (2004). Creating threads of continuity: Helping infants and toddlers through transitions in foster care. *The Source, 13*(2) Berkley, California.

National Sexual Violence Resource Center. (2005). *Preventing child sexual abuse: A national resource director and handbook.* Enola, Pennsylvania, available at http://www.nsvrc.org/about/national-sexual-violence-resource-center Author.

Nelson, E. D. (1994). Females who sexually abuse children: A discussion of gender stereotypes and symbolic assailants. *Qualitative Sociology, 17*(1), 63–88.

Nielson, T. (1983). Sexual abuse of boys: Current perspectives. *Personnel and Guidance Journal, 62,* 139–142.

Nurius, P., Norris, J., Dimeff, L., & Graham, T. (1996). Expectations regarding acquaintance sexual aggression among sorority and fraternity members. *Sex Roles, 35*(7/8), 1–16.

O'Connor, A. (1987). Female sex offenders. *British Journal of Psychiatry, 150,* 615–620.

O'Dell, L. (2003). The "harm" story in childhood sexual abuse: Contested understanding, disputed knowledges. In P. Reavey & S. Warner (Eds.), *New feminist stories of child sexual abuse: Sexual scripts and dangerous dialogues.* London: Routledge.

Ogilvie, B. (2004). *Mother-daughter incest: A guide for helping professions.* New York: Haworth Press.

Olafson, E., Corwin, D., & Summit, R. (1993). Modern history of child sexual abuse awareness: Cycles of discovery and suppression. *Child Abuse and Neglect, 17,* 7–24.

Oliver, B. (2007). Preventing female-perpetrated sexual abuse. *Journal of Trauma, Violence and Abuse, 8*(1), 19–32.

Olweus, D. (1978). *Aggression in the schools: Bullies and whipping boys.* New York: Wiley.

Olweus, D. (1993). *Bullying at school: What we know and what we can do.* Cambridge, MA: Blackwell.

O'Sullivan, L., & Byers, E. S. (1993). Eroding stereotypes: College women's attempts to influence reluctant male sexual partners. *Journal of Sex Research, 30*(3), 270–282.

O'Sullivan, L., Byers, E., & Finkelman, L. (1998). A comparison of male and female college students' experiences of sexual coercion. *Psychology of Women Quarterly, 22,* 177–195.

Oswald, D., & Russell, B. (2006). Perceptions of sexual coercion in heterosexual dating relationships: The role of aggressor gender and tactics. *Journal of Sex Research, 43,* 87–95.

Paine, M., & Hansen, D. (2000). Factors influencing children to self-disclose sexual abuse. *Clinical Psychology Review, 22,* 271–295.

Paludi, M., DeFour, D., Attah, K., & Batts, J. (1999). Sexual harassment in education and the workplace: A view from the field of psychology. In Michele Paludi (Ed.), *The psychology of sexual victimization: A handbook* (1999). Westport, CT: Greenwood Press.

Papon, A. M. (2010, April 9). American University student newspaper issues apology over offensive column. *Global Shift.* Retrieved from http://www.globalshift.org/2010/04/american-university-apologizes-for-column/.

Parrot, A. (1998). Meaningful sexual assault prevention programs for men. In B. Anderson & C. Struckman-Johnson (Eds.), *Sexually aggressive women: Current perspectives and controversies.* New York: Guilford Press.

Pearson, P. (1998). *When she was bad: How and why women get away with murder.* New York: Penguin Books.

Peluso, E., & Putnam, N. (1996). Case study: Sexual abuse of boys by females. *Journal of American Academy of Child and Adolescent Psychiatry, 35*(1), 51–54.

Perry, B. (2000). Traumatized children: How childhood trauma influences brain development. *Journal of the California Alliance for the Mentally Ill, 11*(1), 48–51.

Perry, B. (n.d.). *Aggression and violence: The neurobiology of experience* (available at http://teacher.scholastic.com/professional/bruceperry/aggression_violence.htm).

Peter, T. (2006). Mad, bad, or victim? Making sense of mother-daughter sexual abuse. *Feminist Criminology, 1*(4), 283–302.

Petrovich, M., & Templer, D. (1984). Heterosexual molestation of children who later become rapists. *Psychological Reports, 54*(3), 810.

Pincus, J. (2001). *Basic instincts: What makes killers kill.* New York: Norton.

Plummer, K. (1981). Paedophilia: Constructing a sociological baseline. In M. Cook & K. Howells (Eds.), *Adult sexual interest in children.* London: Academic Press.

Pothast, H., & Allen, C. (1994). Masculinity and femininity in male and female perpetrators of child sexual abuse. *Child Abuse and Neglect, 18*(9), 763–767.

Prescott, D. (2004). Emerging strategies for risk assessment of sexually abusive youth: Theory, controversy and practice. *Journal of Child Sexual Abuse, 13*(3/4), 83–106.

Prevent Child Abuse America. (n.d.). *Fact sheet: Sexual abuse of boys.* Chicago, IL: Author.

Price, B. R., & Sokoloff, N. J. (2004). *The criminal justice system and women: Offenders, prisoners, victims and workers* (3rd ed.). New York: McGraw-Hill.

Quinsey, V., & Lalumiere, M. (2001). *Assessment of sexual offenders against children* (2nd ed.). APSAC Study Guides 1. Thousand Oaks, CA: American Professional Society on the Abuse of Children and Sage.

Ramisetty-Mikler, S., Caetano, R., & McGrath, C. (2007). Sexual aggression among white, black, and Hispanic couples in the U.S.: Alcohol use, physical assault, and psychological aggression as its correlates. *American Journal of Drug and Alcohol Abuse, 33,* 31–43.

Rand, M. (2009, September). *Criminal victimization, 2008* (NCJ 227777). Washington, DC: U.S. Department of Justice, Office of Justice Programs.

Rapsey, R., & Murachver, T. (2006). Adolescent sexuality. In R. D. McNaulty & M. Burnette (Eds.), *Sex and sexuality: Vol. 1. Sexual deviation and sexual offenses.* Westport, CT: Praeger.

Rathus, S., Nevid, J., & Fichner-Rathus, L. (2008). *Human sexuality in a world of diversity* (7th ed.). Boston, MA: Allyn and Bacon.

Reckling, A. (2004). Mother-daughter incest: When survivors become mothers. *Journal of Trauma Practice, 3*(2), 49–72.

Reiss, I. (1993). The future of sex research and the meaning of science. *Journal of Sex Research, 30,* 3–11.

Renaud, C., & Byers, E. S. (2005). Relationship between sexual violence and positive and negative cognitions of sexual dominance. *Sex Roles, 53*(3/4), 253–260.

Rentoul, L., & Appleboom, N. (1997). Understanding the psychological impact of rape and serious sexual assault of men: A literature review. *Journal of Psychiatric and Mental Health Nursing, 4,* 267–274.

Richardson, D., & Campbell, J.L. (1982). Alcohol and rape: The effect of alcohol on attributions of blame for rape. *Personality and Social Psychology Bulletin, 8,* 468–476.

Robertiello, G., & Terry, K. (2007). Can we profile sex offenders? A review of sex offender typologies. *Aggression and Violent Behavior, 12,* 508–518.

Robinson, S. (1998). From victim to offender: Female offenders of child sexual abuse. *European Journal on Criminal Policy and Research, 6,* 59–73.

Rohner, R. (1976). Sex differences in aggression: Phylogenetic and enculturation perspectives. *Ethos, 4,* 57–72.

Rosenberg, A., Abell, S., & Mackie, J. (2005). An examination of the relationship between child sexual offending and psychopathy. *Journal of Child Sexual Abuse, 14*(3), 49–66.

Rosencrans, B. (1997). *The last secret.* Brandon, VT: The Safer Society Press.

Rowan, A., & Foy, D. (1993). Posttraumatic stress disorder in child sexual abuse survivors: A literature review. *Journal of Traumatic Stress, 6*(1), 3–21.

Rowan, E. L., Rowan, J. B., & Langelier, P. (1990). Women who molest children. *Bulletin of the American Academy of Psychiatry and the Law, 18*(1), 79.

Rubin, S., & Biggs, J. (1999). *Teachers that sexually abuse students: An administrative and legal guide.* Lancaster, PA: Technomic Publishing Company.

Russell, D. (1984). *Sexual exploitation: Rape, child sexual abuse and workplace harassment.* Beverly Hills, CA: Sage.

Russell, B., & Oswald, D. (2001). Strategies and dispositional correlates of sexual coercion perpetrated by women: An exploratory investigation. *Sex Roles, 45,* 103–115.

Russell, B., & Oswald, D. (2002). Sexual coercion and victimization of college men: The role of love styles. *Journal of Interpersonal Violence, 17,* 273–285.

Sabina C., & Straus, M. (2008). Polyvictimization by dating partners and mental health among U.S. college students. *Violence and Victims, 23*(6) available on line at http://pubpages.unh.edu/~mas2/CTS53J.pdf.

Salter, A. (2003). *Predators, pedophiles, rapists and other sex offenders: Who they are, how they operate, and how we can protect ourselves and our children.* New York: Basic Books.

Sandler, J., & Freeman, N. (2007). Typology of female sex offenders: A test of Vandiver and Kercher. *Sex Abuse, 19,* 73–89.

Sandler, J., & Freeman, N. (2009). Female sex offender recidivism: A large-scale empirical analysis. *Sexual Abuse: A Journal of Research and Treatment, 21*(4), 455–473.

Saradjian, J., with Helga Hanks (1996). *Women who sexually abuse children: From research to clinical practice.* New York: Wiley.

Sarrel, P., & Masters, W. (1982). Sexual molestation of men by women. *Archives of Sexual Behavior, 11*(2), 117–131.

Sarwer, D., Kalichman, S., Johnson, J., Early, J., & Akram Ali, S. (1993). Sexual aggression and love styles: An exploratory study. *Archives of Sexual Behavior, 22*(3), 265–275.

Saul, J., & Audage, N. (2007). *Preventing child sexual abuse within youth-serving organizations: Getting started on policies and procedures.* Atlanta: Centers for Disease Control and Prevention, National Center for Injury Prevention and Control.

Saunders, B.E. (2003). Understanding children exposed to violence: Toward an integration of overlapping fields. *Journal of Interpersonal Violence, 18*(4), 356–376.

Schewe, P., Adam, N., & Ryan, K. (2009). A qualitative analysis of the temptation to use force in sexual relationships. *Violence and Victims, 24*(2), 219–231.

Schwartz, B., & Cellini, H. (1995). Female sex offenders. In B. Schwartz & H. Cellini (Eds.), *The sex offender: Corrections, treatment and legal practice.* (pp. 5-2 to 5-22). NJ: Kingston Research Institute.

Sgroi, S., & Sargent, N. (1993). Impact and treatment issues for victims of childhood sexual abuse by female perpetrators. In M. Elliott (Ed.), *Female sexual abuse of children.* New York: Guilford Press.

Shackel, R. (2007). The beliefs commonly held by adults about children's behavioral responses to sexual victimization. *Child Abuse and Neglect, 32,* 485–495.

Shakeshaft, C., & Cohan, A. (1995, March). Sexual abuse of students by school personnel. *Phi Delta Kappan, 76*(7), 513–520.

Shea, M.E. (1998). When the tables are turned: Verbal sexual coercion among college women. In P. Anderson & C. Struckman-Johnson (Eds.), *Sexually aggressive women: Current perspectives and controversies.* New York: Guilford Press.

Shook, N. J., Gerrity, D. A., Jurich, J., & Segrist, A. E. (2000). Courtship violence among college students: A comparison of verbally and physically abusive couples. *Journal of Family Violence,* 15, 1–22.

Simmons, R. (2002). *Odd girl out: The hidden culture of aggression in girls.* New York: Harcourt.

Sisco, M., & Figueredo, A. (2008). Similarities between men and women in non-traditional aggressive sexuality: Prevalence, novel approaches to assessment and treatment applications. *Journal of Sexual Aggression, 14*(3), 253–266.

Skrypnek, B., & Snyder, M. (1982). On the self-perpetuating nature of stereotypes about women and men. *Journal of Experimental Social Psychology, 18,* 277–291.

Smart, C. (1989). *Feminism and the power of the law.* London: Routledge.

Smith, A., Saewyc, E., Albert, M., MacKay, L., Northcott, M., & The McCreary Centre Society. (2007). *Against the odds: A profile of marginalized and street-involved youth in BC.* Vancouver: Author.

Smith, D.W., Letourneau, E.J., Saunders, B.E., Kilpatrick, H.S., Resnick, H.S., & Best, C.L. (2000). Delay in disclosure of childhood rape: Results from a national survey. *Child Abuse and Neglect, 24,* 273–287.

Smith, R., Pine, C., & Hawley, M. (1988). Social cognition about adult male victims of female sexual assault. *Journal of Sex Research, 24,* 101–241.

Snyder, H.N. (2000). *Sexual assault of young children as reported to law enforcement: Victim, offender and incident characteristics* (NCJ 182990). Washington, DC:

U.S. Department of Justice, Office of Justice Programs, Bureau of Justice Statistics.

Snyder, H., & Sickmund, M. (1999). *Juvenile offenders and victims: 1999 National Report* (NCJ 178257). Washington, DC: U.S. Department of Justice, Bureau of Justice Statistics.

Snyder, H., & Sickmund, M. (2006). *Juvenile offenders and victims: 2006 national report.* Washington, DC: U.S. Department of Justice, Office of Justice Programs, Office of Juvenile Justice and Delinquency Prevention.

Sorenson, T., & Snow, B. (1991). *How children tell: the process of disclosure in child sexual abuse.* Child Welfare League of America.

Springman, R., Wherry, J., & Notaro, P. (2006). The effects of interviewer race and child race on sexual abuse disclosures in forensic interviews. *Journal of Child Sexual Abuse, 15*(3), 99–116.

State of Delaware, Family Court State of Delaware. (n.d.). *The Child Protection Registry: A Guide to the Child Protection Registry* (available at http://courts.delaware.gov/forms/download.aspx?id=37558).

Stirling, A. (1994). *From generation to generation: Understanding sexual attraction to children.* Tiburon, CA: The Printed Voice.

Straus, M. (1999a). The controversy over domestic violence by women: A methodological, theoretical, and sociology of science analysis. In X. B. Arriaga & S. Oskamp (Eds.), *Violence in intimate relationships*. Thousand Oaks, CA: Sage.

Straus, M. (1999b). Physical assault by wives: A major social problem. In R. Gelles & D. Loseke (Eds.), *Current controversies on family violence*. Newbury Park, CA: Sage.

Straus, M., & Ramirez, I. (2002, July 30). *Gender symmetry in prevalence, severity, and chronicity of physical aggression against dating partners by university students in Mexico and USA.* Paper presented at the XV World Meeting of the International Society for Research on Aggression, Montreal.

Strickland, S. (2008). Female sex offenders: Exploring issues of personality, trauma and cognitive distortions. *Journal of Interpersonal Violence, 23*(4), 474–489.

Stroud, D., Martens, S., & Barker, J. (2000). Criminal investigation of child sexual abuse: A comparison of cases referred to the prosecutor to those not referred. *Child Abuse and Neglect, 24*(5), 689–700.

Struckman-Johnson, C. (1988). Forced sex on dates: It happens to men, too. *Journal of Sex Research, 24,* 234–241.

Struckman-Johnson, C., & Anderson, P. (1998). Men do and women don't: Difficulties in researching sexually aggressive women In P. Anderson & C. Struckman-Johnson (Eds.), *Sexually aggressive women*. London: Guilford Press.

Struckman-Johnson, D., & Struckman-Johnson, C. (1991). Men and women's acceptance of coercive sexual strategies varied by initiator gender and couple intimacy. *Sex Roles, 25,* 661–676.

Struckman-Johnson, C., & Struckman-Johnson, D. (1994). Men pressured and forced into sexual experience. *Archives of Sexual Behavior, 23,* 93–114.

Struckman-Johnson, C., & Struckman-Johnson, D. (1998). The dynamics and impact of sexual coercion of men by women. In P. B. Anderson & C. Struckman-Johnson (Eds.), *Sexually aggressive women: Current perspectives and controversies*. New York: Guilford Press.

Struckman-Johnson, C., & Struckman-Johnson, D. (2003). Tactics of sexual coercion: When men and women won't take no for an answer. *Journal of Sex Research, 40*(1), 76–86.

Tardiff, M., Auclair, N., Jacob, M., & Carpenter, J. (2005). Sexual abuse perpetrated by adult and juvenile females: An ultimate attempt to resolve a conflict associated with maternal identity. *Child Abuse and Neglect, 29,* 153–167.

Testa, M., & Dermen, K. (1999). The differential correlates of sexual coercion and rape. *Journal of Interpersonal Violence, 14*(5), 548–561.

The Crown Prosecution Services. (2009, December 15). *Vanessa George and Angela Allen sentenced* (available at http://cps.gov.uk/news/press_releases/161_09).

The Crown Prosecution Services. (n.d.). *Sexual Offences Act 2003* (available at http://www.cps.gov.uk/legal/s_to_u/sexual_offences_act).

Turner, K., Miller, H. A., & Henderson, C. E. (2008). Latent profile analysis of offense and personality characteristics in a sample of incarcerated female sexual offenders. *Criminal Justice and Behavior, 35,* 879–894.

Turton, J. (2007). *Child abuse, gender and society.* New York: Routledge.

Underwood, A. (2010, April 27). Experts discuss alcohol, sex. *The Harvard Crimson.* Retrieved from http://www.thecrimson.com/article/2010/4/27/people-sexual-alcohol-rape/.

U.S. Department of Education, Office of the Under Secretary. (2004). *Educator sexual misconduct: A synthesis of existing literature.* Washington, DC: Author.

U.S. Department of Health and Human Services, Administration on Children, Youth and Families. (2008). *Child Maltreatment 2006.* Washington, DC: U.S. Government Printing Office.

U.S. Department of Health and Human Services, Administration on Children, Youth and Families. (2009). *Child maltreatment 2007.* Washington, DC: U.S. Government Printing Office.

U.S. Department of Justice. (n.d.). *Uniform crime reports.* Washington, DC: Author (available at http://www.fbi.gov/ucr/ucr.htm).

U.S. Department of Justice. (2000). *Children as victims: 1999 National Report Series Juvenile Justice Bulletin* (NCJ 180753). Rockville, MD: Juvenile Justice Clearinghouse

VanderLaan, D., & Vasey, P. (2009). Patterns of sexual coercion in heterosexual and non-heterosexual men and women. *Archives of Sexual Behavior, 38*(6), 987–999.

Vandiver, D. (2006a). Female sex offenders. In R. D. McNaulty & M. Burnette (Eds.), *Sex and sexuality: Sexual deviation and sexual offenses* (Vol. 3). Westport, CT: Praeger.

Vandiver, D. (2006b). Female sex offenders: A comparison of solo offenders and co-offenders. *Violence and Victims, 21*(3), 339–354.

Vandiver, D., & Kercher, G. (2004). Offender and victim characteristics of registered female sexual offenders in Texas: A proposed typology of female sexual offenders. *Sexual Abuse: A Journal of Research and Treatment, 16*(2), 121–137.

Vandiver, D., & Walker, T. (2002). Female sex offenders: An overview and analysis of 40 cases. *Criminal Justice Review, 27*(2), 284–300.

van Dam, C. (2001). *Identifying child molesters: Preventing child sexual abuse by recognizing the patterns of the offenders.* New York: Haworth Press.

Wahl, C. W. (1960). The psychodynamics of consummated maternal incest. *Archives of General Psychiatry, 3,* 96/188–101/193.

Waldner-Haugrud, L., & Magruder, B. (1995). Male and female sexual victimization in dating relationships: Gender differences in coercion techniques and outcomes. *Violence and Victims, 10*(3), 203–215.

Waterman, C., Dawson, L., & Bologna, M. (1989). Sexual coercion in gay male and lesbian relationships: Predictors and implications for support services. *Journal of Sex Research, 26,* 118–124.

Wechsler, H. (2000). *Binge drinking on America's college campuses: Findings from the Harvard School of Public Health College Alcohol Study* published by the Harvard School of Public Health College Alcohol Study. Cambridge, MA. available on line at http://www.hsph.harvard.edu/cas/Documents/monograph_2000/cas_mono_2000.pdf.

Wechsler, H., & Nelson, T. (2008). What we have learned from the Harvard School of Public Health College Alcohol Study: Focusing attention on alcohol consumption and the environmental conditions that promote it. *Journal of Studies on Alcohol and Drugs,* 69, 1–10.

Weitzman, E., Toben, N., & Wechsler, H. (2003). Taking up binge drinking in college: The influences of person, social group and environment. *Journal of Adolescent Health, 32,* 26–35.

Whitaker, D., Le, B., Hanson, R. K., Baker, C., McMahon, P., Ryan, G. (2008). Risk factors for the perpetration of child sexual abuse: A review and meta-analysis. *Child Abuse and Neglect, 32,* 529–548.

White, J., & Kowalski, R. (1994). Deconstructing the myth of the nonaggressive female: A feminist analysis. *Psychology of Women Quarterly, 18,* 477–498.

Widom, C., & Hiller-Sturmhofel, S. (2001). Alcohol abuse as a risk factor for and consequence of child abuse. *Alcohol Research and Health, 25*(1), 52–57.

Wilcox, C., & Francis, L. (1997). Beyond gender stereotyping: Examining the validity of the Bem Sex-Role Inventory among 16- to 19-year-old females in England. *Personality and Individual Differences, 23*(1), 9–13.

Wolfers, O. (1993). The paradox of women who sexually abuse children. In M. Elliott (Ed.), *Female sexual abuse of children.* New York: Guilford Press.

World Health Organization. (2003). *Violence prevention the evidence: Changing cultural and social norms that support violence.* Geneva: Author.

World Health Organization. (2006). *Preventing child maltreatment: A guide to taking action and generating evidence.* Geneva: Author.

World Health Organization. (2007). *Key facts on the cycles of violence: The relationship between childhood maltreatment and the risk of later becoming a victim or perpetrator of violence.* Geneva: Author (available at http://www.euro.who.int/document/E90619.pdf).

Wright, L., & Hatcher, A. (2006). Treatment of sex offenders. In R. McNaulty & N. M. Burnette (Eds.), *Sex and sexuality: Sexual deviation and sexual offenses* (Vol. 3). Westport, CT: Praeger.

Wuthrich, C. (2009). Reflections on personal responsibility: Sorority members at risk for interpersonal violence. *National Association of Student Personnel Administration (NASPA) Journal, 46*(2), 228–257.

Young, V. (1993a). Self-help for survivors. In M. Elliott (Ed.), *Female sexual abuse of children.* New York: Guilford Press.

Young, V. (1993b). Women abusers: A feminist view. In M. Elliott (Ed.), *Female sexual abuse of children.* New York: Guilford Press.

Zellman, C. (1992). The impact of case characteristics on child abuse reporting decisions. *Child Abuse and Neglect, 16*(1), 57–74.

Zink, T., Klesges, L., & Stevens, S. (2009). The development of a sexual abuse severity score: Characteristics of childhood sexual abuse associated with trauma symptomatology, somatization and alcohol abuse. *Journal of Interpersonal Violence, 24*(3), 537–546.

Index

About the Series

In this series, experts delve into vast psychological perspectives that can be applied to the criminal justice system. The forensic psychology illuminated here includes approaches to law and legislative issues, public policies, police and detective systems and policies, and court issues, including competency and temporary insanity. Forensic psychology can be applied in its various forms to areas ranging from determining treatment for mentally ill offenders to analyzing a criminal's mind or intent to consulting with attorneys on jury selection.

ABOUT THE SERIES EDITOR AND ADVISERS

Series editor DUANE L. DOBBERT is a 38-year veteran of the criminal justice profession. A professor of criminal forensic studies at Florida Gulf Coast University and an adjunct professor in the School of Human Services at Capella University, he is a fellow of the American College of Forensic Examiners and a diplomate of the American Board of Psychological Specialties. Dr. Dobbert is also a juvenile court administrator with the National Council of Juvenile and Family Court Judges and a certified social worker. Also president of forensic consulting and training, he has consulted in more than 300 criminal justice jurisdictions across the United States. He developed and presented training programs pertaining to the nature and identification of sexual predators to law enforcement officers, educators, mental health counselors, and attorneys. Dr. Dobbert has also authored a program and trained thousands in that program, *School Bus Drivers: The 1st Line of Defense against Sexual Predators.* He is also an active member of Child Abduction Response Teams in Florida and Indiana. Dobbert's books produced by Praeger Publishers include *Understanding Personality Disorders* and *Halting the Sexual Predators among Us: Preventing Attack, Rape and Lust Homicide.*

Adviser DANIEL BRUCE KENNEDY is professor in the Department of Criminal Justice and Security Administration at the University of Detroit, Mercy, and principal consultant to Forensic Criminology Associates, Inc., in Troy, Michigan. He is a certified sociological practitioner, a licensed social worker, a certified protection professional, and a certified police academy instructor. In previous roles, Dr. Kennedy was head of research and development at the Wayne State University Criminal Justice Institute and director of the Criminal Justice Program at the College of the Virgin Islands, St. Thomas.

He has also served as visiting lecturer at the FBI Academy at Quantico. Kennedy has been a consultant on crime and security-related issues for media, including CNN, the Associated Press, *20/20*, and the *Detroit News.* He serves as chair of the Ethics Committee for the Academy of Behavioral Profiling and cochair of the Jail Suicide Task Force for the American Association of Suicidology. His work has been widely published in journals including *Crime and Delinquency*, *Professional Psychology*, *Journal of Police Science and Administration, Police Quarterly*, *American Jails*, *Journal of Criminal Justice*, and others. He began his career as a civilian crime analyst with the Detroit Police Department in 1966.

Adviser GARY F. MEUNIER is president of Diagnostics, Inc., a private organization dedicated to providing expert psychodiagnostic and psychiatric assessments in forensic and industrial settings. He is a fellow of the American College of Forensic Examiners and a diplomate in forensic personality assessment of the American Board of Psychological Specialties. He has published widely in the area of forensic assessment and has qualified as an expert witness in local, state, and federal courts. Dr. Meunier is currently Emeritus Professor of Psychology at Ball State University, having served 37 years in various faculty and administrative positions, and he has also served on the faculties of Oklahoma State University (Department of Psychology) and the Indiana University Medical School (Department of Psychiatry). Dr. Meunier has been managing partner of a large private mental health center, staff psychologist at two state mental hospitals, and intake psychologist at a state women's prison. He has created and directed mental health programs in jails and secure adolescent treatment facilities. Dr. Meunier has provided training and consulting services to many different forensic organizations throughout his career and continues to do so today. He has been granted honorary life membership in the Indiana

Sheriff's Association and has also received specific honors for his work at suicide prevention in jails and prisons from the American Correctional Association.

Adviser PAMELA K. S. PATRICK is a clinical psychologist and registered nurse and academic director for colloquia at Capella University. Having worked 15 years as a clinical and consulting psychologist, she also served as executive director/dean and faculty at the School of Human Services, Capella University. She has also served as clinical director for child and adolescent services at Atlantic Shores Hospital, as director of psychological services at Halifax Medical Center, as director of psychological services at North Mississippi Medial Center, and as assistant chief for nursing services at the Veterans Administration at Bay Pines.

About the Author

Karen A. Duncan is a licensed therapist and national speaker known for her advocacy work in the prevention and treatment of sexual abuse and family violence. She received the 2008 Outstanding Mental Health Counselor Award from the Indiana Coalition Against Sexual Assault and was the recipient of the 2005 Social Worker of the Year Award for Region 7 from the National Association of Social Workers, Indiana chapter. Duncan is a member of the editorial board for the *Journal of Mental Health Counseling* and serves on the advisory boards for the Indiana Women's Prison and Indiana Coalition Against Sexual Assault. She has been interviewed by the *Today Show* and the *Tampa Tribune* regarding female sex offenders.